D1101881

Siegfried Hirsch outside Kielortallee 16, Hamburg,
16 July 1978

CONTENTS

FOREWORD

Many books have been written about the Holocaust, about how people got through the war and survived in the camps. Not much has been written about what it was like to live as a Jew in a German city in the final months before the Second World War. This book tells the story of what life was like for Jews in Hamburg from March to September 1939, watching friends and family leave and becoming increasing lonely. What comes across in particular is the despair and the attempt to keep a brave face on what was happening.

The story is told by letters and postcards written by my grandparents Adele and Pincus Hirsch to their son Siegfried, my father, who was later interned in Australia. These letters throw light on very dark times and show the courage and the strength needed to get through each day.

My father was taken to Australia on the infamous ship, HMT Dunera, on which he and his fellow internees had a terrible time, when British soldiers treated the Jewish refugees on one part of the ship in the same way as they did the Nazi prisoners in another part.

I would like to thank my cousin Max Sussman for editing this book, which is very special to me. He has spent many hours of research to be able to write it. I know that if my father were alive today, it would also have meant a lot to him.

I would also like to thank Astrid Louven who transcribed the letters from German script into typescript. She has long had an interest in the Jews of Hamburg, including during World War II; her assistance to my cousin, Max, has been invaluable.

Adele Lustig, Siegfried's daughter

PREFACE

To accept the facts of history is one thing, to understand them is altogether another. The fact of the Holocaust is incontrovertible but how is it to be understood? Philosophers, psychologists, politicians and even theologians have done their best to provide a framework of understanding; it is all unsatisfactory. Magnitude is a central problem. How do we conceive the astronomic number of 6 million? Even the images do not bring one closer to an understanding. It is what I have come to call the 'statistical Holocaust'. It is here that understanding fails. It seems to me that the long path to a real understanding is what I term the 'individual Holocaust'. That is what this book is about

The story behind it deserves to be recounted briefly. When my mother Erna Minden-Sussman née Hirsch died in August 2004 at the age of 98, she left behind a bundle of letters written by her mother, my grandmother Oma, in the year from February 1945, when she was released from Theresienstadt, until March 1946 when she came to us in London. I knew that the letters existed but nothing of the circumstances that gave rise to them or their contents. On my mother's death, in August 2004, the letters came into my possession and with it the opportunity to read them. It was an extraordinary experience, the letters represent the heroic and fascinating story told by a remarkable woman of unshakeable faith. There is hardly a word about the mistreatment she suffered and nothing about her life in the Nazi 'Ghetto Theresienstadt' but there is much else of great interest and meaning about family, friends and acquaintances. Oma's letters are those of a cultured and educated woman with an unusual memory and an extraordinarily sunny outlook on life. I decided to produce an edition of the letters in English translation with supporting background information for my family. For convenience the working title became 'Oma's letters'.

As I was trying to identify the people and the events in Oma's letters, my cousin Adele Lustig née Hirsch told me that she had letters written by her grandparents, Pincus and Adele Hirsch, before World War II, after her father had been made to leave Germany by order of the Gestapo.

These letters were written in the characteristic Deutsche Schrift, which neither of us could read. Fortunately, Astrid Louven, of whom more below, transcribed the letters and commented on their great historical interest. It became clear that these letters, too, were worthy of translation and editing for the family. For convenience their working title is 'the Adele and Pincus letters'. Chronology and convenience determined that the Adele and Pincus letters should be the first to see the light of day and Oma's letters would be second.

While editing the two groups of letters I became acutely aware of people and events about which I knew little or nothing. Most of those who could have enlightened me were no longer in the land of the living. This led me on a long, fascinating, but sometimes sad journey of discovery in which I was assisted by many people, some of who started out as strangers and ended up as friends. First and foremost among these is Astrid Louven of Hamburg. She wrote the history of the Jews of Wandsbek, where my great-grandfather, David Hanover, was the rabbi from 1864 to 1901. An enquiry about my great-grandfather's post-graduate studies was the beginning of the continued help she has given me. She transcribed the Pincus and Adele' letters from Deutsche Schrift, into typescript. Later, during a visit to Hamburg in 2010 she showed my wife, Jean, and me the Jewish sites of the city. Her extensive knowledge of the history of Hamburg was always at my disposal and without her help much in these pages would have remained obscure, unexplained or even unknown.

It soon became apparent that so much family information had been unearthed that a third volume would result. Then the possibility became apparent of a connection between the two sets of letters. A further discussion with Adele Lustig established that she had a bundle of draft letters written by her father while he was an internee in Australia, and these included a further few letters written by her grandparents and a letter written by her father in early February 1945 to a rabbi in Switzerland. This letter proved to be the remote but touching connection between the letters of our respective grandparents. The nature of this connection will become apparent in the volume on the Oma letters.

The research to bring into focus the events and the people referred to in the trilogy, led to the collection of much information and many documents of interest. Some of these had been in the family for many years, while others were provided by various archives, mainly in Germany. These documents will be described and collected in a fourth volume that will include reproductions of some of the more important items and a hand list of documents that cannot on account of their number be included. This documentation volume will not be published but will be placed in the custody of family members and possibly copies will be lodged in a few suitable archives.

The biographical sketches in Appendix 2 of this volume are intended not only to tell of the lives of those who were not members of the Hirsch and Nussbaum families but are mentioned in the letters but also to provide background information about the Jewish communities of which they were part before the Second World War and what happened to them during and after it.

I am deeply grateful to my wife, Jean, for reading and correcting the manuscript of this book with great care.

The title of this volume is derived from the advice about his religious responsibilities Pincus Hirsch gave his son in a short letter of 18 April 1939, shortly after the latter had left home. The final fate of Pincus and Adele Hirsch accounts for the interrogative of the title.

Max Sussman

Chapter 1

INTRODUCTION

When the Hamburg Jewish Community inaugurated its Ohlsdorf (Llandkoppel) cemetery, part of a large municipal cemetery on 30 September 1883, they consecrated an impressive purpose-built Prayer Hall (*Ohel*) (Fig. 1) and expressed their confidence in the future by placing above its portal the words of Ecclesiastes 1:4, *One generation passes away, and another generation comes, but the earth abides for ever* (Fig. 2). It may well be that the 23-year-old bank clerk Pincus Hirsch, a faithful member of the community, was present at the inauguration; after all his father was a community official.

Fig. 1.1. The prayer Hall (*Ohel*) at the Hamburg Ohlsdorf Cemetery

The Jewish community of the great Hanseatic port of Hamburg had been founded in the last third of the 16th century by Sephardi refugees seeking asylum from the Portuguese Inquisition. Ashkenazi Jews arrived in Hamburg a little later and established their own communities. In the years that followed, the community grew, not only in numbers but also in reputation and distinction. Amongst its leaders were great rabbinic scholars and intellectuals, who from time to time also generated great controversies that had their echoes in the wider Jewish world. Indeed, Hakham Isaac Bernays (1792-1849), Chief Rabbi of Hamburg, and his pupil Samson Raphael Hirsch (1808-1888), who was born in Hamburg, were pioneers of Modern Orthodoxy.

Though from the beginning in Hamburg, as elsewhere in Germany, there existed age-old civic and political anti-Jewish prejudice, the community flourished. With its growth in numbers and economic security it became one of the most significant in Western Europe. When the United Synagogue of London established its customs in about 1870, it adopted those of Hamburg as the basis of its own practice.

Fig. 1.2. Inscription above the entrance to the Ohlsdorf prayer hall.

The Hirsch family had lived in Hamburg from at least the middle of the 18th century. During the following 200 years the family had grown and many of its members were in various ways active in the Jewish community, in commercial and business life and had established an economically comfortable life style. The roots of the family in Hamburg were deep and to a great extent forged by the singular traditions of the Hamburg Jewish community.

In 1903 Pincus Hirsch married Adele Nussbaum, whose family had come to Hamburg about a century earlier from Iba in Hessen. Their only child, a son, Siegfried Süsskind Hirsch, was born on 2 September 1904 and educated in Hamburg in a large family who were typical of the observant section of the Ashkenazi community, which afforded them a wide circle of friends and close acquaintances, amongst whom there were rabbis and communal leaders.

By the time Siegfried Hirsch visited Hamburg with his daughter Adele in July 1978 to show her the city of his birth and, as is the Jewish custom, to visit the graves of his ancestors, he will have stood at a biblical inscription, erected after the Second World War, opposite the one his father would long before have seen on the path leading to the main cemetery grounds. This read, *Oh that my head were waters, and my eyes a fountain of tears, that I might weep day and night, for the slain of the daughter of my people* (Jeremiah 8:23). The two inscriptions correspond in sentiment to those of the early and the final generations of the Hirsch family in Hamburg.

By the end of the 1930s only a shadow remained of the proud and confident Jewish Hamburg of Siegfried's early years. He will have been aware of political events and developments in Germany but it will have been unexpected when he was woken early in the morning of the 10 November 1938 by an insistent knock at the door of the home, at Kielortallee 16, he still shared with his parents. The Gestapo had come to arrest him and take him to the Sachsenhausen concentration camp in the Oranienburg district of north Berlin. On his release he was ordered to leave Germany and it will have been a great relief when he was finally able to leave Hamburg. On the way to Britain, he paid a brief visit to Amsterdam.

Siegfried's departure from Hamburg was the stimulus for an intense correspondence with his parents, in which they made valiant efforts to continue, in writing, a semblance of their intimate family life, by asking about his everyday existence in a strange country, by seeking his advice and by advising him about the most personal of matters. The letters and postcards written several times each week during the six months up to 6 September 1939, particularly those by Siegfried's mother, show intense sorrow at his departure and also the increasing loneliness as progressively family and friends leave Hamburg. Interlaced with all this, on the one hand, is Adele's fear of having to move from their home to a *Judenhaus* and, on the other, the ultimately forlorn hope of emigration to safety and a reunion with her son.

Apart from the portrayal of the life of a family under great pressure, there is the theft of Siegfried's insured property in transit to Britain and the refusal of the insurer to pay compensation. Back in Hamburg there is possible evidence that Adele was trying to collect old debts from Siegfried's dentist customers, the auction of Siegfried's property is mentioned and then the difficulty of obtaining the proceeds. Finally, to add insult to injury, long after he had left Hamburg the authorities visited his parents' home to check that Siegfried's business had really been closed down.

To understand the effect of these changes on individuals, it is necessary to look at their personal, social and religious lives. Relatively little is known about the personal lives of individual Jews left behind in Germany during these final months before the war. For a variety of reasons, that are not difficult to comprehend, personal records of such people are uncommon, partly because such evidence was never intended to pass beyond hearth and home and, indeed, may never have been created, or because it may have fallen prey to the destructive exigencies of war. Where such information has survived, it is due to unusual circumstances, as in this case.

The most informative evidence is likely to be found in private narrative accounts, diaries and letters, particularly those which, when written, were intended only for the eyes of close family and friends. By the nature of events at the time, including fear of censorship, much of such evidence is difficult to find and when it has survived, much must be read between the lines.

Siegfried and his parents would have been surprised that anyone should be interested in their lives and letters. Many lives might have given rise to biographies and many letters might have been written with the intention that they be recognised as literature. The modest lives described here and their letters would have remained private, insignificant and unknown were it not for events beyond the control of those who created them - the cataclysmic events in Europe in the 1930s up to 1945 and their aftermath.

This lends the letters great importance. Apart from their intense sadness, the failed attempts of Siegfried's parents to go to the United States are most poignant of all. Amidst all this there is growing evidence of deprivation of civil rights (*Entrechtung*) by increasingly invasive Nazi action, but alongside this there are great faith and heroic attempts to continue age-old family traditions and Jewish communal life.

In spite of all his worries and difficulties, Siegfried believed that he had found a safe haven in London but in early May 1940, there was another early morning knock at the door. The London Metropolitan Police had come to his modest rented accommodation to arrest him as an Enemy Alien; a totally unexpected event probably made more terrifying by the memory of his earlier experience in Hamburg and Sachsenhausen. He was unceremoniously arrested, taken to a detention camp at Huyton near the port of Liverpool and from there to the Isle of Man, from where he was returned to Liverpool. After a very short time he was deported to Australia on a small troop-carrier, the infamous HRT *Dunera*. There followed a frightening journey of some two months. Where in Sachsenhauen Siegfried was a hated Jew, on the *Dunera* he was a hated Enemy Alien.

This book follows in part directly and in part indirectly the lives of Pincus and Adele Hirsch and the journey of Siegfried Hirsch from 1938 in Hamburg, via Australia until his return to London in 1942.

Fig. 2.1. Pincus and Adele Hirsch

Chapter 2

PINCUS, ADELE AND SIEGFRIED HIRSCH

At the centre of this narrative are Pincus Hirsch, Adele Hirsch née Nussbaum and their son Siegfried, members of a family that had long lived in Hamburg. Details of the Hirsch family and their relationships will be described in Volume 3, based on family trees drafted at various times by Siegfried and other sources. The limited information available about Nussbaum family will also be presented in Volume 3. The story of the family emerges through the letters and postcards written by Pincus and Adele to their son between 1939 and 1942. In order to follow the story, it is necessary first to explain what is known about its main protagonists (Lohmeyer, 2012).

Pincus Hirsch

Fig. 2.2. Pincus Hirsch

Pincus Hirsch (1861–1942) (Fig. 2.1) was descended from an old and well-established orthodox Hamburg Jewish family and belonged to at least the third generation of his family to live in Hamburg. Just before his 18th birthday, on 1 June 1879, he started work probably as a trainee at M. M. Warburg & Co. the Hamburg bank. Though he was known in the family simply as Pincus, according to the Communal Tax Record (*Kultussteuerkartei* No. 1567) [StaH, *Jüdische Gemeinden 992b Kultussteuerkartei 1913-1942*] he seems also to have had a second given name, Paul, but in view of handwritten corrections to the record, the second name may have been entered in error. On 1 November 1903, in Hamburg, Pincus Hirsch married Adele Nussbaum.

In 1923, when M. M. Warburg & Co., celebrated its 125th anniversary (*Firmen-Jubiläum*), it recognised the 44th anniversary of Pincus as an employee. In a list of staff members who had been invited on this occasion to a small company party, Pincus Hirsch was the most senior employee (*Angestellte*). On 2 February 1928 he still had a desk in the bank's customer credit control department (*Kundencontrolle*) (Warburg Bank Archives).

Pincus eventually held the office of *Gabbai* (Senior Member of the Board of Management) in the *Vereinigte Alte und Neue Klaus* in the Rutschbahn. The congregation accorded him the honorific title *HeChaver* ('Fellow'), an honour also held by his father before him. This may account for his close friendship with Rabbi Dr Pinchos Bamberger, who was rabbi of the Klaus until his death in 1936.

Siegfried's earliest handwritten family tree describes his father's occupation as '*Kaufmann*' (businessman) but in a later typewritten family tree drawn up in England he described him as a 'merchant banker'. On one occasion, in connection with his father's employment at the bank, Siegfried describes him as *Prokurist* (authorised secretary). In 1913 in the Kultussteuerkartei Pincus is described as a *Buchhalter* (book keeper). The significance of these different descriptions is not clear but they may relate to different positions Pincus held at the bank at various times.

On 15 July 1942 Pincus Hirsch was deported from Hamburg together with many other members of his Hamburg Hirsch family to the so-called "ghetto" in Theresienstadt. The Community Tax record states that on 15 July 1942 Pincus Hirsch resigned his Community membership.

Adele Hirsch née Nussbaum
On her mother's side Adele Nussbaum (1875-1942) (Fig. 2.2) was descended from a very distinguished rabbinic family. Her maternal great-grandfather, Rabbi Jecheskel Joelson (1785- probably 1882), who had settled in Altona from Filehne near Posen, was the interim predecessor of the distinguished Rabbi Jacob Ettlinger of Altona (Duckesz, 1903, 1908, No. 133). Duckesz gives the year of Rabbi Joelson's death as 1885 but states that he died aged 97. Others of Adele's ancestors, who came from Hessen, settled in Hamburg in the first half of the 19th century.

Siegfried told me that his parents greatly enjoyed the operas of Richard Wagner and on occasion went to performances of the complete Ring cycle in a single week. This almost certainly accounts for the name, Siegfried, they chose for their son.

Adele Hirsch was deported to Theresienstadt from Hamburg on 15 July 1942, at the same time as her husband Pincus.

Fig. 2.3. Adele Hirsch

Siegfried Süsskind Hirsch

Siegfried Hirsch (1904-1990) (Fig. 2.4) was born almost exactly one year after his parents' marriage. He attended the Talmud Torah School, which at the time was headed by Dr. Joseph Goldschmidt (1842-1925; Headmaster 1889-1921). In his early years Siegfried came under the influence of Rabbi Dr. Joseph Carlebach, who was headmaster of the Talmud Torah School, before his appointment as the Rabbi of Altona. After his school days, Siegfried was apprenticed in the metal trade to Tobias Feinstein in Hamburg.

Fig. 2.4. Siegfried Hirsch (c. 1933)

Siegfried was active in the religious youth groups, *Hashomer Hadati*, *Ezra* and the *Bar Kochba* Sports Club. In 1936, after his apprenticeship, Siegfried set up a 'Dental Depot', a business that supplied equipment, drugs and other requirements to dental surgeries; his business address was that of his and his parents' home at Kielortallee 16. He was successful in this occupation until the pogrom of 1938, when on 10 November he was arrested by the Gestapo and sent to Sachsenhausen concentration camp. On arrival at the camp his hair was shorn (Fig. 2.4); he was released, on 24 December 1938, the Sabbath of Chanucah, with the order to leave Germany. Siegfried was issued with a German passport in Hamburg on 22 March 1939. On the following day, also in Hamburg, he was granted a visa for entry to the United Kingdom. Siegfried left Hamburg on 28 March 1939 with the permitted 10 German Reichmark. On his way to England he visited his cousin Siegmund Hirsch, his wife Josie and their two children at Geleenstraat 32, Amsterdam, where they had settled somewhat earlier; he would never see them again.

Originally, Siegfried had a permit to stay in Amsterdam for one day but this was extended for a further day and he left Holland on 30 March 1939, arriving by boat in Harwich on 2 April. He finally arrived in London on the following day, 3 April, the day before Passover.

One of the conditions of his entry to the United Kingdom as a refugee was that he was not permitted to take up paid work. Willi Stern and his wife, Betty née Lanzkron, old Hamburg friends, who had arrived from Germany somewhat earlier, welcomed him to their home in North London, and Siegfried lived with them for a time at 84 Queen's Drive, London N4. When, later in 1939, the Sterns moved to Cardiff,

Fig. 2.5. Siegfried in December 1939 on release from Sachsenhausen concentration camp, where his head had been shorn.

Siegfried found accommodation at 356 Seven Sisters Road, London N4. It was here in early May 1940 that he was arrested, interned and deported to Australia on 1 July 1940 (see Chapter 4). He arrived back to Britain at Liverpool on 6th October 1942 and returned to his previous activities organising youth and cultural activities in the North London Adath Yisroel Synagogue. Sometime later he obtained permission to take up employment in the scrap metal business of (now Sir) Siegmund Sternberg, a Hungarian émigré; Siegfried remained in this employment until his retirement in about 1970.

In 1946 Siegfried and Hans (Johann) Sussman, the husband of his cousin Erna née Hirsch decided to move from North London to Hendon in North-West London, where they jointly bought a house at 121 Station Road, NW4. At the same time they both took up membership of the Hendon Adath Yisroel Synagogue, many of whose members were also German Jewish émigrés. On 18 June 1947 Siegfried married his cousin, Rosalind Landau, the daughter of Henny (Henriette) Landau née Hanover. In the 1920s Henny had married Sidney Landau a member of a well-known London Jewish family. She was the daughter of Rabbi Dr David Hanover (1835-1901) of Wandsbek near Hamburg. Siegfried and Rosalind's only child, a daughter, was born on 22 April 1954 and named Adele Sulamith after her grandmother.

The Hendon congregation was expanding and planning to build a new synagogue and Siegfried became a member of the Building Committee. A year later he was elected a full member of the synagogue Board of Management. The rabbi of the congregation was Rabbi Mordechai Knoblowicz, one of the young East-European scholars earlier brought to Hamburg by Rabbi Dr Joseph Carlebach. Rabbi Knoblowicz was in the course of preparing an edition of the important 16th century book *Matte Moshe* ('The Staff of Moses') by the Galician Jewish rabbinic Scholar Moses of Premysl (c. 1550-1606). The book, published in London in 1958, deals extensively with synagogue customs. Thus, Rabbi Knoblowicz had a deep knowledge and interest in Jewish customs and also understood very well the traditions of the Hamburg community in which he had lived as a young man and in which Siegfried had also grown up. This fostered a close and understanding relationship between the two men.

Siegfried loved and was deeply involved in Jewish life and served on many communal committees. With the establishment of the State of Israel in 1948 he began a long-lasting interest in religious Zionism and the Mizrachi Movement in which he held many honorary offices; at the time of his death he was a Vice-Chairman. For a number of years Siegfried was a member of the Board of Deputies of British Jews, the representative body of Anglo-Jewry. Later he was a member of the Shechita Committee of the Board of Deputies. His other interests were the Rabbi Knoblowicz and Rabbi Schonfeld Memorial Trusts and the affairs of the Hasmonean Primary School, a religious Jewish school in North West London. Siegfried was devoted to the Hendon Adath Yisroel Congregation and during a period of some 40 years he held every office in the congregation; from 1977 to 1982 he was its Honorary President. Finally, he was elected a Life Member of the Board of Management. He also worked in an honorary capacity for the Chevrat Bikur Cholim (Society for Visitation of the Sick) of which he was a Vice-President at the time of his death.

In 1985 the Congregation accorded Siegfried the honorary title *HeChaver*, following both his father and his grandfather before him in this distinction. Siegfried Hirsch died in London on 13 February 1990.

Chapter 3

DRAMATIS PERSONAE

This *dramatis personae* lists alphabetically the names of people mentioned in the letters as they appear most frequently. In the case of members of the Hirsch and Nussbaum families, their relationship to Pincus and Adele, derived from Siegfried's family tree of 1985, is briefly explained. For victims of the Holocaust, their final fate is also indicated when known. The relationships in the Hirsch and Nussbaum families will be explained in greater detail in Volume 3. Brief biographies of people who are not members of the Hirsch and Nussbaum families are given in Appendix 2.

Addie Nussbaum, Addi, Adolf, (1923 Hamburg– 2012 California USA), nephew of Adele.

Adolf Levy, first cousin once removed of Pincus (later lived in the USA).

Aly, Rosalie Hirsch, (1867 Hamburg - 1943 Theresienstadt), sister of Pincus.

Auguste, Tante Auguste, Levy, first cousin once removed of Pincus (murdered in Holocaust).

Bella, Badrian née Hanover, Tante Bella, (1866 Wandsbek – 1949 London), sister-in-law of Pincus; not to be confused with plain Bella, whose identity is unknown.

Emil Badrian, Onkel Emil, (1859 Beuthen, Upper Silesia – 1943 Theresienstadt), husband of Bella née Hanover, sister-in-law of Pincus.

Frau Bundheim, Erna, later mother-in-law of Erna Levy, cousin twice removed of Pincus (later lived in Manchester, UK).

Carlebach, Rabbi Dr Joseph Carlebach, Dr. C., (1883 Lübeck –1942 murdered near Riga), Chief Rabbi of Hamburg.

David Hirsch, referred to as David, (1901 Hamburg – 1986 Jerusalem), nephew of Pincus and the husband of Else.

Dora Hirsch née Hanover, Tante Dora, (1870 Wandsbek – 1955 New York), sister-in-law of Pincus, wife of his brother Elkan.

Elkan Hirsch, Onkel Elkan, (1864 Hamburg – 1941 Hamburg) brother of Pincus.

Elsa Hirsch, (1903 Hamburg – 1998 Israel) first cousin once removed of Pincus.

Else Hirsch, (1898 – 1992 Oak Park Mi, USA, buried in Jerusalem), referred to as Else, wife of David Hirsch; not to be confused with Tante Else (Nussbaum).

Else Nussbaum, (1896 Aurich - 1941 Minsk, murdered in Holocaust), Tante Else, née Heymann sister-in-law of Adele.

Erna Sussman née Hirsch, (1906 Hamburg – 2004 London, buried in Jerusalem), daughter of Elkan and Dora Hirsch.

Familie Landau, family of Henny Landau née Hanover.

Fritz Warburg, Dr Fritz M. Warburg (1879-1964), partner in the Warburg bank; brother of Max M Warburg.

Gella de Jong, Tante Gella, first cousin once removed of Pincus, lived in Amsterdam (murdered in Holocaust).

Gottfried Möller, (1899 Hamburg – 1977 London), member of a large Hamburg family.

Gotthelf (Israel) Hirsch, (b. 1933 Hamburg, living in Los Angeles), nephew, son of David and Else Hirsch.

Hanna Hirsch, Hanna H., first cousin once removed of Pincus, one of the 'two Hannas' mentioned in the letters (migrated to New York and later moved to Israel).

Hanna Wittmund, first cousin twice removed of Pincus, one of the two Hannas mentioned in the letters (murdered in holocaust).

Hans Sussman, (1899 Lackenbach, Austria – 1948 London), husband of Erna Sussman née Hirsch.

Harriet Hirsch, Tante Harriet, unmarried sister of Pincus (Minsk, murdered in Holocaust).

Hedwig Nussbaum, Tante Hedwig, Hedchen née Cuder, wife of Max Nussbaum.

Henny Landau, Tante Henny née Hanover, (1875 Wandsbek – 1967 London), half-sister of Dora Hirsch née Hanover.

James Wigderowitsch (1902-1993), a teacher at the Jewish school in Hannover.

Josef Hirsch, (1925 Hamburg, living in Oak Park Mi, USA), son of David and Else Hirsch, great-nephew of Pincus.

Lanzkron, parents-in-law of Willi Stern.

Leo Wittmund, first cousin twice removed of Pincus, brother of Hanna Wittmund (migrated to Chicago).

Lina Nussbaum, sister-in-law of Adele.

Manfred Nussbaum, (1895 Hamburg – 1941 Minsk murdered in Holocaust), brother of Adele and husband of Else.

Max Nussbaum, Onkel Max, brother of Adele.

Max Warburg (1867-1946), Max or Max W., senior partner in the Warburg bank.

Mäxchen, Max Sussman, (1932 Leipzig, living in London), son of Hans and Erna Sussman.

Minden, Ernest Minden, (1898 Hull – 1972 London), a member of the Warburg bank and a younger colleague of Pincus.

Nathan, Dr Nathan Max Nathan, (1879 Emmerich, North Rhine-Westphalia – 23 October 1944 to Auschwitz, murdered), Secretary (Syndicus) of the Hamburg Jewish Community.

Liesel (Alice) Goldberg née Nussbaum, niece of Adele.

Marcus Landau, (1916 London – 2005 London), son of Henny Landau.

Martha Wittmund, later Warisch, (1901 Hamburg – 2010, buried Woodbridge, NJ, USA), first cousin twice removed of Pincus.

Plaut, Dr Max Plaut, (1901 Sohrau, Upper Silesia – 1974 Hamburg), lay head of the Hamburg Jewish community from 1938 until 1943.

Rosalind Landau, (1913 London – 2002 London), wife of Siegfried and daughter of Henny Landau.

Sänger family, Willi (1893-1944, murdered in Auschwitz) and his wife Flora (1895-1944 murdered in Auschwitz); Hamburg friends of the Hirsch family.

Selma Hirsch, first cousin once removed of Pincus.

Siegfried (Fred) Nussbaum, nephew of Adele, son of Max Nussbaum.

Siegmund Hanover, Onkel Siegmund, (1880 Wandsbek – 1964 Haifa), younger half-brother of Dora Hirsch, sister-in-law of Pincus.

Siegmund (later Sir) Warburg (1902-1982), Director of the Warburg bank, later in London.

Siegmund Hirsch, nephew of Pincus, (1905 Hamburg – 30 September 1942 'died', Auschwitz); often referred to jointly with his wife Josi née Levy (17 July 1942 Auschwitz, murdered).

Spitzer, Dr Alexander Spitzer (1897 Hamburg – 1997 London); lawyer, and later rabbi and Director of the Union of Orthodox Hebrew Congregations in London.

Sulamith Hirsch, (1933 Hamburg – 17 July 1942 Auschwitz, murdered), daughter of Siegmund Hirsch.

Streim, Dr Siegfried Streim, (1896 Hamburg – 1944 Auschwitz, murdered, with family), Hamburg dentist and friend of the Hirsch family.

Tina Hanover, Tante Tina, second wife of Siegmund Hanover.

Ursel Hirsch, (1931 Hamburg – 17 July 1942 Auschwitz, murdered), daughter of Siegmund Hirsch.

Warburg, the Hamburg bank M. M. Warburg & co., sometimes given simply as W. or M.M.W. Sometimes W. is a Warburg banker in London.

Warisch, James, and his wife, would later be the parents-in-law of Martha Witmund, first cousin twice removed of Pincus.

Willi Stern (1902 Hamburg – 1961 Cardiff) close family friend.

Chapter 4

THE HAMBURG LETTERS OF 1939

The correspondence at the centre of this book consists of two groups of letters, postcards and draft letters. In this Chapter the first of these, the 'Hamburg Letters', will be described and a translation provided. The second group of letters, the 'Australia Correspondence', will be briefly introduced in Chapter 6 and given in English translation. The original German texts of the letters are to be found in Appendix 1.

The Hamburg Letters were written by Adele and Pincus Hirsch to Siegfried in London from 31 March to 6 September 1939. They consist of 30 letters and 18 postcards and are the property of Siegfried's daughter Adele Lustig of London. In most cases the letters consist of a longer letter by Adele, sometimes with a shorter addition written by Pincus in the remaining space on the page. On occasion, Pincus wrote his letter or the continuation of his letter on a smaller separate piece of paper. The letters and postcards for a given date have here been given a single identification number.

Adele wrote with a fine pen in a clear handwriting that is relatively easy to read (Fig 4.1), while Pincus wrote with a thick soft pencil, which sometimes makes his handwriting difficult to decipher (Fig 4.2). Pincus used soft pencil because he found it difficult to write with a pen on thin air mail paper (David Hirsch to Siegfried, 19 February 1941; Australia Letters No. 50).

The letters and postcards were written in German and, as was common at the time, in a script best described as 'deutsche Schrift' (German script) and are presented here in English translation. The style of German letter writing of the time and particularly that of people of an earlier generation has characteristics that are difficult to represent in modern English translation. Quite apart from expressions that cannot faithfully be translated, the use of punctuation is problematic. Question marks are frequently omitted and where, in English, a full stop would be required, a comma is used. In preparing the translations, a conscious attempt has been made, as far as possible, to preserve the style and the cadences of language of the original. The effect may at first strike the reader as strange but the intention is to preserve not only the sense but also the silenced voices of Adele and Pincus Hirsch.

Hebrew words, transliterated Hebrew words, references to Jewish practices and festivals, abbreviations and contractions are explained in Appendix 3. Abbreviations and contractions that can be identified without further explanation are completed in square brackets.

The many people referred to in the Hamburg letters portray the world of the Hirsch family in the midst of an extended family, as well as many friends and acquaintances. The letters reveal the progressive departure of relatives and friends and the effect on those left behind, who became ever more isolated and lonely. In addition to the extensive and complex network of relatives referred to in the correspondence, many close acquaintances and business colleagues are mentioned. To ease the reader's path through the letters, a *dramatis personae* has been provided in Chapter 3. The relationships of family members to Pincus, Adele and Siegfried, and to each other, will be explained in detail in the third volume of the trilogy. Others mentioned in the letters, who are not family members, are described in a series of short biographies (Appendix 2). Where only a given name is used in a letter, the surname is added, where necessary, in square brackets. When a name in the original is indicated by a single letter, e.g. W[arburg], the name is completed within square brackets. Unfortunately, it has not been possible to identify a number of the people mentioned. Illegible words or phrases are indicated by "....".

While more and more family and friends were leaving Hamburg, normal daily life continued, Shabbat and the Jewish festivals were observed and Pincus Hirsch attended daily and Shabbat services at the New Dammtor Synagogue (*Neue Dammtor-Synagoge*). The maintenance of Hamburg communal life at this time has been described by Miriam-Gillis Carlebach, the daughter of its Chief Rabbi (Gillis-Carlebach 1990, 2009).

In the absence of Siegfried's letters to his parents, it is possible only to surmise what he wrote to them but it is possible to follow, more or less clearly, Siegfried's new life, for the first time far from home. In London he was accommodated by Willi and Betty Stern, old Hamburg friends. After a short time, when the Sterns moved from London to Cardiff, Siegfried found alternative rented accommodation. His life style at this time was very different from that to which he had been accustomed. He had to get used to cold, damp Britain, without the central heating that was at the time already common in Germany. He was short of money and there was a constant search for something to do, when paid work was not a possibility. There are also enigmatic references to the search for a wife. Then there was the laborious effort to learn a new language under the pressure of the forlorn hope that ability fluently to speak and write English might lead to a paid job.

On 3 September 1939, Britain declared war on Germany; the last of the pre-war letters Siegfried received from his parents was written three days later on 6 September 1939.

The Hamburg Letters

[1]
Hamburg, 31.3.39

My Dear Child,

I was endlessly pleased that you phoned in the evening, it gave me a rather good night's sleep, and your postcard of today greatly reassured me, because I saw from it that you obtained permission for the desired stay and that you had a good journey. Often before a journey one is afraid and then one gets over it better than one thought. We, thank God, are well; it is very good that I have much to do these days, so I do not think too much. This morning Bella Petrower said goodbye on the telephone. She is travelling today by boat, you will speak to her there on Sunday. At the jeweller there was a particularly nice man, a Herr Walter, who served us, the tax is 8M and the valuation of the watch an additional 3M yesterday as we thought there was a refusal. At W[arburg] everything was already full, only because Papa is an old colleague, they still accepted it, the gentlemen were all very pleased to see Papa. The discount 10.50, the things must be converted into foreign currency by 31 October, how much they will inform us at the time. Just now your beautiful flowers arrived, a thousand thanks, dear child, I was also endlessly pleased with your dear lines. I will read them again and again and be very reassured and pray to the Almighty that he will fulfil our wishes and soon bring us together again.

Hanna Hirsch is now with us, she arranged the room very nicely, yesterday and today she did many errands for me, which was worth a great deal to me. The parcels from aunty Gella have arrived, I can't write to her anymore today. Give her my warm greetings, I thank her a thousand times. Greetings also to Siegmund and Josi, the children and also Elkeles and wife, have you spoken to the latter, was he approachable? That Nati is not there is a great pity, your letters have been posted. Otherwise there is nothing further to report. Fräulein[1] has not yet been here again.

Now, my beloved boy, I wish you a good 31.3.39, a really good onward journey. Write as soon a possible after your arrival, so that we hear about your journey and arrival. A thousand affectionate regards and kisses from your loving mother.

Kiss

(the two Hannas send hearty greetings)

Hamburg, 31 March 1939

Dear Siegfried!

Yesterday evening there reigned, as you can well imagine, great rejoicing in the Hirsch camp, when your call came. Mama was so happily excited that she forgot to call me to the telephone. I cannot tell you how very pleased I was (and) you did a great Mitzvah by telephoning. It is very nice that you got permission to stay in Amsterdam until tomorrow evening (and) the Almighty will also …. help and grant you *berakhah* and *hatzlaha*. Also many thanks for the beautiful flowers, which we have just received. I wish you no opportunity to ….. Don't forget to fast for half a day[2] on Monday. I wish Josi and …. also …. Elkeles a very good Shabbos and remain with greetings and kiss your loving father.

Also greet dear Siegmund and wife. Convey our thanks to aunt Gella.

Written while Siegfried was still in Amsterdam

[1] Fräulein, lit. Miss, refers to a domestic servant.

[2] The half-day fast was the *Fast of the First Born*.

---

[2]
Hamburg, 3.4.39

My Dearest

I am glad that you landed happily, may the Alm'ghty stand by you that you soon find something satisfying. I hope that you were not annoyed that we telephoned, I am now looking forward to your letter, which will tell us more. We are well, if only longing did not sometimes overtake me, but I master myself, because I have promised you to keep myself healthy. The liqueur chocolates are already much reduced, when I eat one I think of you, since I do this very often each day, you can imagine that they will soon be finished. Yesterday we inaugurated the new gas cooker, it bakes and cooks wonderfully, Else [Hirsch] also baked a cake here, so we were 4 people in the kitchen, that was something for your mother.

When should I actually telephone Mühlenbruck[1] and Nelki[2], let me know some time. I hope in your letter to find out a bit more about cupboard and bed[3], I can probably obtain an iron bedstead. I hear that James Wigderowitsch is also there, does he also live with the Sterns? I also wanted to let you know that the gentlemen at M.M.W[arburg] told us that you should sometime turn to Siegmund W[arburg], who is also in the country, also Mr Minden but I leave that to you. I can imagine that the cold cuts in A[msterdam] tasted so good, we should also get some but Mrs Freundlich kept it all for herself. Today a letter came from Dr. Baer, which I will let you have. This evening Else, Liesel [Nussbaum] and Gotthelf [Hirsch] will be with us, tomorrow for lunch Aunt Harriet [Hirsch], there was much to do but Hanna Hirsch helped me, I would not have managed on my own.

Now my dear I must close for today, more next time, I hope then to be able to enclose a reply coupon. Affectionate regards from me to Sterns and Lanzkrons, also David [Hirsch] and Adolf [Nussbaum]. Have a really good Yom Tov and affectionate greetings and kisses from your mother.

Dear Siegfried

I was really happy to hear that praise God you travelled well and were not sea sick. The dear G-d will also further stand by you. Yesterday I was at the synagogue in Beneckestrasse[4], Carlebach could not speak because he was hoarse, he will speak on the seventh day of Pesach.

I wish you a y"t of blessings, regards from me to Sterns, Lanzkrons, David, Adolf and all dear ones. Keep well and happy and be greeted and kissed by your father who loves you.

Good Yom Tov.

Both Hannas send their regards.

Written on the eve of Passover, hence the intensive activities in the kitchen and the number of relations who will join Pincus and Adele for the Passover meal in the evening.

¹ Egon Mühlenbruck, Eppendorfer Baum 9, was a dentist. It is not clear (see [7]) why Adele was trying to contact him. It may have been that he owed Siegfried money.

² Jul. Nelki, Stuvkamp 9/1, was a dentist who may also have owed Siegfried money.

³ 'Cupboard and bed' is a colloquial reference to domestic arrangements.

⁴ Neue Dammtor-Synagoge (New Dammtor Synagogue), Beneckestrasse, which was functioning again after damage caused during Krystalnacht.

---

[3]
Hamburg 6 April

My Dear Boy

We received your dear letter shortly before Yom Tov, it came very quickly, in contrast to your Shabbos card, which arrived only on Sunday morning. I was endlessly pleased to have heard from you before we sat down to the Seder. How did you, my love, spend the first Yom Tov days? Because the dear little Gotthelf [Hirsch] was at the Seder, we were able to overcome your being far away. He also slept with us and so the breakfast table was also rather lively. For the first lunch Aunt Harriet [Hirsch] was with us and apart from that we had quite a lot of visitors. For lunch today Mrs Oppenheimer ate with us, she brought us a dear letter from Herm[an Möller] and apart from that all sorts from the things he sent. How is it now with your room. David wrote to Else that he had spent a whole day looking with you¹. Did you find anything suitable? I hope it is clean that is my greatest worry. Have you already been able to concern yourself about your luggage, I hope everything arrived in order. If you have your own room with Adolf [Nussbaum], you probably need a great many of your things. I am very excited about your next letter because I think that you will be able to let us know something more about how your life will play itself out in the immediate future. I telephoned Elsa today, the auction will only take place next week after Easter, I will then be notified, I have also enquired at Wissel[2], and as soon as he has notification he will send it to us. I would have liked to enclose a reply coupon but they are only available on Wednesday. Write something about E. Now my dear I must close, because Papa wants to write. Continue to spend Yom Tov well, greet Sterns also Lanzkrons, also Aunty Henny [Landau], David and the children, when you speak to them. Have a thousand affectionate greetings and kisses

From your loving Mummy

My Dear Siegfried!

I hope that you spent *y"t* well. I am curious to hear more about it, I would also have liked to hear whether St. have reported anything about the matter.

Manfred and Else [Nussbaum] visited us on *y"t*, did you speak to David on *y"t*. Did you understand the English sermon? You can well imagine that I am very curious to hear from you. I had a nice letter from Heckscher today. How are you, dear boy, do the English Matzot taste good? It is a pity that one cannot phone every evening. We must be satisfied with the written reports. I hope that these will always be good. Further good *y"t*! With greeting and kiss. Your father who loves you.

Dear Siegfried

As in wakeful dreams your picture hovers

There comes only brightness from deepest darkness!

Sleep in your room, Oh so wonderful,

in the morning at the window twitter finch and starling

At seven Papa raps at the door,

lazy in my bed, I then come to.

Milkman and baker run up and down the stairs.

Yes, I always think: Move out again?

But sunshine and much else compensates

Only goodness the intention of both your parents

Your farewell words are still in mind, with many wishes and greetings,

Hanna H[irsch].

Dear Siegfried, sadly I am not overcome by 'poetitis' like my cousin; so today I send my affectionate greetings, in the hope that you are as well as we. Your Hanna [Wittmund]

The flowers have kept wonderfully. (Adele's handwriting)

---

¹ The search was for accommodation in London, now that the Sterns were leaving London for Cardiff in South Wales.

² Bernhard Wissel, Neuerwall 46, a master goldsmith involved in the valuation of Siegfried's property [see also letters 7 and 8].

---

[4]
Postcard Hamburg 9.4.39

My Dear Siegfried

Many thanks for your dear letter, which we received early to which I will reply in detail after Yom Tov. I hope you received our Shabbat letter. We are well and hope the same of you. Did you get the letter from Dr. B[aer]., will you answer from there or shall I do that from here. Placing a box for the telephone into the bedroom will cost 17-18M. I would like your opinion whether I should have it done, but you must answer immediately in your next letter, because I must give the order.

Now, for today my dear child, good Yom Tov, affectionate greetings from me for Sterns and also Mrs Lanzkron and have affectionate greetings and kisses from your mother.

Many greetings from the Hannahs and Else [Hirsch], who has again baked a cake here.

My Dear Siegfried

I want quickly to send a Yom Tov greeting. Spend the days really well and be greeted and kissed by your father.

Answ. 14/4/39

Mr. Siegfried Hirsch c/o Stern, London N. 4, Queens Road 87

---

[5]
Hamburg 12/4 39

My Dear One

I hope our short card has reached you and also hope that you spent the last Yom tov days as well as we did. We had many visitors again, I believe this news will give much pleasure. Your dear letter was read with a tearful eye. How can it be possible that carriage and customs can cost so much money, who gave this to you. Willi [Stern] or Addie [Nussbaum], tell me this please. It would perhaps have been more correct if we had stored the boxes in the Freeport, but that can no longer be changed. I hope that the further storage will not cost such an awful amount of money. That rooms there are so dirty, I had already heard and worried about. Can you at least take your cases into your apartment or how have you arranged it? How is it with your washing and repairing socks, I wish I were with you to be able to do everything for you.

How is it, have you yet spoken to W[arburg] about business matters or did you not manage to do it because of Yom Tov. Always inform us about everything, whether happy or not, we would like to bear everything with you. Today the enclosed letter from the Association[1], shall I now send the notice of withdrawal to the trade police and what should I tell to the Association? When you write again have my letters to hand, so that you can answer all my questions. Today Miss Gerson was here, she could not come sooner, because her father was ill. She has taken all the 'Platten'[2] to the attic for us and also attended to several matters. She took the packet to Poulson[3] with her, she sends greetings for you, from the 15th she has accepted a position in a household. The day before yesterday a postcard arrived from Rita Nachum, she is well, I will give her your address. Then, when she is in London, she can telephone you. In 8 days also Else [Hirsch] will be leaving us, I am pleased for David [Hirsch], also for you, then you will have someone more with whom to talk matters over. We though are becoming ever lonelier. What is the weather like over there, here at present it is warm and summery, quite unusual for the time of year, if it is like this with you, you will at least not have to freeze. About aunty Lena we laughed heartily. Adolf had already written about it. How is it now with 'cupboard and bed', I would like to hear from you about it. I just remember that Kugelmans are also travelling today, you will probably speak to him over there one day soon. Berta Polack also wants to give me the address of Henry, who is at present in London, she was very sorry not still to have been able to speak to you. That Uncle Emil [Badrian] was 80 today, you will have known from David. We have donated 5M to the Community. You will think, what confusion mother chattering, but I write as things occur to me.

Now, beloved boy of my heart, I must finish, Päppchen wants to have the final page for himself. In case I cannot write again before Shabbos, I already send today affectionate Shabbos greetings. Also regards for all over there and affectionate kisses from your Muttchen

Is it actually Queens Road or Drive?

My Dear Siegfried

Now y"t is over and the time for work begins, if one can get permission. Let us hope for the best, that also this will in some way come true *Bimharo Bjomenu*[4]. You have probably much to tell me and I am really curious about your next reports. Who is the cashier to whom you have to turn for the time being. For the time being going to the synagogue is somewhat….. I hope, dear boy, you are really well and that you have spent the Yom Tov days really well. As Mama has already written, Uncle Emil was 80 years old today. Write him a few good words, he will be pleased with that. In expectation of your Y[om] T[ov] report I remain with greeting and kiss. Your Papa

---

[1] The Association was a professional or trading association.

[2] The meaning of 'Platte' in this letter is not clear.

[3] Poulson was A. Th. Poulson, a Hamburg shipping agent.

[4] The German pronunciation of the Hebrew bimhera beyamenu, meaning "soon in our days".

---

[6]
Postcard Hamburg 16.4.39

My Dear Siegfried

Your dear letter arrived here yesterday Saturday afternoon at 6.30, we were immensely happy with it and with reading it we could chase away time. As long as your time permits, please always write to us in as great detail, you can imagine how every detail interests us, how much we long for your letters. We are well, I hope the same is true of you. The weather here has also changed again, that was predictable. Uncle Manfred and Aunt Else [Nussbaum] have just been here, I believe that in the matter little is to be done. You write that it is so cold I your room, can you not use your lovely camel hair cover and your pullover to keep warm. I hope it will soon be warmer, then this worry will end. Now for today I must end, next time in greater detail. Greet everyone heartily and have affectionate kisses from your mother.

Dear Siegfried

We were immensely pleased that your card arrived before nightfall. Greeting and kiss Papa

---

[7]
Hamburg 18.4.39

My Dear Siegfried

I hope that our postcard of Sunday has reached you and I want to reply to your dear letter in greater detail. I hope that you are well as I can report of us. Your description of London has interested us greatly, I have long read of the great deal of traffic there. Just now I once again have a book in which one can read much …… about England. I am infinitely sorry that you are so cold, my darling, would that I could send you some of the lovely warmth of our apartment. I have already written to you that sending on of your housecoat will not work, perhaps this was as with the old raincoat, which unfortunately Else could not take with her anymore. I gave her the dictionary to take, as also a thousand fond kisses for you. Now she is probably just on the boat, I only spoke to her on the telephone yesterday, the farewell once again hurt me very much, so one dear person after the other leaves and one stays behind lonely. I hope that at long last you have received your belongings, then you will have your lovely warm donkey jacket. I think a lot about your living and domestic arrangements, it is certainly a big change for you, unfortunately many have to suffer this, let this be a consolation to you and don't take it too badly. It is only sad that you are backward with the language but with a little effort you will soon master it. Have you actually spoken to any of the many from Hamburg, and please let us know whether there is any prospect for the plan initiated by *St[ern]*. It will probably not come to anything, otherwise you would have given an indication. I have telephoned Mühlenbruck, I should send in advance on Friday, I shall telephone Nelki this evening. Herr Grunert of Elsas[1] told me that the auction has been deferred, I shall phone again next week, Herr Wissel is waiting for a decision from the currency authority, then we will be sent written postal instruction. Today we will receive the first reduced salary payment, it will be RM 28 less per month, nice isn't it? The chamber of commerce has called to enquire whether your firm has already been liquidated, which we confirmed. Today an invoice came from Sallinger by way of Mühlenbruck, over RM 3.80 from November and January, which surely cannot be correct, you will surely have noticed this when closing your books. I wrote to Mühlenbruck, that you are no longer here, that there must have been a mistake. Still every day pamphlets and recommendations arrive, shall I keep these or can they be disposed of. Papa asks that I should leave space, so for today I must finish. By the way the letter of Good Friday arrived on Sunday morning. Well, now many affectionate greetings and kisses from your Mummy.

Dear Siegfried!

I am pleased to hear that you are well, praise be to God. I hear today that Herr Iska Emanuel has also left for there. It would be very nice if you could learn[3] with him, if he does not live too far away. He learns very well also was ……. very clear. Dear Siegfried I would also request of you, as I have already told you, to deal with everything immediately and not delay, whether it is a business matter or a mitzvah, then know that for every mitzvah one does an angel is created, who supports that person and protects him. I hope always to receive favourable reports from you and remain with greetings and a kiss Papa

Good Shabbos

Dear Siegfried!

With God's will y"t passed for this …time. My thoughts really accompany you always and I hope that you courageously overcome all crises then h"y[4] will also be with you. Thanks to my 'pleasant' presence your dear parents are very lively and Mama is very courageous. I feel very well here and it is reassuring for me to be at the side of your parents.
With many wishes Hanna H[irsch].

[1] Adolf L. Elsas, Rodingsmarkt 82, an auctioneer and valuer with an office in Kaakswiete 1, a small alleyway that no longer exists

[2] These were connected with Siegfried's business interests

[3] In German and Yiddish, the formal study of Jewish religious texts is called 'lernen' (literally, To learn)

[8]
Postcard Hamburg 21.4.39

My Dear Siegfried

We received your dear postcard on Friday morning, because yesterday there was only one delivery. In the meantime I hope that Else arrived there well and you will now have heard by word of mouth about our wellbeing. The letters were immediately written by Hanna today and will be sent together with this card. The matter of Wissel was settled today, about M(ühlenbruck Eppendorfer Baum[1] I will write soon. I hope to hear in detail in your letter of tomorrow how you spend your days and how you spend your time. I know of nothing further for today to let you know. I wish you a really good Shabbos, regards to Sterns, Mrs Lanzkron, David and Else and affectionate greetings for you too from your mother.

I am pleased that the weather is better, as it is here also.

Dear Siegfried

I confirm receipt of your dear letter of the day before yesterday and hope that these lines reach you in the best of health. I do not know for certain whether we have given Kugelmann your address, I believe he was just here for y"t. I am looking forward to the detailed Shabbos letter and, for today, wish you good Shabbos and remain with greetings and a kiss Papa

[1] Egon Mühlebruck, Eppendorfer Baum 9, was a dentist. Adele occasionally used an initial with a street name to identify people, e.g. M. Eppendorfer Baum as in letter 9 below.

[9]
Hamburg 27.4.39

My Dear One

Yesterday evening at 6 o'clock your dear detailed letter arrived, many thanks. Since you wrote in your Shabbos card that you may write on Sunday, Papa was already terribly excited on Tuesday that no letter from you had yet arrived. You know our Päppchen, to imagine something is writ large with him. The letter you received so promptly was posted at 8 o'clock in the morning. In order to obtain a reply coupon, one has actually to be at the post office in Hansastrasse at 8 o'clock on Wednesday morning, there is a colossal rush there. At 8.30 they are all sold out. This week it did not work, because we wanted to wait with the letter writing until your letter arrived. The desired small consignment will leave for you today. Tante Else will attend to it. The other thing was not to be done, I could not force her, perhaps it will soon work with the old raincoat, why do you actually need it? I am very pleased that your appetite is so good and that it tastes so good, it is only a pity that when you are on your way at lunch time you can't have anything warm, I hope that with time you will be able to arrange it.

How do you feel otherwise, do you sleep well and is everything else in order. Oh, my darling, how much I would like to care for you again, the longing overcomes me mightily sometimes, but I always say to myself, keep your chin up. As far as your reports about the particular matter is concerned, we will leave it to the Alm'ghty, he will determine the correct thing for you. Is the correspondence that you have to deal with, business matters or private?

From M. Eppendorfer Baum we received RM 20 last week, I do not know exactly how much he still owes us. Only an arrangement about RM 25, 80 und 100 has to be found. Did he give you anything for us during your last visit. If not, with the last RM 20, he has paid RM 225, so there are still RM 98 to be paid.

I telephoned N. Oberaltenallee[1], he promised to send but did not do so, I will speak to him very severely. Also Elsas is making excuses, nothing more has been sold. I shall go there myself next week. Besides I cannot find a schedule of what is still to be sold. Do you possibly know where I can find this, also I would like to know where Kaakstwiete is, where he lives. The business with your luggage is hair-raising, I would, where

I can, advise against Gärtner[2], it is outrageous that he connected with such inferior firms. Besides, do you think that I should write to Sterns personally and express my thanks. Did you get anything from Addie before his departure? Now on 15 May Elsa Hirsch will travel with the Manhattan and at the beginning of next week Rudolf Glückstadt will be in London with his family. He took his leave of me yesterday, I gave him regards for you. Uncle Elkan and Aunt Dora often come to us in the evening, Aunt Dora read us Else's letter. Hearty regards for David and Else from me, also Sterns and Mrs Lanzkron, Petrowers and also Adolf [Nussbaum]. Papa would like to add something to this sheet of paper, so I must now close. I am already looking forward to your next report, the nicest for me is when I just see your handwriting. So, for today be well my darling, take a thousand greetings and kisses from your Muttchen.

Hamburg 27/4. 39

My Dear Siegfried

Your dear letter gave me particularly great pleasure yesterday, since you notified us of it for the beginning of the week and the same arrived only on Wednesday, you can imagine how pleased I was when it arrived yesterday evening. This week Uncle Erich ....., he told how grandly he was celebrated, first in the synagogue of the orphanage, festive service with sermon by Carlebach and then all sorts of written and personal congratulations, *inter alia* Max Warburg wrote a nice letter and Dr Fritz Warburg sent wine. Surely you also wrote, he already wondered that your congratulations were still missing. How was it with the *aumer* this year, did you forget as often as in Hamburg or was it better. When dear Mama thinks of you, I must always give her something from the nice box and as you can imagine, since she thinks of you often, the box has developed may gaps. As all good thoughts must be reinforced by an act, so it is also with this. Uncle Emil [Badrian] also gave me the address of Max Warburg and I pass it on to you, perhaps you can make use of it.

The address is as follows: M.M.Warburg

London E.C.2 Gresham House

24 Old Broad Street

You probably fill your time with language practice or what else do you get up to?

(Continuation on an enclosed sheet)

Dear Siegfried

Did you by any chance take the Zionswächter[3] with you amongst your books. Mr Kahn would have liked to borrow it, I could not find it. You write that you have so much to tell us that you do not know where to begin. So we still hope to hear many good and interesting things from you. Do you still have the dental business in the programme of future projects or has it been ruled out? Well, dear boy, be very punctual in writing, best greetings and kisses from your Papa

Good Shabbos

---

[1] N. Oberaltenallee is unidentified.

[2] Erich Gärtner a shipping agaent of Altstädter Strasse 17.

[3] Zionswächter, 'Der Treue Zionswächter'. an orthodox Jewish periodical, founded and edited by Rabbi Jacob Ettlinger (1798-1871) of Altona.

---

[10]
Postcard Hamburg 30.4.39

My Dear Siegfried

We received your all too short postcard yesterday afternoon, I hope that you are well. You don't write anything about it. We are well praise G-d, only we have not been out a lot, because the weather was cold and rainy here. Today it is warmer, Papa has just taken a nice walk. I hope that you are not too cold, I would gladly have sent something warm but do not know how I should do this. Else writes that she lives in a room that cannot be heated, this must be very hard with the little children. How is it with your things, are they still in a somewhat usable condition, I hope to hear more about this in your letter. I would also very much like to know how you arrange your time and how it is with progress with your language. Have you not received the parcel from Aunt Else. I hope to have answers to all my questions in your next letter. I must actually already write my letter on Tuesday, because, as I have already written to you, because only on Wednesday can I get a reply coupon, which must immediately be enclosed with the letter. Well, for today again an end. Many, many affectionate greetings and kisses from your Mother.

Send the letter in good time.
Greeting and kiss Papa

[11]
Hamburg 2/5 39

My Darling.

It is now 6.30, I thought that perhaps post, which I can answer immediately would come from you today, I do not want to delay writing, because early tomorrow morning I want to go to Hansastrasse to get a reply coupon. How are you my love. Your last card did not satisfy me, were you annoyed about your things? I hope to hear about it in your next letter. How is it actually with the prospect of a work permit, is there any possibility? You write that you have to be on the road so much and have much correspondence to deal with, is this all about business matters, do St[erns] take an interest in this. I would also once like to know something about your landlady, is she a somewhat nice and clean woman. It is hardly to be believed, that in as big a city as London the arrangements for heating and warm water are still so primitive. Is this so only in your part of the town or also in the better parts. How are you able to get your crockery clean with cold water. Do you at least have washing cloths and towels. Now when you have all your own things, you will find everything, I gave you everything to take. I am worried that you cannot satisfy your appetite as you would like could you not in the morning prepare something, so that you can eat before you leave, or do you not get enough bread. If only I could send you something, I often do not like to satisfy my appetite, when I think of you. I really wonder whether you received the parcel from Aunt Else, as the latter told me, also for Adolf [Nussbaum] not everything arrived. On Friday afternoon, go to Bella, perhaps she has something for you. You should write to me once again how it is with your washing and your socks, whether you have found anyone to do the darning. Have you already seen something apart from the City of London or don't you have time and desire for this. On Shabbos aunt Hedwig will be 70 years old, if you have some spare postage, write her a little card, otherwise I will convey congratulations from you. Siegfried Nussbaum got his visa on Friday, he telephoned us immediately, he will travel on the Manhattan on Friday 15th. Petrowers will follow, probably on 2 June, could you not get some of his agencies or is there not much to be done. Mrs O. would very much have liked your room, she was very disappointed when she heard that it is already occupied, I prefer it this way.

For today, my dear child I must end, I really hope to hear from you tomorrow. Regards to all and you take a thousand affectionate kisses from you Mummy.

Tomorrow it is already 5 weeks that you are away.

Dear Siegfried

Last week I gave you the address of Max [Warburg]. I wanted only to let you know that I heard that several lifts to New York were standing in front Max's apartment, it may be assumed that he will make his permanent residence in New York. I know nothing further about this. I just still want to tell you what Mama has also written to you, that in the morning you should take a piece of bread with you, so that you do not become faint when you go into the City. I am curious to hear more from you about how you are occupied. I remain with greetings and kiss. Papa

---

[12]
Postcard Hamburg 5.5.39

My Dear Siegfried

We received your detailed card of 2 May, since I want to await your detailed letter to reply in detail, for today only that we are thank G-d well and I hope that this is also the case with you. Is Addie still in London, then give him greetings from me and the same to all dear relatives and acquaintances. I certainly hope to hear from you tomorrow, I wish you a really good Shabbos and send you affectionate greetings and kisses. Your Mother

Henry P. is no longer here but he is coming again, his mother will then give me his address.

Dear Siegfried!

I wish you a really good Shabbos   Kiss   Papa

---

[13]
Hamburg 9/5 39

My Dear Siegfried

We received your letter of 5.5 on Shabbos afternoon, heartfelt thanks.

I hope that you also received our Shabbos postcard as well as a parcel, please let us know. I hope that you are well, we too thank G-d are well, only my arm is still giving me trouble, hence my bad writing, tomorrow after a long time I shall go again to Mrs Battenfeld, perhaps she will give me something for it. Naturally, I was shocked that you have been so much robbed, I certainly believe that this occurred at the shipping agent, it is outrageous that something like that can happen, if one hands a firm one's keys on trust. Let us know immediately about the attitude the insurer is taking. I am very pleased that you make a meal in the morning, I have recently had a sample bag from the Reformhaus[1] and arranged it for myself, it tasted extremely good and particularly it is very nutritious. That Adolf [Nussbaum] so quickly got a work placement is marvellous, he is writing home very enthusiastically. You have probably heard how awful for me is the thought of the change and the disturbance[2] I have to suffer here, particularly to dispose of everything and all the work rests on me, since in this respect Papa can give me little help. Now I hope it will not come so soon. Today I bought a nice warm housecoat, which I want to give to Papa for his birthday, I think that he will like it and he will be pleased with it. There was actually at present not much choice, there are more towards winter. On Sunday I am going to the cinema with Tante Else, for the first time since you left, Bel Ami will be shown. Hanna H[irsch] gave a farewell coffee for Elsa [Hirsch], the enclosed card from the participants of the same. Now John and Bella will soon be leaving England to move on, perhaps John can leave behind something warm for you. You can ask him. How is progress with your language, will you soon write us a letter in English. Uncle Manfred and Aunt Else are taking an intensive course, particularly Aunt Else already seems to be well ahead. Today Oberaltenallee sent the first RM 5, after I had telephoned twice, regarding my enquiry about M. and Elsa I hope to hear in the next letter also about your prospects there. We wanted to go to Wilhelminenhöhe[3] over Shavuot[4], but it is still too cold for us, we still have some heating, I want now to book for 14 days in mid-June, what do you think? Is Max W[arburg]. still there, do you want to speak to him before he leaves, or write to him later, naturally in the first place it depends on what your prospects are. As I have heard here, many from Hamburg are moving to Cardiff[5], life there should be much cheaper. Have you already spoken to Kugelmann? Aunt Harriet has just telephoned, she sends greetings and asks whether you have received her parcel.

You now have many questions to answer. Stuff for the next letter.

Well, my beloved boy, for today be well. Have many affectionate greetings and kisses from your Mummy

Many greetings for all there. Our neighbour sends hearty greetings.

Hbg. 9/5 39

My Dear Siegfried

That is a nice business with the Genäwe[6] of your things, hopefully these will be replaced.

I am curious about your next letter, because I hope to learn something of your business prospects. Has David something in prospect? If you don't want to go to Max yourself, you can ask [Ernest] Minden whether he knows whether M[ax Warburg] will stay in London or whether he will go to America. I am surprised that Kugelmann has not visited you. I don't actually know whether he knows your address. Have you spoken to anyone about a possible Shiur?

It is already 10.15, so for today greetings and kiss Papa

---

[1] A vegetarian or health food store.
[2] The prospect of having to move into a Judenhaus.
[3] See Appendix 1
[4] The festival of Pentecost
[5] A reference to the Stern family.
[6] Theft

---

[14]
Postcard Hbg. 12.5.39

My Dear Siegfried. It is 6.30, so far the letter of which you gave notice in your postcard of yesterday has not arrived. I can't wait any longer and want briefly to send my heartiest Shabbos greetings. We are thank G-d well and hope the same of you. Mrs Battenfeld was thank G-d satisfied with my heart, also with Papa. Since she is away for 5 weeks, she has prescribed for almost 13 Mark, very nice, isn't it, it is for my breathing, with Papa for his things which he always has, well, the main thing is that it helps. Hanna Hirsch is just writing to David, that one of you should be concerned for Elsa [Hirsch], who will come from Southampton on Wednesday and then goes on to Manchester, Hanna [Hirsch] sends her greetings to you. I hope for certain to hear from you tomorrow in detail, to get answers to all my questions. You must have much to do, that you always defer writing. For today, again, affectionate greetings and kisses from your Mother.

Many greetings to Sterns and Mrs Lanzkron

Dear Siegfried

I would have many questions. I want to await your letter of tomorrow and for today send affectionate Shabbos greeting Papa

---

[15]
Hamburg 15/5 39.

My Dear Siegfried!

I am writing to you earlier, apart from the Shabbos letter, since dear Mama will still write an extra letter, because I want to raise various questions with you, which I ask you to answer. Your dear Shabbos letter I read with pleasure, from the same of which I saw that you are thank God well, which is most important. Now comes the business aspect, about which you are silent in seven languages. It is nice that you take to heart the saying, 'Silence is golden', but in relation to parents it must have its limits. I know that in England it is very difficult with work permits and therefore one must get used to the idea that for the time being you will not be able to earn anything. I have heard from others that one can make a start with foreign agencies. You have written nothing about whether the other matter has any prospect. Dear Siegfried you must not misunderstand, it is in no way an inappropriate curiosity of mine, rather an expression of fatherly interest. Otherwise, have you found out what the prospects are with respect to your stolen possessions.

Siegfried Nussbaum leaves tomorrow. Has Mr Kugelmann been with you yet? I was pleased to hear that you have been with Dr Spitzer[1] for a shiur[2]. It would be very nice if you could get a permanent shiur, you could not find a better teacher. I would try to have a shiur in Schulchan Aruch[3] or Tenach[4]. Have you spoken to Petrower about his agencies?

45

I ask you please, dear Siegfried, to write something about those of the above mentioned subjects, about which you can give information, I would be very grateful.

I remain for today, with affection greeting and kiss. Your Papa

My Dear Siegfried. I wanted to write to you in detail today but Leo [Wittmund] was with us and I did not get round to it, since, because of the reply coupon, the letter must go off tomorrow morning, I must be brief, more G-d-willing for Shabbos. I hope you are well and cheerful, we too are thanks to G-d well. Naturally, Papa is impatient, he wants to know more about your prospects, he will not be persuaded that this will not go quickly and is altogether difficult, so I let him write, you will know best what you can say. I hope to hear from you again tomorrow, very soon and in detail, it is the nicest thing for me if a really long letter like the last arrives. Today a Feodora[5] left directly from the shop, Elsa may also have a bar for you, write when your stores are exhausted, otherwise it will become too old.

It is 10 o'clock and soon bedtime, so for today most affectionate greetings and kisses from your Muttchen

---

[1] Rabbi Dr Alexander Spitzer, Hamburg lawyer, later a rabbi in London
[2] lit. 'a measure', a study session
[3] Standard code of Jewish law
[4] The Hebrew bible.
[5] A brand of chocolate

---

[16]
Hamburg 19.5.39

My Dear Boy. Your dear postcard arrived at just at 10 o'clock on Friday, it was probably delivered only today because of the holiday, I hope that in the meantime you received our letter with reply coupon. Your last detailed letter arrived on Shabbos at half past 6 with the last post, we hope that tomorrow we will hear from you again in detail. I hope that you are well, we too thank G-d are well and happy. My arm has improved, this week I saw Professor Hansen about my eyes. He said that these are good thank G-d, I only have a severe conjunctivitis for which I got drops, and apart from that my spectacles are no longer strong enough. I bought very modern spectacles with very good Zeiss lenses, if you could see me with them, you would like me a lot, I surely look like an English lady. I hope that I will still become one. In any case keep us in continuous touch, whether in a foreseeable time there is a prospect for us. I am very pleased that you can occupy yourself in an honorary capacity, it will give you satisfaction, I hope that soon there will be a prospect of other jobs. How is it now with the insurance, will you get everything replaced, write to me again how it turned out with the handkerchiefs, Aunt Dora [Hirsch] is not here at the moment, if you get it replaced, I would buy some over there. They are surely better than your old ones here. How is it with your typewriter, is something wrong with it seemed to me that Aunt Else made a remark about it. The business with the washing is really a catastrophe, it would be a shame if your good things were so quickly ruined, here Mummy would be in her place. How is it with the language, are you making progress? I thought it nice that you already made a small outing, was it together with Germans or English people? That Addie helps you so much pleases me from my heart. He is really an upright friend. You wanted to let me know some time whether I should write directly to the Sterns to thank them. On Sunday afternoon we were for coffee at Uncle Max [Nussbaum] in order once again to be with Siegfried, the latter left reasonably cheerful. Incidentally, Uncle Max will be 60 years old on Tuesday, if you can send him a little postcard, it would actually have to be here on Tuesday morning, because they, as also Uncle Manfred and Aunt Else are going to Wilhelminenhöhe for Shavuot. If Uncle Elkan and Aunt Dora do not come back from Leipzig[1] by then, we will be alone for Yom Tov. As I have already written to you, I was at the film Bel Ami with Aunt Else, it was very charming and for two hours we were much amused. Unfortunately there are also moments when one is very sad and depressed, when in summer one is on the street, so it was this week when I passed David's earlier apartment and I saw extensive scaffolding. Also many things go through my head, oh my darling, I miss you at every step. Have you in the last few days been at Bella, otherwise go to her and ask whether she has anything for you. Let me know about that immediately. Regards from both the Hannas. Yesterday Aunt Bella brought the enclosed letter. Papa said today that the father of Max Levin died suddenly, I assume that he knows, in any case show your concern for him. This week I bought myself a nice blue hat and a Turkish scarf, I had great need of both. I hope to hear from you again in detail tomorrow and to have answers to various questions. Since Papa also wants to write, I must finish for today, about linen prices, Elsas etc. in the next letter. Well, good Shabbos and a thousand affectionate kisses from your Muttchen.

Dear Siegfried

Dear Muttchen has written everything today, also I also only send affectionate Shabbos greeting and Kiss. Papa

---

¹ They were visiting their daughter, Erna Sussman's family in Leipzig in anticipation of their emigration to England

---

[17]
Hamburg, 22.5.39

My Dear One

We received your dear letter still on Shabbos afternoon, I hope that also our Shabbos letter was in your possession in good time. With regard to Papa's enquiries, I have already written to you that these were not in my mind, because I knew that you will not keep anything secret from us and, as you did here, will tell us everything. I was, as you can imagine, rather downcast by your lines, though I have already heard here, that for persons who have come under guarantee, permission to work is difficult to obtain, so I thought that it might be more possible through Willi St[erns] connection to obtain it for you. Apart from that you are quite right, you must first know the language properly, and then we must not loose courage, trust in G-d, the Almigh'ty will stand by you and let you find the right thing. The main thing above all is that you are and remain healthy, I am happy, as I have already written to you, that you can occupy yourself in an honorary capacity. We are thank G-d well, I am pleased when I have a good deal to occupy me, so that my thoughts cannot 'walk about' so much. Last week we got 3 packs of butter and cheese, it is really generous of her and, think of it, on Friday morning, addressed to Hanna Hirsch a package with the contents that you always [illegible] get on Friday evening. We ate it immediately on Friday at lunch with tossed potatoes and cucumbers, you can imagine how invigorated we were. Have you already heard anything from Lotte Solling and have you been to see Professor Türkheim, has Mr Kugelmann been in touch? This evening Mrs Oppenheimer is with us and on the second day for lunch Martha

Wittmund[1]. We congratulated Uncle Max by telephone, he is at work this afternoon and he goes to Wilhelminenhöhe. We gave him 6 linen handkerchiefs. Far too generous isn't it? Have you written to him? He told me on the telephone that he had a postcard from Adolf [Nussbaum] in fabulous English, don't you sometimes speak English to him. Have you delivered the handmade things, do the things fit the children.

I telephoned Elsas last week, he has sold for about 19 M for us, after the holidays I shall go there personally to compare what is still there. Now I want to let you know the desired linen prices, as far as I know them at present.

Shirt, white 45 (Pfennig?) white collar 10, stiff collar 15, pyjama 60, handkerchief 5, 17 socks 10, (duvet)case 40, sheet 30, coffee table cloth 45, about wool and net underwear, pillow case I have still to enquire, will tell you later.

The weather here is lovely today, I hope it stays like this for the next few days. After the holidays let us agree a telephone call, I must hear your voice again.

For today beloved boy I must close. Have a really good Yom Tov and have a thousand affectionate kisses from your Muttchen.

Dear Siegfried!

I thank you for your the answer to my questions. I am sorry that Mama was not satisfied with it but I had to hear from you about it. Now I also wish you a right good *y"t*. If there is cheese cake there, really enjoy it but don't eat too much of it. G-d-willing I hope to hear from you tomorrow. For today, hearty greetings and + y"t kiss. Papa

---

[1] The guests were for Shavuot [Pentecost] on 24 and 25 May 1939.

---

[18]
Postcard Hamburg 26.5.39

My Dear Child. We received your two dear postcards and I also hope that our letter and that to Sterns arrived there in good time, the latter had already left when your card with reference to it arrived. We spent Yom Tov well and are today thank G-d well. This morning a number of things have given me cause for concern. Aunt Else told me on the phone that Adolf [Nussbaum] had written that you would now eat in the public canteen. How did this happen, did Sterns require this of you. Naturally I am very worried, whether the food is sufficient for you, whether in this way you can maintain your strength, because one does not know whether you can earn anything at all over there and how long it will take until you can afford other food. He also wrote that you have to sleep together and that you have mice. Oh, it is a tragedy about you there, one does not like to afford oneself anything when one thinks of you out there. Is Max W[arburg] still there, can you not some time speak to him about yourself. Write to me in detail how you are getting on, whether you get satisfied and whether you feel strong. Soon Liesel, David and Else are coming there. If possible I shall give her something for you. On Tuesday, G-d willing, I will again send you something to nibble, has that from the shop now arrived. I await soon your detailed information, good Shabbat and a thousand kisses from your worried about you Muttchen

Dear Siegfried

The matter is also inconceivable for me. How does it make sense? For today greeting and Kiss   Papa

Good Shabbos

---

[19]
Hamburg 30.5.39

My Beloved Siegfried

Hearty thanks for your dear Shabbos letter, which as always arrived here by the last post. I hope that also our letter is with you and excitedly await your reply to the same, I also hope to receive replies to my other questions, I would very much like to have a picture of your life over there, also as far as I can remember I asked various questions. Also my dear take some time and write to us about all that we would like to know. As I have already written to you we spent a good Yom Tov, I received lovely flowers such as lilac, lilies and tulips, I also baked a nice cheesecake of which I would have liked to send you a piece, in this respect it was as always, and so it was also in your mind, wasn't it? In the first day we were with Dr Carlebach and on the second at Parkallee[1] and so it was for us, since we also …. table visitors, not all so lonely. You also write to me how you spent the days, whether you were invited and so on.

Now to the contents of your last letter. The refusal by Dr. [Fritz] W[arburg] I had actually expected, even if there was a small glimmer of hope to the contrary. I only cannot understand, if he has made the prospect of a possible guarantee for a home for 12 pounds a month, he could give this sum in another way (besides, which I find very high for a home, since here one can get a private hotel). One can naturally not judge at all from here and as you have already written, the whole thing is for the time being only plans, you will surely keep us continuously informed, when it is safe to speak about it one can further correspond about it. I would be infinitely pleased if you could achieve something profitable for yourself, I ask the Almigh'ty daily that he support you.

This morning Liesel took her leave of us, she travels tomorrow, perhaps you can speak to her, I gave her something for you to nibble, I myself similarly sent something off for you. Have you once again been to see Bella, ask her whether she has anything for you. We have written to Max Levin, I hope that the card has arrived, also the letter to the Sterns. Now, at 5 o'clock, I continue to write the letter. In the meantime I was at Warburg with Papa, we had an answer by telephone but should one of these days collect currency from Jeweller Hintze[2] in exchange. It was valued all together at 385 Marks, so by 31 October about Pounds 20 should be sent, I don't know how exactly it is calculated, in any case this is not possible, and it will then be sold, only with the difference that in the meantime we had RM 60 expenses. If we had known that the redemption had to be so soon, you would probably not have advised the deposit. Well, what has been done can no longer be changed. I have also been to Elsas, were paid the RM 19.40. Mr Grunert told me that he had a lump sum offer for the remaining things, he very much advised me to accept, because he cannot get rid of the things separately, as a result of standing around for a long time they would not improve, so I agreed. Cupboard and bedstead etc., will be collected next week. I am sending the letter already today because I would like to close, since for the reply coupon one has to send it open to the post office. Papa will write you an extra few lines, we then want to enclose the coupon. Now, my dear boy, the four pages are soon full, so for today the end. I await your news soon and send you a thousand kisses

Your Muttchen

Hamburg 30/5 39

My Dear Siegfried!

For your dear letter heartfelt thanks, I am pleased that praise God you are well and that you had a good Yom Tov. Dear Mama already wrote that thank God we are well and that we praise God spent the days well. Also about the matter of M.W. Mama has already written to you, nevertheless, that we await soon a detailed letter about our diverse questions. Look over the letters received from us and you will remember the questions you still have to answer. My gold watch was valued at RM 100, I would very much like to exchange it but it will not be possible. The Rav[3] spoke very well on Yom Tov about Megillat Ruth[4], we also visited him on the second day. I look forward with pleasure to your detailed letter and remain with greeting and kiss your father who loves you.

I wish you a good Shabbos

---

[1] The address of Pincus's sisters, Harriet and Rosalie
[2] Otto Hintze a long-established (1866) Hamburg jeweller
[3] Term for a rabbi, here refers to Chief Rabbi Carlebach
[4] The biblical Book of Ruth that is read in the synagogue on Pentecost

---

[20]
Postcard Hamburg 2.6.39

My Dear Siegfried

We received your dear postcard yesterday Thursday afternoon and the contents somewhat reassured me. I expect more detail in your next detailed reply letter. I would ask you always to write your postcard on Tuesday, so that we have it on Wednesday. Papa always makes such a fuss if there is no post here on a Wednesday afternoon. You know your Päppchen. Also you might start your Shabbos letter on Thursday, then you would have more time to write in detail. You can imagine that we would like to have everything answered. We are thank G-d well, also the weather here is lovely. I hope it stays like that when we go to Wilhelminenhöhe next week. During Yom Tov the food there was simply fabulous, the people were all enthusiastic. Uncle David and Aunt Else went there today to help. We had a postcard from Else, we were surprised that David did not add anything. Have you been to Bella and were you pleased. Chocolate left here, Liesel probably brought some too, Bella also has some, enjoy it. I wish you a really good Shabbos and send you affectionate greetings and kisses Mama

I wish you a right good Shabbos

Greeting and kiss   Papa

Answ. 6.6.39

---

[21]
Postcard Hamburg 9/6 39

My Dear Siegfried. Your dear postcard arrived yesterday Thursday morning, I hope that our letter of Wednesday is in your possession. We are thank G-d well, only I am an unlucky person, I have a root infection and am being treated by Dr Streim[1] (who sends his best regards). I have rather a lot of pain. We are due to go to Wilhelminenhöhe on Wednesday but I will probably not be able to travel. Dr Streim thinks that it will not be better by then. That one calls really bad luck. I will write to you on Monday where to address the post. I am pleased that Bella gave you so many presents. She intended to give you her old black raincoat with an embroidered frieze lining, ask her about it sometime. It is good that you received the chocolate, perhaps you will get some more this week. We gave Uncle Elkan [Hirsch] a nice basket of Cigarillos, also Cognac, chocolate, and various conserved fish etc. Hanna Hirsch decorated it very nicely with crepe paper. I am very pleased that you once again played tennis. If your time permits do it more often. I hope to hear from you tomorrow. For today I wish you good Shabbos and send my affectionate regards and kisses Your mother

Dear Siegfried

I wish you a right good Shabbos

Affectionate regards and kiss Papa

---

[1] A dentist and close friend of the family

---

[22]
Postcard Hamburg 12/6 39

My Dear Siegfried

As always we received your dear letter, many thanks, I was very pleased that my fears were groundless. The purpose of our card today is to let you know that unfortunately we will only be able to travel on Thursday. Dr Streim hopes by then to be able to put in a temporary filling. At least since Shabbos I no longer have any pain. But it is bad luck all the same, because we will probably also have expenses, because out there there is a great demand for rooms and we will have to compensate Mr Frank, but that cannot be changed. Dr Streim was here twice on Saturday to have a look at me. I thought it simply remarkable. By the way we have just been to Uncle Elkan to congratulate, after that he came (to us) again in the afternoon. Since yesterday the weather has changed, it is cool and rainy, it is probably the same with you. Your last card reached us only on Thursday morning, you really wanted to know. Tomorrow, G-d willing, I will write again, so for today also affectionate greetings and kisses from your mother.

(*written up side down above the address*)

Mrs Oppenheimer will telephone John from here at half past 7, if possible be there.

Dear Siegfried!

I am glad that dear Mama's pains have stopped

Greeting and kiss   Papa

---

[23]
Hamburg 13. June 39

My Dear Siegfried. I hope that my card of yesterday has reached you and praise be to G-d today I can report that the improvement in my teeth has fortunately been maintained, I hope it stays like that, so that we can travel on Thursday, then we will be able to keep the room for 14 days, from the 29th it is occupied again. The various information in your last letter interested me a lot and I await with excitement your further report about your undertakings. In your next letter let me know what happened about the insurance, whether you had everything replaced and whether you bought anything again. I would also like to know how you actually accommodated your suits, whether they get so creased. Was the outing on Sunday nice, have you already once been in Hyde Park? I would also like to know how it is with your health, whether everything, digestion etc. is in order. Now the curious Muttchen has again posed so many questions, how should they all be answered. Stop, here comes another one, how is it with the language, can you make yourself better understood? Leo [Wittmund] has just been here, he and Martha [Wittmund] have been summoned to be informed about a visa, which also means to take leave of these two. I hope that you can arrange to be with John tomorrow evening, then we will, if you get this letter, have spoken personally. Are you sorry that the two are leaving, or have you not been together with them, I hope to hear something from you about his farewell gift. Last week we bought a Lüsterjacket[1] for Pappchen and similarly we had him measured for boots. Mr Falke, our foot doctor, has recommended a shoemaker. The birthday evening meal for Uncle Elkan was very nice, we had fried plaice with mixed salad, bread butter and cheese and lemon pudding with strawberries. In 14 days James Mathiason will also come there, I always spoke to him at the dentist. Have you by any chance spoken to Dr Nathan, he brought a Kindertransport over there. We now chatter a lot in English, because Hanna wants to practise the language and we join her. The weather has probably also changed for you, there it is usually as it is here. At Uncle Elkan there were a lot of visitors on Shabbos, that was really something for your uncle, less so for your aunt, by the way I gave the latter something. How did David's apartment turn out, did he somehow get the furniture together, regards to the two of them from me. This week we got to read a letter from Mrs Simreich, she is not very enthused, making a living is very difficult there, she asks after us and you, I should send regards for you from Mrs Markus, Alice's mother and from the neighbours on our floor, who constantly enquire after you, similarly from the lady upstairs. So, now the material for today is finished, a little space must be left for Päppchen. Keep well and have affectionate greetings and kisses from your Muttchen. (If you hear nothing further, send your next letter to Wilhelminenhöhe, Rissener Landstr. 127.)

Dear Siegfried!

Apart from matters about which you have already been informed, I have been measured for an overcoat and will have the same made when

G-d willing we return from Wilhelminenhöhe. What is studied with Dr Spitzer? Write to me about it. Have you already heard the rabbi and did you understand something of it? Is it Minhag Ashkenaz[2] or Minhag Polen[2] in London?

It was rather cold here today and one should probably take winter clothes to Wilhelminenhöhe. You Papa greets and kisses you

Shabbos and Sunday is Rosh Chodesh[3]. Don't forget to say Hallel[4]

I wish you a right good Shabbos.

---

[1] Probably a jacket made of a shiny material

[2] Minhag, custom. Minhag Ashkenaz is the liturgical custom of Frankfurt-on-Main. Minhag Polen, literally the custom of Poland, which was widespread in Germany and Britain.

[3] Rosh Chodesh, the first day of the lunar month

[4] Joyous prayer consisting mainly of Psalms recited on Jewish festivals and dating from Temple times

---

[24]
Postcard Blankenese 16.6.39

My Dear Siegfried

It was a great joy finally when I heard your voice again, if it were not so expensive I would telephone more often. Since yesterday afternoon we are now here in Wilhelminenhöhe. We have a nice sunny room, naturally the first night I hardly slept. But instead this morning I lay for 3 hours in a deckchair under pine trees, it was simply wonderful. Many visit here, very many acquaintances, introductions are hardly necessary. Hardly had we ended the telephone conversation on Wednesday, Uncle Elkan and Aunt Dora came and told us about David, we had a great shock. I hope he will achieve satisfaction. Just as we were sitting comfortably at supper, he had an operation. Heartfelt greeting to both of them. I wish a recovery, I will write myself next week. I hope that instead of the omitted card we will have a detailed letter from you, though the same will probably only arrive on Sunday. Did Petrowers leave in good order. Mrs Oppenheimer was very nervous. Now my dear I wish you a good Shabbos and send you affectionate kisses   Your mother

My Dear Siegfried!

You can imagine, that I too was very shocked, when I heard of David's operation. I am now a *Kurgast*[1] Wilhelminenhöhe. I hope the weather remains good. I wish you a right good Shabbat affectionate greeting and kiss   Papa

---

[1] Kurgast, visitor at a watering place

---

[25]
Blankenese, 20.6.39

My Dear Siegfried

We received your dear letter at the same time as your postcard on Sunday morning, hearty thanks for your dear lines. I hope that you received our postcard and also our last letter of the previous Tuesday with the reply coupon. You mention nothing about it. Thank G-d we feel very well here, the food is very good and plentiful and we spend almost all day in the open, mostly we lie in our chairs and look at the air, for me this is an ideal. In the morning for first breakfast we get 2 rolls, as much white and black bread as we want, butter and marmalade, cocoa or coffee and every day fruit, apple banana or orange, at lunch there are three courses, in the afternoon tea and cake and in the evening plentiful cold cuts, fried potatoes, vegetable salad etc. so you can see that one can stand it here very well. About the quota number (Wartenummer) I immediately telephoned Aunt Else but up to today have not received any forms. When I think that we may not see each other again until you can one day invite us from America, I could despair, I hope that it will be successful in another way. We wrote to David yesterday, I hope that he will improve further. It is very nice of aunt Henny that she often invites you for a meal, Rosalind has surely become a nice girl. Have you got to know anyone else of the family Landau? Or do you not have the opportunity to pay visits. That Gertrud W. is over there I had already heard, she was lucky, in Antwerp she was not allowed to work. My dear, you will not be cross with me if I do not write more today, it is soon time for coffee and before that I have to shave Papa. I hope to hear from you soon, for today affectionate kisses from your Muttchen

My Dear Siegfried!

I was very pleased to hear that Gerhard W went to [Ernest] Minden, one can see again the value of patronage, since so many cannot manage to get permission to work. I have not given up hope that you too will one day get it. Well further to trust in God.

We like it very much in Wilhelminenhöhe. I hope that the stay will do Mama good.

Affectionate greeting and kiss   Papa

---

[26]
Blankenese, 23.6.39

My Beloved Siegfried

We received your dear yesterday and I also hope that our letter is in your possession. We are thank G-d well, we are relaxing, *unberufen*[1], excellently here, we spend all day in the open in a deckchair (my ideal), food good, have pleasant company, so what more do we want. As you wished we are staying a few days longer, that is until Sunday in 8 days, from Monday the room is booked, there is great demand, there are even various people here from Berlin, I hope the weather will continue as wonderful so that we can further exploit it. Dr Plaut has just been here, he told us that he spoke to you over there, that he found you looking well, about which we were naturally very pleased. Aunt Harriet was very glad that she had a response to her advert, through Aunt Else she was able to have both matters settled, she thanks you very much and will write next week, I would be very pleased if she is successful. One does not know how long it will last here, it would be a crying shame if it were to end. You have probably heard that Herm has had a boy. Mrs Oppenheimer wrote to me from Frankfurt, I still want to congratulate both of them today. The form[2] has been sent to the consulate, the number will not be a very low one. I think they are already at 19,000. We had a card from David [Hirsch] today, have you read same, we were greatly amused. Thank G-d that he does not lose his sense of humour, give him and Else our heartfelt regards and tell him that we were very pleased. It is nice that you were pleased with the things from John, it is a pity that you don't like the handkerchiefs, he probably could not get others, it is silly that he had to pay so much customs for his cousin's things. This week chickens were distributed as a donation by Mr Bialoglowski, we were also entitled but had to do without. On Monday the first holiday children arrive, a number of 80, it will probably become quite lively.

I hope that tomorrow we will get the promised detailed letter with answers to all our questions. What I would also very much like to know is whether you still have any connection with the respective family, you will know what I mean, please write about it sometime. Päppchen is just making a wonderfully beautiful snore concert, he can do this here particularly well, I get up as often as 3 times a night to nudge him, our beds are not side by side.

I also wish you a right good Shabbos and send you many, many affectionate kisses your Muttchen

My Dear Siegfried!

At the moment there are so many gentlemen here that we can pray with a minyan every day, which, as you can imagine, pleases me very much and is also very convenient for Mr Frank, who is again an *ovel*[3] and so has the opportunity to lead the prayers.

It speaks for itself that I am very pleased about the report by Dr Plaut of which dear Mama has already written to you, and I hope that your opinion of the prospects corresponds. I had real pleasure from David's postcard, one can see from it that despite all the unpleasantness he has not lost his humour and has kept his *ḥen*[4].

I must still change for Shabbos, so send only most affectionate Shabbos greetings and remain with greeting and kiss, Papa

Mazal Tov for the birth of the little Oppenheimer

Soon with you Amen!

---

[1] 'Let it be unsaid', has the meaning, lest it bring bad luck.

[2] Application to immigrate to the United States

[3] Avel, a mourner, ovel is the German pronunciation

[4] Hebrew for *charm, grace*

---

[27]
Blankenese 27.6.39

My Dear Siegfried

Your Shabbos letter of this week we already received on Shabbos morning, which gave great pleasure, I hope that you received our letter in good health. We are as before also thank G-d well, everyone finds us looking very well thank G-d. Until Shabbos the weather was simply wonderful, it is now cooler, nevertheless in spite of that well wrapped up we always spent almost 4 hours in our deckchairs. This morning we had a wonderful walk with Mr. and Mrs. Warisch and Mrs. Bundheim to Sonneneck through pine forests. From there we had a splendid view of the Elbe. I had no idea that this is such a beautiful area, it is sometimes just as in the Harz. Since yesterday 80 holiday children are here, because of this naturally it is noisier but one gets used to it. On Sunday evening, G-d willing, we are returning home, together with Mr and Mrs Willi Sänger, who have already been here for several weeks, we will hire a car that will take us and our luggage home. On the way here we had a carrier recommended by Mr Frank for our luggage while we travelled by tram, Hochbahn and car, which cost us even more. Apart from the guests already mentioned, there are also here Mr Siegmund Cahn and wife, the present Oberkantor[1], Mr Aron, various young girls from Hamburg and guests from Berlin and Frankfurt. Tomorrow Aunt Hedwig's sister Toni and her two children, they were here yesterday to rent. How is it that you have still not heard from the insurance, perhaps Elkeles who, as I have heard from Miss Rosskamm, is once again in Amsterdam, can undertake something in the matter. A very nice man from the business police visited us, who wanted to see your office, whether there is anything in it, when he saw that it was arranged as a bedroom, he laughed and was reassured. When I asked him about confirmation for the (trade) association he said this would come directly from him. Apart from that in the newspaper your firm was officially notified as dissolved. I have not heard from Berta Polack for long time, when I enquired from her, she told me Henry is in America but would once again come to Europe. That I have to draw on the reserves for our use is natural, because as much as it comes to in a month, I can with the best of will not reduce (expenditure) but for the time being it is thank G-d still enough. The Salinger firm apologised, they had made a mistake. I telephoned Eppendorfer Baum again, he wanted to send something one of these days, I don't know whether in the meantime he has done it, similarly N. Oberaltenallee. I have in the meantime found all the dispositions and I am fully in the picture. With Elsas I could achieve nothing further, it agrees exactly with your list, I could have refused but nothing very different would have emerged, when I am back I will call again. The report about your landlady does not exactly fill me with enthusiasm but for the time being you must accept it.

Now, my dear I must close for today, the postman who takes the mail with him is coming now. So, for today have affectionate greetings and kisses from your Muttchen who thinks a lot about you

Dear Siegfried!

Today I can only send you an affectionate greeting, because Mama is urging that the letter goes.

So greeting and kiss Papa

---

[1]   The communal official who leads synagogue prayers, The hazzan or reader, was called the Kantor in Germany, a term probably derived from its use in the Church. When there was more than one Kantor, the most senior was the Oberkantor (lit. 'chief Kantor').

---

[28]
Blankenese 29.6.39

My Dear One

Your dear detailed letter we received yesterday Wednesday morning, a lady brought it to us when we were already lying in our deckchairs and then we had a nice job to read it. Naturally it interested me very much, I now get a better picture of your life there. I am pleased that you can afford yourself better food and occasionally an egg. So at least you will maintain your strength. I cannot tell you anything yet about strawberry prices, because there are no shops here and so I cannot find out. How very much I would once again like to eat Knackwürste[1], during last Shabbos we had meat, everyone a slice, tasting very good, the first time since Josef's Barmitzvah Shabbos. I believe that I have put on a lot of weight, I eat and drink a lot more than at home, particularly every afternoon tea and cake. We have to pay 9 Mark per day for us both, so we would rather make an end, rather G-d willing perhaps to come here again for Succot[2]. I also don't know whether the filling in my tooth can stay for longer, it now and again draws attention to itself. Since yesterday Toni and children

61

are here, the boy will go to Sweden on hachsharah[3]. Toni will take him to Berlin next week, he is a nice boy, you will also know him from Hamburg times. By the way, did you hear that Siegfried Nussbaum's job came to nothing, when he arrived, Mr Stern had just had to dismiss 15 people and so could not take him on. He has now found something, I believe in a hotel, I cannot quite make sense of Toni's account. You write in reply about your suits that I think of everything, you cannot imagine my dear child, how often and how much think of you, may the Alm'ghty allow, as you also write, that our separation does not last too long. I forgot, by the way, to tell you in my previous letter that we have already had a reply from the American consulate and namely the numbers 17,333 and 34 and that our turn will come in an unforeseeable time, with G-d's help we hope that we will not have to wait for an unforeseeable time before we see each other again.

How is David, is he home again and what reply did they get at the consulate? As much as I would be pleased for him if Else could soon follow David, I would be sorry for you. It is so nice that from time to time you can eat with her, she cooks so well, also that she does your washing and the darning of your socks, it is altogether for me reassuring that you have a home life with them. Hans and Erna will also probably come over there, we had a postcard from them in reply to our birthday wishes. Why have you not yet written to Uncle Elkan, I think that he is very offended, if you have not yet done it, make up for it immediately. I am sorry that the language does not work for you, you usually grasp things so easily. You must overcome your inhibitions when speaking, just chatter on, in that way you learn most quickly, it does not matter if you are sometimes laughed at. Here everyone is learning English, everyone is speaking of emigration possibilities, the public here is changing very much, because many people stay here for only 8-10 days, today Dr Carlebach is coming with several children, have you spoken to Frau Dr.[4] over there. To come back to your information about the lunch, I think it simply fabulous, what you can get over there for 2 pennys, I would advise you if your time and money permit always to go there, I would note again that first of all the main thing is that you further look after your health. It is silly that your landlady does not place much value on cleanliness, anyway it is something that at least she is not economical with bed linen. I hope to hear from you again tomorrow, the next news you should again send home. If you can, always write in great detail, I am interested in every triviality, it is my greatest pleasure, to reread your letters and postcards over and over again. Well, for today an end. A really good Shabbos and affectionate greetings and kisses from your Muttchen.

As you may imagine your chocolates are long finished but in the meantime I have had others but they do not taste as good as those you gave.

Dear Siegfried!

We received a postcard from Uncle Elkan today in which he writes, Siegfried seems completely to have forgotten about us. Write to him immediately on Sunday. You know that he places great value on such things. I still have to change for Shabbos, so for today only hearty greetings and kisses from Papa.

About the Zionswächter I was mistaken, the paper is called the Orient, which I have in the meantime found.   Good Shabbos

---

[1] Saveloy

[2] The festival of Tabernacles

[3] Literally, *preparation*, agricultural training for emigration to Israel

[4] Mrs Carlebach, wife of the Hamburg Chief rabbi.

---

[29]
Hamburg, 4. July 39

My Dear Siegfried

Since Sunday evening we are again at home. It was very nice in Wilhelminenhöhe. The food was excellent and apart from a few cool days we had good weather. On the last Shabbos we were honoured to have Chief Rabbi Dr Carlebach with us and he also pleased us with a sermon, namely on account of the Bar Mitzvah of Johannan Levisohn's son in Antwerp. The parents were in Wilhelminenhöhe. The Rav also spoke at table and because of that Shabbos was particularly hallowed. In the afternoon the Rav went with our gentlemen to Hamburg to the Oneg Shabbos[1] and on Sunday evening at 6 o'clock there was a wedding in the synagogue, so the rabbi had to travel back. We then travelled back to Hamburg at 9 o'clock with Mr and Mrs Sänger. It was very comfortable and at 9.30 we were again at home. We have not yet bought the material for the overcoat but will do it in the next days, I will have it made at

Rappaport, he got permission to work for an Aryan tailor. It is 12 o'clock, so far the fast is good, I think that I will be able to complete the fast. For today I remain with greeting and kiss   Papa

My Darling. This time we received your dear letter on Shabbos morning, hearty thanks. Now we are again at home and I like to think back to the lovely days in Wilhelminenhöhe. It was so nice that we were favoured by the weather, even if it was a bit cooler, I lay in the deckchair well wrapped up. Last Shabbos Papa has already written, in the evening after Shabbos we sat with many other guests around Dr. C[arlebach] until round 12 o'clock, he told Dontjes[2] and funny things that had happened to him, we all laughed heartily. On Shabbos there were, including staff, 55 adults and 70 children to feed. Aunt Harriet is completely exhausted, she does not have the right help, it is time that she gets something else, unfortunately she has so far not had a reply to her application. Toni went to Berlin with Hans and Aunt Hedwig, tomorrow the boy travels to Sweden and Aunt Hedwig will go for several days to Wilhelminenhöhe. What you write about the matter with the family referred to, I would ask you under no circumstances in any way to consider out of concern for us to go into the matter if she does not accept. Too much would depend on it, if one ties oneself for life and is not completely satisfied, so no hurried decisions, you are right, it all happens as it is determined by G-d. That there are so many fires over there is awful, you have probably not seen anything of them, I assume it is far away from you. On Thursday Erna comes here, in the meantime Hans has gone to his mother in Vienna, if it works out they will still travel over there on the 12th. Do you sometimes speak to Siegmund Hanover and have you written to Uncle Elkan? That citizenship for Hanna Hirsch did not work, I think I already wrote to you, she once again turned to Mrs Witter over there, whether she achieves anything, I do not know, everyone has his own worries. I hope to hear from you again soon. Greetings to the Sterns and all relatives and acquaintances and you take a thousand affectionate kisses from your Muttchen.

Tomorrow a parcel leaves, please write whether it has arrived.

---

[1]   Literally, *Sabbath delight*, term for informal gatherings on Shabbat accompanied by singing, light food and drink

[2]   Funny stories in Plattdeutsch, a West German language descended from early Old Saxon, spoken in northern Germany and the eastern Netherlands.

---

[30]
Postcard Hamburg 7/7. 39

Dear Siegfried

Hearty thanks for your dear postcard. I am pleased that praise be to G-d you fasted well. Papa broke his fast at 2 o'clock, you know don't you that already last year Dr Neufeld didn't allow a whole *tanis*¹ on this day.

I hope our letter is in your possession and also the parcel. Erna is here since yesterday evening, she is sleeping in your bed, and also Hans who is coming on Monday will live with us for one night, because they are already travelling² on Tuesday. On Sunday Uncle Elkan, Aunt Dora and Aunt Auguste are here for lunch, also yesterday evening Uncle E[lkan] and Aunt D[ora] were with us for supper. At present great activity reigns here, apart from the sitting room, several rooms were occupied by people sleeping. I am to send you hearty greetings from Dr Streim, unfortunately he did not get further with his matter. Erna brought various things and so Hanna and I were occupied all morning to arrange everything for Sunday. Tomorrow I hope again to receive a detailed letter. For today good Shabbos hearty greeting and kiss Mama

Adr. Fr. Oppenheimer Frft a/M. Gaustraße 16, Hamburg, Bornstr. 24   b. Schloss

My Dear Siegfried

I was very pleased that you were able to deputise for me on the *tanis*, since I did not complete the fast. For today hearty greeting and kiss

Good Shabbos Papa

---

¹ German pronunciation of *ta'anit*, Fast day, The Fast of Tammuz.
² Hans and Erna Sussman were moving to London. Their son Max had been in London since February 1939

---

[31]
Hamburg 11/7 39

My beloved Siegfried

For your dear Shabbos letter and also your dear postcard of Sunday hearty thanks, the latter was a particular pleasure as today Tuesday we receive nothing from you. We are thank G-d well, I hope the same is true of you. Yesterday we were at Mrs Battenfeld, she was satisfied with both of us, she also found that we had a good rest, nevertheless again we had medicines for RM 10 but we are used to these. We then went straight to town and bought material, an overcoat a pair of striped trousers and also a very nice material for the suit, which you wanted to give Papa for his birthday, you know the same is on Sunday. It is strange that the Aryan with whom R is allowed to work is Mt Levien of Michaelisstrasse. I then immediately did some shopping for Hans, I hope this has his approval, the saleswomen in the shop helped me to choose, when I mentioned the name of Hans they said that they still knew his taste. They were a few lovely days with Erna, now at midday there is once again the bitter farewell. The weather is very stormy, I hope that E will not have to suffer so much on the journey. The two are of good courage, have not lost their humour, are naturally happy to see Mäxchen[1] again. Naturally, Uncle Elkan and Aunt Dora are very sad that now their last children are leaving them but in the end it is the same whether one child or three leave, one stays alone and the only hope is that in not too long a time one can come together again. Hanna H. has not yet heard anything again, Marta and Leo can collect their visa on Friday, the examination was in order, they are going to Chicago. A postcard has just come from Max and Hanne Dörte Levien, they write that they also have many difficulties. To our pleasure they tell us that you thank G-d are well and look good, I wish and hope with all my heart that it will further stay like this. You intended to tell us something about your conversation with Kezi and Mrs. Graham, or did nothing positive emerge from it. M. Eppendorfer Baum has again sent us RM 20, (In spite of promising) N. has not been heard from. Henry Polack is still in New York, his mother will let me know when he is again in London. Dr Streim again sends his regards, he has not made progress in his matter, I must go to him again, I hope for the last time. The matter with Elsas has again given me a knock, I am due to get an answer from him in the next days and will then let you know. David now always gets the *Nachrichtenblatt*[2], I assume that you also read the same. I have not again been to the Kulturbund[3], after the 3 weeks I will G-d willing go again, only films are now shown there. Concerning your trip to Siegmund[4], I would dissuade you, I believe it is better if you stay there, after all you can discuss things in writing, so rather leave it. Erna will also tell you of my concerns, she can also tell you about our lovely Sunday meal.

Now the material for today is finished, the letter must also go to the post because of the reply coupon. With regard to the 2 tables [Tafeln] you were right, you will probably receive them at the end of the week.

For today take it easy my darling, have affectionate greetings and kisses from your Muttchen. Greetings to all, also Aunt Henny, also for Leviens. Don't forget Papa's birthday.

Hbg 11/7 39

Dear Siegfried

We have now returned to our home from our summer holidays.

On *motze shabbos*[5] really comfortable in Wilhelminenhöhe. After *havdoloh*[6] we sat in the dining room and Dr Carlebach told various Dontjes, about which we laughed with delight. Amongst other things he told how a year ago he had officiated at the marriage of Hermann Bacharach's daughter. On a neighbouring balcony stood a man and Dr Carlebach heard him say, "That Pollack over there looks just like Dr Carlebach." You can imagine how we laughed. Also we have heard nothing from Kugelmann since their departure, which surprises us very much. It confirms the truth of the saying, "out of sight, out of mind". The day after tomorrow, G-d willing, you will speak to Erna and Hans, they will leave this evening.

For today greeting an kiss from Papa

---

[1] Max Sussman

[2] *Jüdisches Nachrichtenblatt* 'Jewish Newssheet'. See Appendix 2

[3] The Jüdischer Kulturbund Hamburg, (Jewish Cultural Association of Hamburg) was part of the cultural 'resistance' of Hamburg Jews to Nazi oppression.

[4] Siegfried was planning a trip to his cousin Siegmund Hirsch in Amsterdam.

[5] Should be *motzoei Shabbos*, the conclusion of Shabbat

[6] Should be *havdalah*, a short ceremony to mark the end of Shabbat

---

[32]
Postcard Hamburg 14/7. 39

My Dear Siegfried

I hope that our letter of Tuesday has reached you, in the meantime you will have heard by word of mouth from Erna and Hans about our wellbeing. I hope they both had a good journey. Great will have been the joy when they saw Mäxchen. I was also in the Ferdinandstraße[1], there were a colossal number of people there, it was rather stirring for me. On Tuesday evening Mrs Oppenheimer came back, she was with us on Wednesday and told me that she had heard from a cousin of the Spiers that they are also in London. Betty has established herself in medical practice and her parents are with her. She asked the cousin to get the address, as soon as have this I will let you know. Perhaps you can already get this over there, since Betty as a doctor is surely registered. On 17 August Leo and Martha are travelling on the New York, on the other line everything was already taken for August and September and they did not want to wait any longer. Leaving will be particularly difficult for Martha, she would, I believe, have been happy if not everything had worked. Yesterday Berta Polack was here, she is imminently awaiting her permit for Africa, then another good friend is gone. Henry is staying for longer in Europe. He is also once again coming over there, she will then give me his address. For today I wish you a right good Shabbos and send affectionate greetings and kisses   Mama

(up side down on first page) Dear greetings for all

My dear Siegfried

I hope Hans and Erna arrived there well. Prima[2], now the circle of relatives in London will soon be greater than here. Affectionate greeting and kiss Papa

Good Shabbos

---

[1] The Hamburg headquarters of the Warburg bank
[2] 'First class'

68

[33]
18/7/39

My Dear Siegfried!

I confirm receipt of your dear letter of 14 July and today want to send you a report of the celebration of my birthday and the nice presents I received. Above all I say a hearty thank you for the lovely suit material, which we bought on your instruction. Dear Mama gave me handkerchiefs, cigarette holder, cigarillos, cigarettes etc. flowers, umbrella, 3 ties and cake. Hanna Hirsch honoured me with an English poem, which is really admirable; apart from that the two Hannas gave me 2 books by M. Bergmann about the peculiarities of the English language. Yesterday evening Uncle Elkan and Aunt Dora, ... , Aunt Else, Mrs Oppenheim were here, it was very comfortable. Now I would still like to count a religious, nice, daughter-in-law amongst my presents, but for that I must probably be a bit patient, I hope not too long. With the difficulty in England associated with obtaining work permission, perhaps the only way to achieve this quickly is to marry into an existing business. This Shabbos Dr Carlebach spoke in the Home for the Aged, yesterday Mama was at Frau Dr Carlebach and collected the once again intended regards for us. Enclosed is a copy of the poem composed by Hanna Hirsch. Now I think that I have told you everything and remain with greeting and kiss your Papa

We were very pleased with the various English regards also those from Rosalind [Landau], it seems to me that you are making progress, not much of R. needs to be changed.

My beloved Siegfried

We also received your dear English postcard from your outing, I am very pleased that you use your free time to spend time outdoors. We are now limited to our own balcony, it was good that in Wilhelminenhöhe we could spend so much time in the open air. Papa has already written to you about his birthday, we had visitors all day, in the evening we were together in comfort, then there was bilberry cake, *Zuckerkuchen*[1] and my lovely cake with currants and raisins, for me only one thing was missing, that you my dear were not there. We heard from various people about the early arrival of Erna and Hans, they write enthusiastically about their journey, how nice that you are now all there together. You can now mutually advise one another. David wrote very funnily to Papa, he thinks that if we also one day arrive in the middle of the night, we only need to whistle *Azlo Geresh*[2] and then we would get a more or less hard bed for the night. Isidor Isaak and his wife have also got their certificate and will leave us in the near future, he was very ill for a few days, he is thank G-d better again. Papa visited him yesterday. Mrs Markus Möller, Herman's mother is coming to you soon in order to wait for her immigration to Palestine. You will already have heard that Bob de Jong will get married on 15 August, don't forget to send congratulations. There will be a Bar Mitzvah at Dr. Neufeld on Shabbos Nachamu[3], we will write to him soon. Last week Mrs Gerson telephoned again to enquire how we and you are, she is still faithful. Write her a few lines. John's mother-in-law told me about the presents he gave when he left, it was cakes, biscuits, marmalade, preserved fish and apart from that 4711 and cigarettes, write to me some time whether this was really the case. Have you already heard anything from him in New York, they have already sent pictures from the boat. Finally, yesterday the cartons from the loft were collected, I had to pay something extra in order to get rid of them. As Adolf, with whose English postcard we were very pleased, probably told you, reply coupons are now available on Tuesday so I am writing to you today immediately after coffee time. Now I must go into the kitchen to make rote Grütze[4], have you had any over there. It is a pity that I cannot send you any. I hope to hear from you again one of these days, greetings to all dear ones and you again also have many, many greetings and kisses from your Muttchen.

Send a postcard to Parkallee.

---

[1] Sugar cake, also known as Hamburger Butterkuchen (butter cake)

[2] A very characteristic cantillation note used in the Pentateuchal reading in the synagogue. It was whistled by the Hirsch family to identify themselves to each other and to friends

[3] The Shabbat after the Fast of Av, when the prophetic reading is Isaiah Chapter 40, which begins, *Nahamu, Nahamu ami...* "Comfort thee, Comfort thee my people"

[5] Literally, "red groats", mixed red fruit set by cooking with crushed oats

---

[34]
Postcard Hamburg 22.7.39

My Dear Siegfried

We received your dear postcard yesterday afternoon and I hope that our Tuesday letter has reached you. We are thank G-d well and I hope the

same of you. Aunt Harriet has not had a reply to her letter. I had wished it so much for her, since it is so awfully difficult for her here. Hanna has also had a letter from the consulate, which is probably sufficient for her affidavit but that she has to wait for several months. It is probably the case, as you wrote, that the numbers of the consulates are thrown together and that as a result the turn of one is sooner and the other later. It is naturally a pity for her, because she no longer has proper existence. Our concerns are really the same. Just today I wanted to enquire whether you have written to Adolf [Levy] in Chicago. Please don't put it aside. As soon as I have Spiers address, I will naturally let you have it. In this connection, Mrs. O. will make enquiries in Frankfurt. Don't you have any English lessons at present. It is important that you make progress. Kauders have probably also arrived over there, soon old Mr Kugelmann is going to his [old] home. He will see whether he can find out anything about Spiers.

For today a right good Shabbos and affectionate kisses   Mama

Regards to Uncle Siegmund and Aunt Tina from me

[upside down on p. 1] Have a good fast[1]

Lieber Siegfried

I am pleased that you made such a nice outing and has such pleasure. I wish for t"b[2], a right good fast. Affectionate Shabbos greeting from your Papa

---

[1] The reference is to the Fast of Av

[2] Abbreviation for *tisha be'av, the 9th of Av*, the Fast of Av

---

[35]
Hamburg 25.7.39

My Dear Siegfried

Once again we received your dear letter on Shabbos afternoon, just this once, in the week in which Erna was here it arrived on Sunday morning. I hope that you have received our Shabbos postcard and also that the remaining …. parcel which we sent arrived promptly with everyone. It is surprising that you already know all the news that I send you, it seems to me that Hamburg and London have become a single community. The most recent news you probably don't know, that on Friday Mrs Oppenheimer received her permit and will still leave us before Yom tov. She is, however, not going to London but to a small place to her nephew Julius Sickel, as already said, our circle is becoming ever smaller. Have you not yet heard anything from the insurance, it would be a shame if for all your good things you did not get any replacement. How did you like the gloves and the tie that Hans got as a present from Erna? Have you in the meantime ordered "rote Grütze", by the way strawberries were not cheap here either. Aunt Else told me that Adolf had twice been invited for meals by a family Bier, is that the family in question, you will know what I mean. How is it that A[ddie Nussbaum] is invited there. Have you already undertaken anything to obtain work permission. Please write about it. The address of Dr Neufeld is Tel Aviv Frug Street 8 II., the Bar Mitzvah is already this Shabbos, yesterday we wrote an airmail letter. Apart from that in the near future Dr. Wertheimer is also leaving. Can we again find another doctor. We bought the material for Papa at Siem and Sievers, I hope that next week first of all he gets his overcoat. I hope that by the time you receive this letter you will have got over the *tanis* well and that you broke the fast well. The letter must go, so for today a thousand kisses from your loving Muttchen.

Today only affection greeting, because I no longer write in the morning.

Greeting and kiss   Papa

---

[36]
Postcard Hamburg, 28.7.39

Dear Siegfried,

We received your postcard yesterday Thursday afternoon, many thanks. Could you not already write on Tuesday, so that we have news on Wednesday, without post from you the week is so long. I hope that you are well, once again I have pain in my right knee, it seems that a nerve has become inflamed, I have already tried heat and cold on it, so far nothing has been useful. Today Hanna H[irsch] been summoned for 28 August, which is good for her, because she now has hardly any income. There is no purpose in my sending you any news from here, because you get know everything as quickly over there. Today Dr. Liepmanson visited me, he goes to Los Angeles in September, he wanted to have the address of Fips(?), to sell several things, he sends you his regards.

I find it remarkable that Herm[an Möller] and John have not been in touch, I will ask Mrs O. what that means. Papa thank G-d fasted and broke his fast very well, he was in bed from 1- 6, which was very good for him. Tomorrow I hope to be able to read a really long letter from you.

For today good Shabbos man, many affectionate kisses from you Mother

Dear Siegfried,

I hope that also your *tanis* was good. I wish you good Shabbos

Greetings from me for all dear ones

Very affectionate greeting and kiss

Papa

---

[37]
Hamburg 31. 7. 39

My Dear Siegfried

Hearty thanks for your dear postcard, you were right that we were somewhat disappointed, because for us Shabbos only begins to be pleasant if we have a really detailed letter from you. You cannot believe how despondent I am on days when I am not distracted by work. It is lucky that Uncle Manfred and Aunt Else are still here, when they come to us I am always somewhat more cheerful. We have already agreed that for Rosh Hashanah[1] we will G-d-willing be together, provided that they are not asked to go to help in Wilhelminenhöhe, for Succot we have already notified to be there. My knee is, thank G-d, somewhat better, but if I walk a lot it is still painful. On Shabbos and Sunday it was very hot here, today it is thank G-d cooler. Lotte Solling was probably very pleased when she spoke to you, because for September she has a new job when she comes to London. I have not been able to find out anything about Spier's Address, you know Mrs O. she likes to talk without there being anything behind it, in spite of that I am very sorry that she is now leaving. Toni Singer, Aunt Hedwig's sister also wants to take a domestic job in England, her boy is in Sweden and the daughter is further to be educated here so that she can then go over there. We heard that Gottfried Möller got permission to work, is that correct? So it does happen, I hope that you will also be successful, I pray every evening to the Alm'ghty about it. I spoke to Mrs O. about Herm[an Möller] and John, she also has no explanation for their silence. Today I spoke to Dr. Wertheimer, I gave him greetings for you, he told me that he will not stay in London, rather he goes to a small place at the sea, he finds parting from here very difficult. Papa tried on his overcoat today, I hope that it will fit him well, one cannot see much at the first fitting. Aunt Else has just phoned, her farewell call, from tomorrow they will no longer have a telephone, so I will have to do without nattering. She told me that Adolf had written, it was very nice and comfortable at David and Else and it tasted very good, also that you have to find a new fellow tenant, I hope you find a nice person.

Now my beloved, I must make an end for today, when will we again have a little hour to natter by word of mouth. Write soon and take a thousand affectionate kisses from your Muttchen.

A parcel is leaving today, let me know whether it has arrived.

Dear Siegfried

Mr Boninger, who is going to Chile, leaves today, since he is going via London, I have given him your address and asked him to speak to you and to pass on regards from us, I hope that he does. Have you submitted the prescriptions you took with you, whether there is possibly a prospect on account of them to get work permission. I would very much like to know about it. Today I ordered my *arba minim*[2]. The congregation has a number available. How are the other members of the family David, Else, Hans, Erna and children. Give them all my regards and for you dear Siegfried particular regards and kisses from your Father.

---

[1] The Jewish New Year

[2] The 'four species', the palm, citron, myrtle and willow paraded ceremoniously in the synagogue during Tabernacles

---

[38]
Hamburg 4.8.39

My beloved Siegfried

We received your dear letter yesterday, many thanks. We are thank G-d well, I hope that the same is true of you. What you write about the insurance is very deplorable, you are right, when it comes to paying It is the same everywhere. I hope that you still get something. That the marriage matter seems so hopeless, I am in a way sorry, you might in this way have got a foothold, but such a matter is determined by G-d, there we humans can do little. It is a very hard blow for me that Uncle Manfred and Aunt Else are leaving so soon. As I have written to you, they are the only ones with whom I could talk about everything and who gave me some diversion. One cannot speak sensibly to Uncle Elkan and Aunt Dora is so dejected by the loss of her independence and her need to stay in the Home for the Aged, that a conversation with her brings no consolation. I am pleased that Uncle Manfred and Aunt Else will now find an existence and above all that they will be together with their young ones, when will we have this luck? Concerning a doctor, who one must have for all good things, I am at a complete loss. Dr. W. recommends Dr Wolffsohn but I do not know whether I will take him, it could be that after a time we would have to change again, what do you think if we take Dr Henneberg, write about is sometime. I bought several materials in the sales, yesterday and the day before the dressmaker was here and made me 2 dresses, I had to downgrade 3 of my dresses as house dresses, they are now about 12 years old and have become far too tight for me. The two have turned out very beautiful and together cost RM 26. I mould be very interested with who and about what you have discussions and correspondence with regards to a work permit, you were going to write about it. Now I wish you a very good Shabbos and greetings and kiss you affectionately your Muttchen

My Dear Siegfried

I would like to return to the matter concerned of which you write in your dear letter. Above all I wish to remark that nothing is further from me than to influence you in so important a matter. I would only like to know from you whether you like the girl and whether the business is of such a kind that it can eventually support a family. The first point only you yourself can decide, about the second one would have to make enquiries. If you have no objections, I would write about it to Kern. How is it with the religious aspect? That the son has not come back to you about the matter is not a proof that he does not want to go into the matter at all. The language is after all something that will improve with time. Well let us trust in G-d, if this is nothing, that something else will be found. Study English industriously so that you will soon master the language. I wish you a very good Shabbos and remain with greeting and kiss your Papa

What do you say to Uncle Manfred and Aunt Else? I wanted to remind you that Monday in 8 days is the birthday of dear Mama

Again greeting and kiss Papa

I could not prevent Papa from writing about the matter. He gives me no rest, you know your Päppchen, when it concerns marriage, he cannot be persuaded that it is nothing. So again affectionate greetings Muttchen

---

[39]
Hamburg 7.8.39

My Dear

Hearty thanks for your dear letter which again this time we received on Sunday morning. I am very sorry that you were dejected about my letter, you know me, I can often not go against my mood and with whom can I speak, if not with you. You can feel for me that I am sad, if now after you siblings and all good friends (also Berta Polack has her permit) leave, one gets so lonely and has too much time to think. But I will pull myself together and always remember to keep myself healthy and ask the Alm'ghty that he further support us and reunites us in happiness.

Berta Polack told me today on the telephone that Henry was here briefly, he is now in Sweden, she does not know whether he will come to London again, she is coming to me on Thursday and will tell me in greater detail. Have you by chance heard where Bob's wedding will take place, we want to send a telegram, write the address to us immediately, don't forget to send congratulations. In the meantime you have probably had an answer from Mrs Oppenheimer, she has requested your address, Herm's boy is called Lucien, Margot is better again, at the moment they are on summer holidays. For the time being John has a post as chauffer, you probably heard this from Eschweges. I have always wanted to ask whether you hear anything from Aunt *Lina* and the children, let me know sometime. Now I would like to have your advice in the following mater. The bed surround in our bedroom is completely finished. I am completely undecided what to do. Without such it is too dangerous for Papa and whether it is advisable to buy a new one, the price is probably at least RM 50, I don't know, it is uncertain, whether later we can use one. Write to me what you think about it. Similarly I do not know whether to buy a case, here we have no need for one and if we really still go away, we would need crates, I don't know what to do. The weather here was very bad in the last few days, powerful thunderstorms with heavy showers. Have you both got a new room mate yet or are you not trying, the rent will certainly be more expensive. Has Hans any prospects or is it equally difficult for him? Now you have several questions to answer, when you write have this one in front of you. Apart from that has the parcel arrived? Now my dear I must finish for today. The two Hannas send their regards. From me have greetings and kisses your Muttchen

My Dear Siegfried

It is important for you to have spoken to Gertrud, even if at the moment she cannot do anything about it. I would put an advert about marriage in the Jewish Chronicle[1], perhaps you will have luck. If one can book the advert here it may be possible. I don't yet have my overcoat the tailor was to come today for the second fitting.

For today affectionate greeting and kiss Papa

Good Shabbos

---

[1] The most widely read Jewish newspaper in Britain

---

[40]
Postcard Hamburg, 11.8.39
Dear Siegfried,

We received your dear letter only today Friday morning, many thanks. We are thank G-d well, also praise G-d my knee is improving. I have bought a light box, which did me good. I hope it will no remain better. I suffered quite a lot of pain. I have not spoken to Mrs O. all week. The lady is a cousin by marriage of Mr Spier. Mrs O. has written to her again about the address. Yesterday Berta P. was with us, Henry was here on Sunday morning with his young wife, they are now in Sweden, whether he will come to London again is doubtful, also she herself will not come there. Her permit is still on its way, it will probably take a few weeks before she travels. On Sunday Aunt Auguste [Levy], Martha and Leo were with me for lunch, because they are leaving on Thursday. So we will also send our telegram to Aunt Gella's [de Jong] address. Aunt Dora [Hirsch] told me that Ursel [Hirsch] and Sulamith [Hirsch] are bridesmaids. On Friday will be Erna's and Hans' wedding anniversary, congratulate them on our behalf, I thank Erna for her lines for my birthday.

For today now only good Shabbos and affectionate greetings and kisses

Mama

My Dear Siegfried

I wish you a very good Shabbos and remain with affectionate greetings

Your Papa

---

[41]
Hamburg 15.8.39

My beloved good child

Yesterday it was the loveliest birthday joy to hear your dear voice once again. Thank you for your dear lines and for the lovely pralines, it stirred me deeply that already before your departure you thought about my birthday. May the Alm'ghty grant that everything you write will be fulfilled and that G-d-willing we will be together again next year.

Though I was feeling rather melancholy, it was really pleasant yesterday evening, because most of the dear guests will soon no longer be here but nothing of that can be changed. Also on Sunday at lunch it was very nice, it was delicious. We had asparagus and peas with potato croquette, stuffed eggs garnished with slices of salmon and gherkins and potatoes with mayonnaise and cider pudding with raspberry juice, isn't that really excellent? Martha doesn't like fish and she was enthused that I took account of her taste. Naturally, the parting after that was not easy but what can one do. Coming back to my birthday, I was given many presents. Aunt Auguste embroidered a very nice handkerchief for me, from Leo and Aunt Dora I got chocolate, the two Hannas gave me a rubber bag, one in blue, like one I got from you, which is done for, with a very nice poem from Hanna Hirsch. From Uncle Manfred and Aunt Else I got a very nice tablecloth, from Berta Polack a waxed cloth bag with a zip, very tasteful, also in blue, from Mrs Oppenheimer 4711 perfume and soap and from Parkallee writing paper. For the evening I baked my raisin cake and flaky pastry and had a wonderful Kranzkuchen[1] from Hellmann, now you are completely in the picture. Not to be forgotten is that post from everyone, also from Siegmund and Josi, Aunt Henny Landau und from Eli and Goldine Leers in Rotterdam. Now to various reports in your letter.

Dr Wertheimer is still here on Thursday he will come to us again to have another look at my knee which is thank G-d better, I will then speak to him about who might succeed him. His arrangement there is really fabulous, I wish also that it will work for us. I hope to be able to deal with your matters in the desired manner. With regard to the purchase of a case for us, write to us about the measurements of our old ones, I have forgotten them. Please tell Erna that some time ago I gave the poem by Blumberg to Uncle Elkan, I thought she had received it long ago. I always wanted to ask whether Nati and Martha have gone to Holland and also whether and how you get anything from Addie [Nussbaum] and Ernst and in what manner they arrange this, whether in any way they let you feel it. Please write how it is with Betty St., has she had her operation and how is she, then I would like to write. I have received nothing from Oberaltenallee in spite of much telephoning. It is difficult for me to do anything there. Have you written to Adolf [Levy] in Chicago, don't delay it any longer. Tonight after a long interval I want to go to the cinema again, it is already 6.15 and I must end. Don't be cross that today no reply coupon is enclosed, this time I could not have the letter ready at the right time. Well, my greatly loved, again hearty thanks and a thousand affectionate kisses from

Your Muttchen.

My Dear Siegfried

I was very pleased yesterday evening to hear your voice on the telephone but I could not answer much because I was too excited. The main thing is that I heard, that God be praised you are well. I hope that you can soon let us know that you can engage in business. This week I should get my overcoat and trousers, Liselotte will make the suit. I must now go to *mincha*[2], still adding affectionate greetings and remain with Papa

(the following added in Adele's handwriting)

Uncle Emil and Aunt Bella, who we visited on Shabbos send their hearty greetings as also the two Hannas

---

[1] 'Wreathcake'

[2] The afternoon prayer

---

[42]
Postcard Hamburg 18.8.39

My Dear Siegfried

I confirm receipt of your postcard of the 16th with hearty thanks. I hope that in the meantime you have received our letter as well as that from Nick. Yesterday was a miserable farewell, Hanna still looks very miserable today, also Dr. [Fritz] W[arburg] said farewell, but he is not going via London but asked for your address. On Tuesday also Mrs Markus is going, if I can in any way, I will visit her tomorrow. Here too at present the weather is very nice, I hope it will stay like this for a bit. The film this week "Frau am Steuer" with Lilian Harvey and Willi Fritsch was quite good, only it was not very full, and I don't much like that. The pralines are the same kind, they are only in a different packing of ½ pound, so I have 2 packs, I think that they will keep until Rosh Hashanah, if I eat too many I will get too fat. Aunt Henny also still wrote to me, also Marcus. They are now probably home again. For today I send affectionate greetings and kisses and wish you a very good Shabbos.

Mama

Dear Siegfried

Dear Mama leaves nothing for me to write. So I must restrict myself to send you affectionate Shabbos greetings. With greeting and kiss Papa.

---

[43]
Hamburg 21.8.39

My Dear Siegfried

This time we received your all too short postcard only on Sunday. We are well, I hope the same of you. Today Hanna Hirsch received a letter from Selma in Holland, the same wrote that Aunt Gella [de Jong] is not at all well, have you heard anything about that from Siegmund? I wanted all along to ask you, whether you have arranged to have your papers sent over there from the American consulate here, write to me about it in the next letter without fail. I was at Elsas last week, something has been sold again, but there is still something there. Mr Grunnert sends his regards. Leo and Martha have already sent a postcard from the ship, they write that they are still affected by the farewell but are now trying to adjust. Have you written to Chicago, otherwise do it soon. Uncle Manfred and Aunt Else are occupied eagerly with preparations, I believe that they will not have it easy when they are there but can always look for something else. They are taking their paraffin oven that has been serviced, it is one like we have, do you think that paraffin will be cheaper than gas. Aunt Else will give me her sewing machine that is electric and then I will again be able to sew something myself. Today Papa got his overcoat and trousers, they both fit well, the master tailor wants to make the suit himself, then we would have to pay 20 Mk more for the work, as at Sinnreich, that is too expensive for us, I will first speak to him, and make enquiries elsewhere. Otherwise I have nothing more to tell you for today. I hope that in the next days we hear from you in detail. Further keep well my dearest and have affectionate greetings and a thousand kisses from your Muttchen.

The pralines taste excellent. Regards to Stern, Mrs Lanzkron and all relatives.

My Dear Siegfried!

We had to be satisfied with one postcard last week and hope to receive a detailed letter this week. Have you enquired how it is with synagogue seats for Yom Tov, will you be able to get one for a low price. Speak to Mr Stern about it.

I believe I have asked once before whether you have spoken with Mr Minden about a work permit, one must see whether anything is to be achieved through influence.

With affectionate greeting and kiss Papa

---

[44]
Postcard Hamburg 25.8.39

My Dear Siegfried

We have received your dear letter, hearty thanks, I hope that our letter of Tuesday is in your possession. We are well thank G-d, I am pleased to hear the same of you. Your wishes I shall as far as possible fulfil. Just a few days before I was at Henkels to buy a breadknife, next week I shall go to enquire about the adapter. About the pralines it is correct, they are 1200 gr in 2 packages, is also the same quality only the previous presentation is not available. A quarter is already finished, you know, I have too often to think of you. Mr Kugelmann is not too bad, only he should not have visitors in hospital. Sadly a very sad thing happened the day before yesterday. Mrs Klier, née Schlesinger died after a short serious illness. Today I have already dealt with a lot of correspondence. I have written to Siegm. and Josi, because yesterday was the birthday of the latter, then Adolf [Levy] and Liesel [Nussbaum] to Rio, you have probably heard that the latter has also sent off the papers for her parents. Next week G-d-willing I will write more, for today hearty Shabbos wishes and affectionate kisses

Mama. I would like to know whether the letter from Nick has arrived.

Dear Siegfried!

Yesterday the Rav gave a *hesped*[1] for Benny Meyer Z"L[2]. I was there we, Elkan and I, said *kaddish*[3] afterwards, because we had Jahrzeit[4] for Mama Z"L.

Affectionate Shabbos greeting and kiss   Papa

---

[1] Eulogy

[2] Abbreviation for *Zikhrono Liverakha*, "May his memory be a blessing"

[3] Doxology said in memory of the departed

[4] Literally, "year time", the anniversary of a death

---

[45]
Hamburg 28.8.39

My Dear

We received your dear letter yesterday Sunday morning and I thank you very much also for the photo you sent with which I was infinitely pleased. It occurs to me that you have put on some weight, or am I mistaken? I am writing to you immediately on Monday morning to tell you that we are well thank G-d, I hope that this is also true of you, if at all possible reply immediately. Today for the first time it is somewhat cooler, the heat was rather burdensome for me. I will enquire about the iodine pencil today, if I cannot get them, I will ask Dr. St[reim] who I have to see about my tooth, I will then if possible give you information. The paraffin oven was always completely free of fumes, each requires some work, it must be filled and the wick cleaned, I shall in any case enquire whether there is anything else but I think not, because nowadays paraffin is obsolete. The last letter had only just been sent, pity that you did not get it. Schneider L. was here last week, he sends his regards, he cannot make the suit for less than RM 75, I have enquired with another tailor, who even asked for RM 85. Where your information concerns Minden etc. I would have liked to know whether your information about the gentlemen concerned your or our affairs, I would understand better if it was ours. Write immediately about it, you can imagine how much I depend on it to hear something about it. This morning Hanna H went to the consulate for the examination, we wait anxiously for the result. The auction at Uncle M. should only be on 5 September, the two are, as you may imagine, are very depressed. Eppendorfer Baum don't say anything, I must always first telephone. I will wait to see how everything develops, then I will get to grips with Oberaltenallee. Now my dear beloved I must end, I would like the letter to leave soon. I pray to the Alm'ghty always that all goes well and that we can further hear from one another. All the best my golden one, remain well, we too want to stay strong. A thousand affectionate greetings and kisses.

Your Muttchen

Hanna has just telephoned that everything is in order, that she can collect her visa on 6 September. I hope she can now travel.

That Betty [Stern] does not yet need an operation pleases me, give her greetings and I wish her all the best.

My Dear Siegfried

What you write about Minden very much surprises me, here one can see again the truth of the Psalm *Al tiftechu bin Divim*[1]

Let us hope that everything will turn out for the best.

Hearty greeting and kiss   Papa

---

[1] Should read *Al tivtechu benedivim*, usually translated 'Place not your trust in princes' (Psalm 146:3) but a more literal translation for '*nedivim*' is 'benefactors'.

---

[46]
Hamburg 29.8.39

My Dear One

Today only briefly a few lines that we are thank G-d well. I hope that you have received our letter of yesterday and also the trial sample of Jodo-Muc[1]. May G-d grant that everything goes well and that we will further hear from one another, I dare not think if it could be otherwise, for me above all everything is still too lively in my memory. Martha and Leo telegraphed that they arrived at Adolph, a great good fortune. I must go to Dr Streim again, perhaps he will decide to extract the tooth, it would be better if it continues to cause pain. That everything worked for Hanna is nice I have already written, now it depends on whether she can leave, as I hope.

My darling if G-d determines otherwise than we hope and wish and I cannot write to you, so I send you already today my most heartfelt wishes for your birthday. May all your wishes be fulfilled, that you very, very, very soon reach the desired goal. Keep well and may the Alm'ghty ensure that we meet again very soon. I still always hope to G-d that I will be able to write to you for the day.

For today be well my darling a thousand affectionate greetings and kisses

In love, your mother

Dear Siegfried

I also want to be sure and I already today send you for your birthday (22 Ellul), 6 Sept. my heartiest good wishes,

May the future be a right happy one for you and change for the better. At the same time I wish you a really good, healthy and happy year, in case we are not able to write again before that.

For today hearty greeting and kiss   Papa

---

[1] An iodine-based antiseptic

---

[47]
Hamburg 31.8.39 Thursday

My Dear Siegfried

Just now at half past 6 we received your dear letter, which came very quickly, many thanks. I hope that in the meantime you have received our Tuesday letter and the Jodo-Muc. I write again this evening, perhaps then you will still receive this letter on Shabbos. We are thank G-d well, only naturally very anxious, because one still does not know how everything will turn out. May G-d only grant that everything goes well, I ask hourly for this. What you write about our matter is very, very regrettable, do you think it right that Papa, if everything remains quiet, writes to M[ax] W[arburg]. Apart from us, a disappearing small number of people are still in question, because most are no longer here. Mrs O. was here yesterday, she has still not been able to get the address. If possible she will go to Herm next week, then over there, I have invited her for Shabbos lunch. Uncle Manfred phoned today, G-d willing we want to be together for Rosh Hashanah, because they are still here. Today the tailor came for the first fitting, I was not yet satisfied with the fit, I hope it will work out well. Is it still so warm with you, I perspire quite colossally. Last week we had a letter from Dr. and Mrs Neufeld, they thanked for our good wishes and send their regards to you, they are well but they still have little income. It is nearly half past 10, I would like Papa to post this letter tomorrow morning. So, my beloved, all the best, I hope to hear from you in the next days. Good Shabbos, a thousand affectionate kisses from your loving Muttchen

Dear Siegfried

How is it now with the English, do you understand people better, I hope it will soon come. I wish you a good Shabbos and remain with affectionate greeting and kiss Papa

[48]
Hamburg 6.9.39

My darling Siegfried

Hearty thanks for your dear Shabbos letter, I hope that also our postcard has arrived. I asked you already in my last letter to start earlier with your writing, so that you can answer all our questions and you also can deal with our news. I have the feeling my dear that you do not have the courage to write, or am I wrong, but you would be wrong, you must keep your chin up and trust in G-d, he will grant you his help. You know that my thoughts are always with you and how pleased we are if we can take part in all your concerns but that is only possible if you write to us in detail. And now to your news about meals. I was very surprised, particularly the turns of expressions others are able to use, you too must be able to use these, because if one has undertaken something one must fulfil one's duty. Naturally one must not judge in a one-sided manner, it is really much for B[etty Lanzkron] always to have two guests at her table but they knew that before. Nevertheless you are duty-bound to thank them otherwise you would still be here. With respect to the financial aspect, I do not believe that they bear it all alone or is that not the case. For me the main thing is that you remain strong, weigh yourself from time to time, if you lose weight you must absolutely do something about it. On the days that Adolf [Nussbaum] does not go to the canteen you might go to eat in a restaurant, Sterns would not notice this or do they pay the canteen directly, in any case you must consider it exactly, for goodness sake you must not offend them, in any case write to me about the matter. Yesterday Mrs Quandt who made me the nice coat was here, the material you still sent me last year. It fits very nicely and today in the Ost-Indienhaus[1] I bought a very fine summer dress, dark blue with little white dots, a small white high-buttoned waistcoat with a skirt and dark-blue belt – ¾ length sleeves, it suits me very well. Yesterday Elsas had the cupboard, bedstead, bicycle and Leitz lever arch file collected, I am curious what comes of it. Miss Gerson wrote the enclosed postcard, in view of the capital matter we really had to calculate, I will give her your address, Lotte Solling also wrote me a postcard and asked for your address, I was also to give hers (*overleaf*). Please let me know whether your chocolate arrived, also whether you were pleased with Bella's present. John wanted to give you something before his departure to the U S A, he will probably telephone you, whether you should go there next week, please let me know what he gave you, I am interested. The next page must be left for Päppchen, so I must now close. I hope that you can fulfil our request for details, have a thousand kisses from your constantly thinking of you Muttchen

(*overleaf*)

Lotte Solling c/o Mrs Parkinmoore

Rosetrees Portinscale Keswick/Cumberland/England ("England" was crossed out)

Should we rather send the letters to your home, let us know

My Dear Siegfried

Also I would like to ask you from my heart to answer our various questions. Particularly I would like to know whether you go to the *shiur* by Dr. Spitzer. When does one go to Shul[2] there the morning, if you could go regularly you would gain time. Is there not a synagogue near you? Uncle Elkan will be 75 years old on Shabbos, I imagine you will send him congratulations. We have invited Uncle Elkan and Aunt Dora for supper on Shabbos evening. Everything else you have heard from Mama, so today only heartfelt kisses and greetings from your Päppchen.

---

[1] A Jewish clothing store at Neuer Wall 13/15, owned by Heinrich Colm [see Appendix 2].

[2] Derived from Schule, school, used for 'synagogue' in everyday speech in Germany.

Chapter 5

DEPORTATION TO AUSTRALIA

Early one morning at the beginning of June 1940, the Metropolitan Police came to arrest Siegfried at the address where he was living; it was the beginning of a nightmare. The reasons are to be found in the political developments in Germany in the 1930s. Increasing anti-Semitism and persecution encouraged many refugees to leave Germany and many came to Britain, with the result that by September 1939, before the outbreak of the Second World War, some 80,000 German and Austrian refugees, were living in Britain. Under the Aliens Restriction (Amendment) Act 1919, which derived from Aliens Registration Act 1914, they were all, including the Jewish refugees who had fled persecution in Nazi Germany, regarded as Enemy Aliens.

The day after the signature of the Treaty of Non-Aggression between Germany and the Soviet Union (the Molotov–Ribbentrop Pact) on 23 August 1939, the Emergency Powers (Defence) Act 1939 received the Royal Assent. This gave the British Government wide emergency powers, including Defence Regulations designed to regulate everyday life in the country. These Regulations were finally repealed in 1959.

Under the Defence Regulations, enemy aliens over the age of 16 were classified into three groups. Class A Aliens, of whom there were less than 600, were in principle regarded as a high security risk; they were arrested and interned. About 6,500 of the aliens were classified as Class B Aliens and were regarded as persons of doubtful risk, who were to be supervised and subject to restrictions. The remaining Aliens of Class C, of whom there were some 64,000, were regarded as 'Friendly Aliens' who did not constitute a risk. The majority of these were Jewish refugees, and they were to be left at liberty.

Increasing concern was expressed about the large number of German and Austrian Aliens, including Jews, coming to Britain. With the German invasion of France and the Netherlands in the spring of 1940 there was a press campaign that demanded the internment of all refugees in view of Britain's dangerous military position. Assessment of the security risk represented by the refugees was made by Metropolitan Police tribunals that included magistrates, some of whom were biased and sometimes allegedly, frankly anti-Semitic. As a result the decision of whom to round up was sometimes biased, arbitrary and occasionally prejudiced, particularly in the case of Jewish refugees from Nazi Germany many of who could not speak English and could not easily explain themselves. The result was that many of these refugees, who should have been in Class C, were placed in Class B and interned.

Later, in response to official concern about the large numbers of Germans in Britain, the security services considered the immediate problem and Winston Churchill, the Prime Minister, when consulted, is reputed to have said "Collar the lot". Increasingly aliens of Group C were interned, so that by mid-1940 some 8000 people had been arrested. What was to be done with such a large number of internees presented a problem for the British Government. The decision was taken that families and women should be sent to the Isle of Man. In consultation with Commonwealth Governments a decision was taken that internees without dependents should be sent to Canada or Australia.

After his arrest, Siegfried Hirsch, who was unmarried, was taken to the Huyton Alien Internment Camp near Liverpool, which had first been occupied in May 1940. He was given the United Kingdom Prisoner Number 76193. At Huyton the internees were housed in the Woolfall Heath Estate, a recently built group of council houses and flats. The camp was surrounded by an eight-metre high barbed wire fence and the large number of internees lived in unfurnished houses and tents. Many had to sleep on mattresses on the floor and the conditions in the camp were very poor. Food was limited and morale amongst the inmates was low.

At the same time, Siegfried's 17-year-old cousin Adolf Nussbaum, usually called Addie by his family, was also arrested. He had come to Britain on a Kindertransport in 1939 and was living at an address in London. He too was interned and taken to Huyton. Other internees were taken to Lingfield Race Course in Surrey that had hurriedly been converted into an internment camp. Some of the internees were survivors of the ill-fated *Arandora Star*, which had been sunk on 2 July 1940 by a German U-boat with a heavy loss of life. The internees were then taken to Liverpool and from there by boat to the Isle of Man, where they were held in Douglas and elsewhere. For some of the internees the stay on the Isle of Man was very brief before they were returned to Liverpool. Here 2,542 internees, including Siegfried and his cousin Addie, were embarked on *HMT Dunera*.

This turned out to be the only transport of internees to Australia and it left Liverpool on 10 July 1940. Also among the passengers were 200 Italian Fascists and 251 German prisoners of war. It seems that all the deportees on board, irrespective of the grounds for their deportation to Australia, were treated as if they were enemy prisoners of war. The overcrowding on the ship was severe, the hygiene facilities were minimal and the passengers suffered considerable privation. Many were robbed of their belongings, some of which were thrown overboard and they suffered brutality and physical abuse at the hands of their British guards. The poorly trained soldiers who guarded them belonged to the Pioneer Corps. They were under the command of Lieutenant-Colonel William Scott. A junior officer was First Lieutenant John O'Neill, V.C.

The *Dunera* was shadowed by a German U-boat for part of the journey. It was established later that torpedoes had twice been fired at the *Dunera* by a German U-boat but both missed their target. Apparently, the U-boat had picked up some of the prisoners' belongings that had been thrown overboard and, under the impression that the ship was carrying German prisoners of war, did not press home its attack. Accounts of the journey and the later internment in Australia, based in part on reports by some of the internees, has been published by Patkin (1979) and Pearl (1983).

It has to some extent been possible to reconstruct Siegfried's movements in Australia based mainly on records in the Australian National Archives (www.naa.gov.au). The *Dunera* arrived at Freemantle, Western Australia on 26 August 1940 and in Sydney on 6 September 1940. On arrival in Sydney the first Australian to go on board was Alan Frost, an Australian army medical officer, who was appalled by what he saw and the condition of the internees. He subsequently wrote a report that led to a court martial of those responsible. Lieutenant-Colonel William Scott was later severely reprimanded and a Regimental Sergeant Major was court-marshalled, imprisoned, reduced to the ranks and discharged from the army. The British Government later paid £35,000 compensation for the losses suffered by the internees.

On arrival in Sydney, on 6 September 1940, the arrivals were sent to Hay on four trains and a formal 'Order for the Detention of an Enemy Alien' was made in respect of Siegfried (Fig. 5.1). This was a formal legal document, under Regulations pursuant to the Australian National Security Act 1939-1940, to authorise the detention of enemy aliens.

At the same time a 'Service and Casualty Form' was begun, in which the heading 'Prisoner of War' was deleted and replaced by a rubber stamped 'Internee'. In this way Siegfried was formally registered with the Identification No. E39770. The 'Service and Casualty Form' usefully details Siegfried's movements throughout the period of his internment up to 17 July 1942 (Table 5.1; Fig. 5.2).

Table 5.1 - Siegfried's journey from England to Australia and Back

10 July 1940	Departed England for Sydney
6 September 1940	Arrived Sydney
6 September 1940	Departed Sydney for Hay
7 September 1940	Arrived in Hay
19 May 1941	Transferred from Hay to Tatura
17 July 1942	Departed Tatura
22 July 1942	Departed for United Kingdom
6 October 1942	Arrival in Liverpool

On 16 October 1940 a Report form was completed in which, once again, 'Prisoner of War' was deleted and 'Internee' was written in (Fig. 5.3). This form contained personal details, including his address at 356 Seven Sisters Road, N4, from which Siegfried had been arrested. He described his occupation as a 'Wholesaler Exporter Dental Articles'.

The internees had arrived at Hay on 8 September and, according to Siegfried's 'Service and Casualty Form', he was then marched from the railway station to the Hay Camp. This was at the site of Hay Gaol (prison), which during World War II served as a prisoner of war and internment camp. The camp had been constructed in 1940 as a group of high security camps under the guard of the 16th Garrison Battalion of the Australian Army. Camp 6 was for Italian civilian internees and Camps 7 and 8 were for Jewish internees. Siegfried was housed in camp 7.

COMMONWEALTH OF AUSTRALIA.

Order for Detention of Enemy Alien.

WHEREAS by Regulation 20 of the National Security (Aliens Control) Regulations it is provided that if the Minister or any person authorised by the Minister to act under that regulation is of opinion that it is necessary or expedient in the interests of the public safety, the defence of the Commonwealth or the efficient prosecution of the war to detain any enemy alien he may make an order directing that the enemy alien be detained :

AND WHEREAS the Minister has, pursuant to the provisions of section 17 of the National Security Act, 1939-1940, delegated to me, Captain Albert Richard Heighway, an officer of the Adjutant-General's Branch at Army Headquarters, the powers and functions conferred upon him by Regulation 20 of the National Security (Aliens Control) Regulations insofar as the exercise of those powers is necessary for the purpose of making Orders for the detention in Australia of those persons on board His Majesty's Transport " Dunera," who have been sent from the United Kingdom to Australia for internment in Australia in accordance with arrangements entered into by the Government of the Commonwealth and the Government of the United Kingdom :

AND WHEREAS I am of opinion that it is expedient in the interests of the public safety, the defence of the Commonwealth, or the efficient prosecution of the war that **Süsskind** **Siegfied/HIRSCH**   , being an enemy alien on board His Majesty's Transport " Dunera," who has been sent from the United Kingdom to Australia for internment should be detained.

NOW THEREFORE I do hereby order that the said   **Süsskind** **Siegfried/HIRSCH** shall be detained.

Dated this **Sixth**   day of   **September**   One thousand nine hundred and forty.

(Sgd.) A. R. HEIGHWAY
Captain

L 2612/40

Fig. 5.1. The Order for Siegfried's Detention dated of 6 September 1940 (N.A.A.).

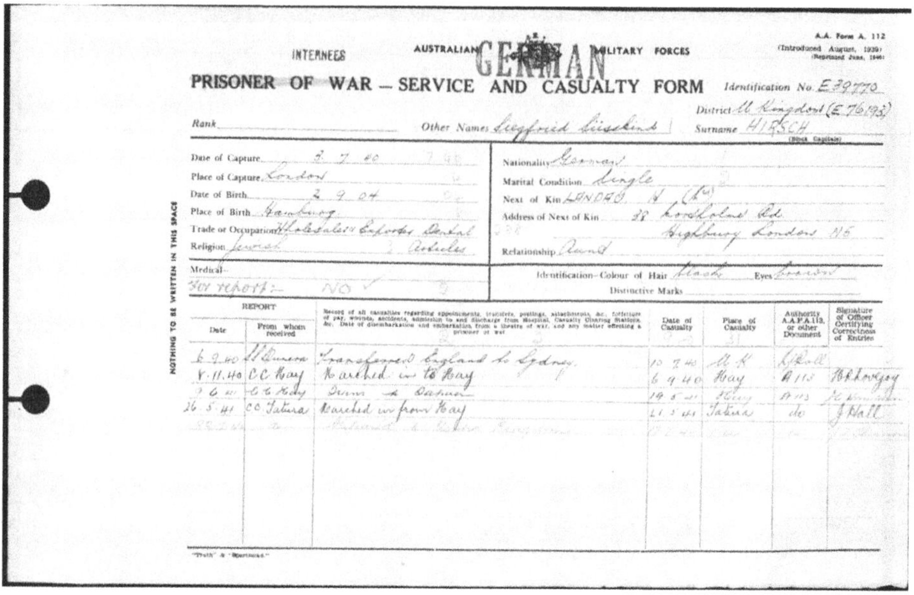
INTERNEES AUSTRALIAN GERMAN MILITARY FORCES

A.A. Form A. 112 (Introduced August, 1939) (Reprinted June, 1940)

PRISONER OF WAR – SERVICE AND CASUALTY FORM Identification No. E 39770

District U Kingdom (E 76193)

Rank ______ Other Names Siegfried Süsskind Surname HIRSCH (Block Capitals)

Date of Capture 3 7 40

Place of Capture London

Date of Birth 2 9 04

Place of Birth Hamburg

Trade or Occupation Wholesaler Exporter Dental Articles

Religion Jewish

Medical – 30V report:– NO

Nationality German

Marital Condition Single

Next of Kin LANDAU H (Mr)

Address of Next of Kin 38 Lordholme Rd, Highbury London N5

Relationship Aunt

Identification – Colour of Hair Black Eyes Brown

Distinctive Marks

NOTHING TO BE WRITTEN IN THIS SPACE

REPORT Date	From whom received	Record of all casualties regarding appointments, transfers, postings, attachments, &c.	Date of Casualty	Place of Casualty	Authority A.A.F.A. 113, or other Document	Signature of Officer Certifying Correctness of Entries
6 9 40	HT Dunera	Transferred England to Sydney	10 7 40	U K	[illegible]	
8 11 40	CC Hay	Marched in to Hay	6 9 40	Hay	A 113	[illegible]
19 6 41	CC Hay	[illegible]	19 5 41	Hay	A 113	[illegible]
26 5 41	CC Tatura	Marched in from Hay	21 5 41	Tatura	do	J Hall

Fig. 5.2. Siegfried's Service and Casualty Form (6 September 1940-17 July 1942) (N.A.A.).

Although it was recognised that the Jewish internees in Australia were not strictly-speaking prisoners of war, they were in some ways treated as such. Thus, on 4 February 1941, Siegfried completed a pro forma requesting that his name and details not be communicated to the German government or the International Red Cross (Fig. 5.4) as would have been required for Prisoners of War under the Geneva Convention.

The climate at Hay is very hot and dry and it was a difficult environment for many of the European internees. So, on 19 May 1941 Siegfried and other internees were transferred from Hay about 260 km south to Tatura, New South Wales, where they arrived on 21 May. In Tatura arrangements were made for a group of some 300 observant Jews to organise a kosher kitchen and they were visited by Rabbi Jacob Danglow from Melbourne but, from the evidence of one internee, it appears that he was not very co-operative; Rabbi L.A Falk who visited a little later was somewhat more helpful (Patkin, 1979; Pearl, 1983).

While awaiting release, the Jewish internees, who eventually became known as the "Dunera Boys", developed a rich cultural programme, including concerts, and they established an unofficial university.

GERMAN

A.A. Form A.111.
(Introduced August, 1939)
(Reprinted June, 1940)

AUSTRALIAN MILITARY FORCES.

REPORT ON PRISONER OF WAR *INTERNEE*

1.

Identification No.	Surname	Other Names	Nationality
E 39770 (E 76193)	HIRSCH	Siegfried, Süsskind	German

2. Date of Birth 2 Sept. 1904   Private Address 356 Seven Sisters Rd, N4 London

Place of Birth Hamburg   Business Address

Occupation Whole saler Exporter Dental Carticles   If registered, State Place London

Religion Jewish   Registration No.

3. Place of Capture London   Date of Internment 6.9.1940

Date of Capture 3. July 1940   Place of Internment HAY

For Report - NO   From whom received BRITISH GUARD

Height	Weight	Complexion	Hair	Eyes	Marks and Peculiarities
5'6"	8½ stone	Dark	Black	Brown	None

4. Reason for Internment:—

ENEMY ALIEN
Jewish Refugee

5. If medically examined? Yes   6. Personal Effects:— 1 golden Ring, 1 wrist watch

Medical Report No.

7. Marital Condition:—
Married or Single Single   Next of Kin aunt Mrs. H. Landau

Name of Wife   Her Address 38 Northolme Rd Hyo Highbury London N5

Children ✓ Male ✓ Female

8. How long resident in Australia

Date of Entry 26 8 40   Ship Dunera   Port of Disembarkation Sydney

If any property in Australia (if so, specify place and extent)

9. Statement of Service:—
(Reserve, Colour, Naval, &c.) NONE

10. Special Observations 3 Interned   A.H.Q. 2nd ECH. 23 OCT 1940 RECEIVED

Father's Name (in full) Pincus Hirsch

Mother's pre-marriage name (in full) Adele Nussbaum

Signature of Siegfried Nussbaum   Adjt.

Date 16/10/40   Camp Commandant. Date 16/10/40

Defence Print, Sydney.

Fig. 5.3. Siegfried's Internee Report (N.A.A.).

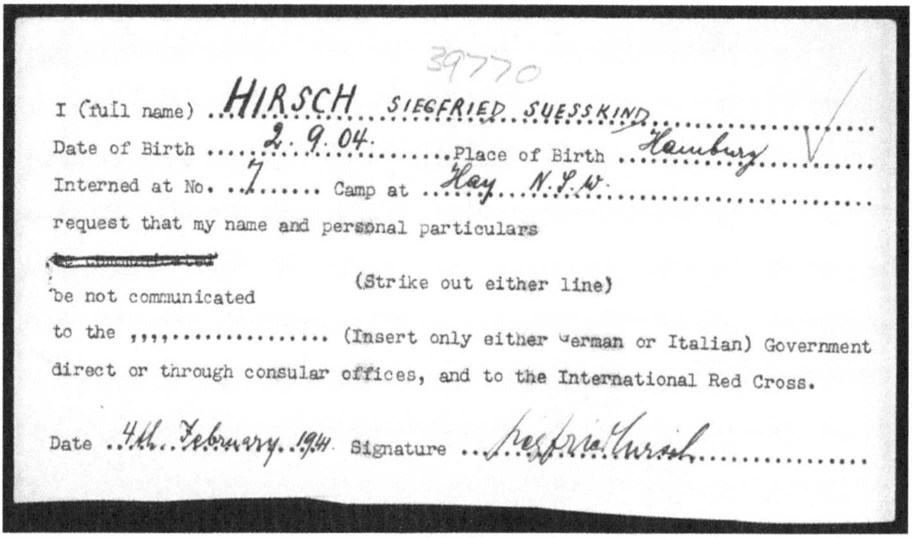
39770

I (full name) HIRSCH SIEGFRIED SUESSKIND

Date of Birth 2.9.04 Place of Birth Hamburg

Interned at No. 7 Camp at Hay N.S.W.

request that my name and personal particulars

~~be communicated~~

be not communicated (Strike out either line)

to the ,,,,............... (Insert only either German or Italian) Government

direct or through consular offices, and to the International Red Cross.

Date 4th. February. 1941 Signature Siegfried Hirsch

Fig. 5.4. Siegfried's request that the German Government and the International Red Cross should not be informed of his internment (N.A.A.).

The last entry on Siegfried's record as an internee in Australia was made on 17 July 1942 (Fig. 5.2) and he finally arrived back in Liverpool on 6 October 1942, two days after Rejoicing of the Law (*Simchat Torah*). In due course the injustices suffered by the internees were recognised and by the end of 1942 most had been repatriated, though some chose to settle in Australia permanently.

Adolf (Addie) Nussbaum

Addie Nussbaum, Siegfried's cousin, was born in Hamburg on 7 March 1923 and came to England in March 1939 on a Kindertransport, having been sponsored by Willy and Betty Stern friends of his parents who came from Hamburg and were living in London; he was 16 years of age. At first on arrival in Britain he lived with the Stern family but soon found a job and found another place to live.

Addie was also deported to Australia at the same time as Siegfried. His experiences between the time of his arrest in London and the departure of HMT Dunera from Liverpool on 10 July 1940, were similar to those of Siegfried. On arrival in Australia on 6 September Addie was detained as an Enemy Alien in the same way as Siegfried and he was registered as internee number, E40324.

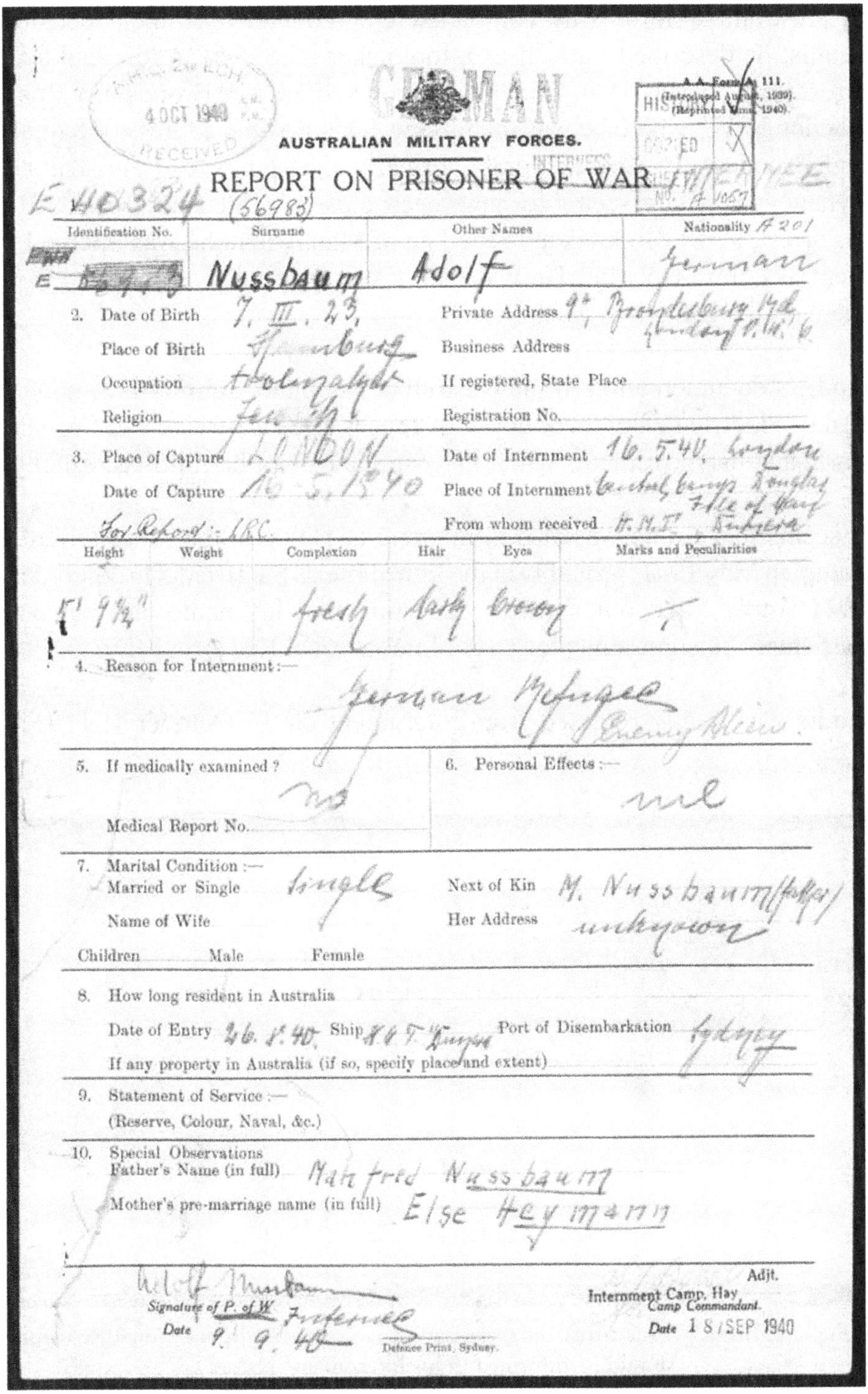

GERMAN

A.A. Form A. 111.

HIS

COPIED

AUSTRALIAN MILITARY FORCES.

INTERNEES

REPORT ON PRISONER OF WAR

E 40324 (56983)

Identification No.	Surname	Other Names	Nationality
E	Nussbaum	Adolf	German

2. Date of Birth 7. III. 23.
Place of Birth Hamburg
Occupation
Religion Jewish

Private Address
Business Address
If registered, State Place
Registration No.

3. Place of Capture LONDON
Date of Capture 16. 5. 1940

Date of Internment 16. 5. 40. London
Place of Internment
From whom received

Height	Weight	Complexion	Hair	Eyes	Marks and Peculiarities
5' 9½"		fresh	dark	brown	

4. Reason for Internment:— German Refugee Enemy Alien.

5. If medically examined? no
Medical Report No.

6. Personal Effects:— nil

7. Marital Condition:—
Married or Single single
Name of Wife
Children Male Female

Next of Kin M. Nussbaum (father)
Her Address unknown

8. How long resident in Australia
Date of Entry 26. 8. 40. Ship H.M.T. "Dunera" Port of Disembarkation Sydney
If any property in Australia (if so, specify place and extent)

9. Statement of Service:—
(Reserve, Colour, Naval, &c.)

10. Special Observations
Father's Name (in full) Manfred Nussbaum
Mother's pre-marriage name (in full) Else Heymann

Signature of P. of W. Internee
Date 9. 9. 40

Adjt.
Internment Camp, Hay
Camp Commandant.
Date 18 SEP 1940

Defence Print, Sydney.

Fig. 5.5. Addie's Internee Report (N.A.A.).

In Australia a form was completed that contained Addie's personal details; he described himself as a toolmaker (Fig. 5.5). Addie had been arrested on 16 May 1940 from his London address at 9 Brondsbury Road, London NW6, where he was then living. This was the address of Kilburn and Brondesbury Chevra Torah, formerly the Hampstead and Kilburn Synagogue, which seems to have been closed in the late 1960s. After his arrest, he was first taken to the Isle of Man, where he was interned in Central Camp, Douglas. He was then taken back to Liverpool and from there on the Dunera to Australia.

Addie's documentation in the Australian National Archives is similar to that of Siegfried's but there does not appear to be a Service and Casualty Form and his movements while in Australia cannot be followed exactly.

It seems that Addie was at first interned at Hay and then transferred to Tatura in May 1941, probably at the same time as Siegfried. On 3 February 1941 Addie filled out a form requesting that his name and personal particulars be communicated to the International Red Cross (Fig. 5.6).

Addie was finally released from internment on 13 October 1941 (Fig. 5.7).

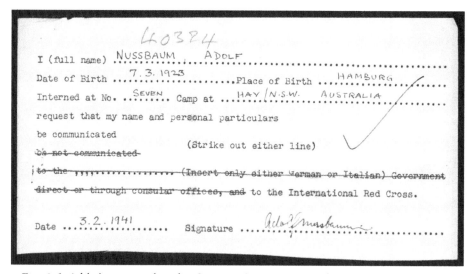

Fig. 5.6. Addie's request that the German Government and International Red cross should be informed of his internment (N.A.A.).

GERMAN

AUSTRALIAN MILITARY FORCES.

A.A. Form A.111A.
(Introduced September, 1939)
(Revised August, 1940)
(Reprinted September, 1940)

RELEASE
Report No. _____

REPORT ON INTERNEE PRISONER OF WAR

FOR INFORMATION OF

International Bureaux of Relief and Information

ITEM	DETAIL.	REMARKS
1	Identification Number . . .	E. 40324
2	Name (Surname)	NUSSBAUM
3	(Other Names) . .	Adolf
4	Nationality	German
5	Date of Birth	
6	Place of Birth	
7	Regimental Number	
8	Place of Capture	
9	Date of Capture	
10	Place of Internment	
11	Rank	
12	Unit	
13	Surname (Father)	
14	Name of Mother	

15

REMARKS:

This internee was released from internment on
13.10.1941.

Next-of-kin:-
(Father) Manfred NUSSBAUM.
Unknown.

Date _____

_____ Captain,
Officer in Charge Prisoners of War Information Bureau

"Truth" & "Sportsman" Ltd

Fig. 5.7. The Report of Addie's release from internment (N.A.A.).

The Jewish internees who had been deported to Australia became known as the 'Dunera Boys' and eventually became an important milestone in Australia's cultural history. About 900 of those interned at Hay eventually remained in Australia and their contribution to subsequent cultural, scientific and business developments in Australia was significant. The Dunera Boys became an integral and celebrated part of Australian cultural and intellectual life; in 2010 some fifty still survived.

Chapter 6

THE AUSTRALIA CORRESPONDENCE
1941 AND 1942

The circumstances and conditions under which the Australia letters were written were very different from those of the Hamburg letters; for this reason explanatory headnotes rather than foot notes are provided. Only few of the items of the Australian correspondence are the letters as sent, most are drafts. The texts of the letters are reproduced exactly as written, except that material of no consequence and repeated text, particularly in the drafts addressed to 'Peter' and 'Musch', has been redacted between brackets "(......)" but no attempt has been made to correct grammar or spelling. Illegible text is indicated by question marks (?......?). The numbering of the Australia letters follows on from that of the Hamburg letters.

Siegfried thought very carefully about what he wrote to Germany, probably fearful that a misplaced word or phrase picked up by a censor might become problematic for the recipient. He drafted all his letters with great care and kept the drafts of these letters for the rest of his life. In most cases he did not receive a reply and these drafts represented the unfulfilled duty to write to his parents that he took so seriously.

Particularly enigmatic is a group of drafts addressed to a 'Peter' and 'Musch', who it has not been possible to identify. In a letter from Switzerland, dated 25 April 1945, after her release from Theresienstadt, Siegfried's aunt, Dora Hirsch née Hanover, refers to 'Uncle Peter' as having been in Theresienstadt but she does not mention anyone by the name of 'Musch'. It is reasonable to assume that Musch was also there but their identity and fate remain unknown. In the context of this correspondence, these drafts provide little information and are of limited importance but partially redacted extracts are included because they give an insight into Siegfried's relationship with Peter and Musch as well as evidence about his life as an internee in Australia.

The drafts include a number intended for Siegfried's parents and were sent by prisoner of war mail. Some may have been sent via the United States, but of these in most cases there is no further evidence. Also included is a number of very brief draft messages to Pincus and Adele that were probably intended for transmission by the International Red Cross.

Amongst the letters Siegfried received in Australia were some from his cousin David Hirsch, who by this time was in the USA and living in New York. Before the United States entered the war in 11 December 1941, postal communication between Germany and the USA continued. David Hirsch received letters from Pincus and Adele and sent details of their contents to Siegfried but apparently not the original letters. In some cases, possibly because the original letters were passed on to other family members, Siegfried made partial typewritten transcripts of those parts of David's letters that reported news from his parents. These transcripts are included here, because they provide interesting background information. Also included are two letters from Pincus and Adele to Siegfried, dated 27 April 1941 and 10 November 1941 that probably came via the United States. These are the last letters Siegfried received from his parents.

The Australia Letters

[49]
A draft made while Siegfried was in the Hay internment Camp, New South Wales. It was sent via a censor.

Siegfried Hirsch, Hut I, No. 7 Camp
Eastern Command, c/o District Censor
45 Reservoir Str., Sydney

6 February 1941

Dear Musch, Dear Peter

I hope confidently that when you receive these lines that all is well with you and that you are in the best of health. I can also report about myself that I am healthy and have been since my last letter to you and it is well with me. I was worried that some time ago you dear Peter were not very well. What was wrong was it a cold? In any case I hope confidently that you have completely recovered and that I will hear about it from you. If my daily thoughts about you were lines, you would have as many letters as the week has days. It is the great longing on which one lives here, always the same thoughts and prayers that one will soon again see ones dear ones. One has much time to think and also determine the conversations between Addi and myself about the same matter. When will we see our dear ones in the USA and we hope confidently in G-d that this will be soon. I am constantly looking forward to the moment when I can start again to work for my dear ones and to repay all the good you did for me. To return you all the goodness, which I feel because of the present distance from you. The main thing is that you keep yourself healthy, as I have written before, you need have no worry about me and can be in good spirit. With hearty kisses and much love, your

Siegfried

---

[50]

The first of three typewritten extracts made by Siegfried of letters received from David Hirsch in New York. The other extracts are dated 6 April 1941 (No. 53) and 8 May 1941 (No. 54). David Hirsch reports the contents of letters he had received from Pincus and Adele, who appear to be aware of details of Siegfried's life though considerably after the events.

(From) *David Hirsch*, 19/2/41

73 Keap Street, Brooklyn.

I have two letters from your parents of 21/1.and 30/1. They would be glad if you could join us soon to have one care less. They got information that your papers have been transferred to the Consulat in London since July of last year. They want, to know if your address is the same as that of Addy because your uncle Max of Rio wanted to-write you. I asked why your father did not write so much. It is because he cannot work on the thin air mail-paper. Always his pen hooks on it. Now he has written with ink pencil. He is well th.Gd. He does not walk so much because it is very cold and snowy. But regularly he attends the services in the morning end in the evening. Your mother comes daily to my parents to bring them the newspaper.

---

[51]

The letters from Hamburg that Siegfried is acknowledging here will have come to him via the USA.

28 February 1941

Dear Musch, Dear Peter

With the contents of your letters of 10 December 40 which I received on 7/2, I was immensely pleased and I hope that in the meantime my lines of 6 February have arrived. (......) Each day I take part in the public prayers in which an increasingly large number of people take part. More frequently I lead the prayers and on the Shabbat before last I was called up for the Torah reading and then read the weekly portion of the Prophets. (......) I am pleased that Uncle Manfred and Aunt Else can visit you more frequently, give them my best regards and also Aunt Harriet and Hanna.

I wish you already today a very pleasant Easter holiday and am with hearty kisses and affectionate love

Your Siegfr.

---

[52]

The letter, of which this is a draft, appears to have been sent to Martha Wittmund in Chicago for onward transmission to Hamburg.

21 März 1941

Mrs M Wittmund
Chicago

Dear Musch, Dear Peter

I hope that in the meantime you have received my February letter and that you are in the best of health. (......) By the way how are Aunt Henny and Aunt Aly, I hope that they have survived the winter well, do they still live in the same boarding house? Convey my hearty greetings to them.

(......)

I too am occupied with studies speaking, shorthand and office work and sometimes with assisting a dental surgeon. I make sure that I always have something to do in order to fill the day. I have also had practice with cleaning and doing the washing.

(......)

(......) with hearty kisses and much love your S

---

[53]
See headnote to No. 50. Siegfried's letters seem not to have reached
Pincus and Adele but they were receiving his news through David Hirsch.
This letter gives an insight into conditions in Hamburg.

From David Hirsch
6/4/41

I have got 2 letters from your parents of February 26th.and March 11th.
They are glad to have heard about you and that you are allright. They hope
you will go on this way. They regret that your things have gone lost, but
you should not be discouraged because it is the fate of many of us. Please
Gd. better times will come for you too. They always thought how you
will care that they have not heard from you. Now it is good that you are
quiet. The news that your coming to the States may be delayed has them
rather dejected. They think that would delay at the same time to meet you
one day but they hope that the Almighty may improve conditions that life
may be worthwhile bearing. They are glad that Adolph and the other ones
take care of you and thank them. It may be better perhaps if your coming
will be delayed for some time, They think we are in a better position to
judge the matter. They are th.Gd. in the best of health, although other
sorrows are plenty. Your mother comes every day to see my father, she
wished she could give more help. Also your mother is convinced that
Elkeles has too much cares of his own, otherwise he would help more
as he did in former times. She advises me to communicate with Ernst,
though he also did not show much interest when your mother saw him
the last time. Your mother's siblings (*Geschwister*) hope to come over
here still this year so that they will have the pleasure to see again their
Addi. They do not know if they can live during the holidays according
the dietary laws. They send their most cordial regards for you and hope to
hear about you very soon again. Your father adds some lines telling that
he feels happy to read about your wellbeing. He is okay and hopes same
from you. He wishes you all the best especially that you may meet us
soon.-In the other letter they regret that the informations are lying so far
behind. Some weeks ago your mother went with your father to his former
business. It was affecting to see the joy all former colleagues displayed
when they met and shook hands with your father.

---

[54]

See headnote to No. 50. The first two sentences are addressed by David Hirsch to Siegfried. The remainder of the letter was transcribed by David Hirsch from a letter dated 16 April 1941 mainly by Adele and responding to a letter from David Hirsch.

From David Hirsch
75 Fort Washington Ave., Apt. 42., New York City. 8/5/41.

(16/4/41.)

Many thanks for your letters of 26.2.and 3. I wanted to answer them before the holidays but I was too tired and exhausted by the work that fatigued in this year more than ever because I did not have the real help.

I was pleased to hear again from you and your dear ones, hope they will be allright. As to your report of Siegfried's passage it is regrettable in every respect if it has to be delayed, but it is up to you of course as you are in a better position to judge what will be good. As you write it is hard for both sides to put up with it but we almost do not mind for more or less hardship. I am confident that you all will hasten whatever and whenever something can be done. I hope, Siegfried will understand it, even if it is special bad for him to have setbacks again and again. Hope he will follow your advice to write more personally and that he is okay. So far we have spent the holidays well. The first nightsi we were alone, we could not have visitors. We thought back with woefulness of the fine nights in your house. The first day at lunch Gustav Heineman was with us, Berta is in the Hospital for some weeks to be observed. Yesterday Loebels have left for there, next week Zinners will leave. I hear that also your mother-in-law may leave soon, so it gets more and more lonesome round us. The dear Papa is somewhat better during the last days. Hope it will last this time a little longer. Now, dear D. hope to hear from you soon again. Love for all your dear ones and for Siegfried as well.

Your auntie Adele.

The most cordial regards for you and Siegfried, yours uncle Pincus.

---

[55]

This letter appears to have come to Siegfried in Australia directly from Hamburg, probably by prisoner mail.

Hamburg 27. 4. 41

My Dear Siegfried

Through Sally Cohn who is also there and who wrote to his father, we got to know your address and we hurry to let you know that we are thank G-d well. We also thought sometime to hear from you. You can well imagine how worried we are about how things are with you, I hope that you are cheerful. We were very interested to learn something of your life there from the letter to Mr Cohn. We spent the Easter holidays well, I assume and hope that you could keep everything in the accustomed manner. My dear father, as before, goes into the neighbourhood and also several times in the week to his sisters, and according to the wish of my doctors take a daily walk.

I hope my dear child that you will answer immediately after receipt of these lines otherwise it will be a long time before we have your reply. Be well for today and have affectionate greetings and kisses

From your

Mother

My Dear Siegfried

Also I would be infinitely pleased to receive a sign of life from you. I am thank G-d well and hope the same of you. Write <u>immediately</u> after receipt of these lines.

For today most affectionate greetings and kisses

From your father who loves you

6.1 Draft letter [No. 56] to Peter and Musch, probably dated 30 April 1941 and posted on 2 May 1941.

[56]
The significance of the two dates at the beginning of this draft [Fig. 6.1]
is not clear.

2/5.41 30.04.41

My Dear Musch, My Dear Peter

I was again very pleased with the contents of your lines of the end of
January, which I received at the end of March. (.....) I hope that you spent
the Easter holidays[1] well. That was also the case with me as far as it was
possible this year, in any case all religious requirements were satisfied.
As I already mentioned earlier, I am always together with Addi[2] and we
again live under the same roof, albeit together with others. I was very
sorry to hear from David that Uncle Elkan's illness[3] is not at all trivial. In
his last letter he wrote that he is a little better. (.....)

(.....) I was pleased to hear dear Peter that in spite of the end of the
cold (illegible) you attend the divine services morning and evening and
that you dear Musch go daily to visit your siblings ?....? also Else and
Manfred[4] ?.....?. (......) in the hope of hearing from you soon I am with
hearty kisses in love your Siegfried

---

[1] A reference to Passover.

[2] Adolf Nussbaum,

[3] Pincus's brother, at the time suffering from cancer of the bladder

[4] Addi Nussbaum's parents.

---

[57]
The new address referred to in this letter, is to Siegfried's move from Hay
to Tatura. The nature of the documents Siegfried needed, possibly for his
or his parents immigration to the USA, is not clear.

5/6.41

My Dear Musch, Dear Peter

I hope confidently that you are both very well. (....) As you will see from
the address I am now in another place. I live under conditions similar to
before, only the climate is a better one. (.....) From Uncle Adolf Salomon
I urgently need new documents because the old ones are valueless. So far
I am not in possession of the same, though I wait impatiently. Without the
same I will not be able to travel. (.....)

Let me hear from you immediately by Air Mail and be affectionately kissed

By your Siegfried

---

[58]
Draft letter dated 11 June 1941 omitted as almost identical to other letters.

---

[59]
Redacted draft of a letter to Peter and Musch

Siegfried Hirsch
Camp No.3, Sector B
Tatura, Victoria, Australia
17 June 1941

My very dear ones, I am still waiting to hear from you and so am writing by Clipper Post.

I am very worried that the Consul has not yet confirmed receipt from Chicago of the new affidavit. I hope that finally it reaches there so that the matter will be speeded up. I think that my lines of 21/3 and 30/4 have in the meantime arrived that shortly I will receive a reply to my letters.

(……..)

This week finally I had the first letter from Elkeles and a reply regarding immigration to the USA. He confirms receipt of my first two letters

(……..) Today be affectionately greeted and kissed by

Your loving Siegfried

---

[60]
Undated letter to David Hirsch in New York, probably of October 1941.

Dear David

Many thanks for your lines and your good wishes we were happy after a longer interval. According to what you write to your mother you have a lot of work, in my opinion work is a blessing, so one does not have the opportunity to think too much about everything difficult. We spent the holidays well, I am glad that I now also have more to do, for the reasons mentioned earlier. We are thank g-d well, I hope this is also the case with all of you, for this one must already thank the Almighty. On the last festival day Uncle Pincus together with his earlier business colleague Aron was nominated for the honoured office of this day[1]. In the afternoon we were all together with the men entrusted with these offices and there were nice addresses framed by choral song. That for the time being nothing will come of the visit of your cousin is very regrettable, now it means once again to come to terms with it. That my brother Max wrote to you with an enclosure we already knew, we recently had post from him.

Now dear David I send both of you as well as your dear ones, also Hans and Erna the most heartfelt regards, we hope soon again to hear something.

For today be well and all the best

Your Aunt Adele

Dear David

Also I thank you heartily for your dear lines, I was very pleased with the same and send you both very heartfelt regards

Your Uncle Pincus

---

[1] Probably a reference to Simchat Torah. See Appendix 3

---

[61]
This draft letter was written in English – marked at the top "letter David".
The passage marked X - X was probably omitted from the letter that was
sent.

27/10/41

My dear Peter and Musch, I confidently hope that you are quite healthy, thank G'd I can tell you the same about me. I have not heard about you since the middle of August and I trust to get your news very soon again. With David's last letter I got the grievous notice that uncle Elkan passed away, redeeming him from great suffering. I am very upset by this report. I still hoped all the time it will be possible to cure his illness. It may be comforting to you all that he didn't know he was seriously ill. I learn that he has been buried at the side of his Selma, that many friends attended the funeral and that our Rabbi, who was a sincere and ardent friend, delivered the speech. Dear Peter please tell also dear Aunt Dora, Siegmund and the aunties that I am very sad with you over the bereavement which all of you have sustained. I heard that you, dear Musch, were present almost every day during uncle Elkan's sickness and I am sure you will further on assist Auntie Dora and be at her side as she is so alone now.

I hope you spent the autumn holidays as well as possible and that both of you got well over the Fast. On those days I had only one prayer to the Almighty that he may give you a constant health and that we can join again before long. I also trust that my hearty wishes for your this year's birthday, dear Peter, arrived in time and I am waiting to hear whether this was the case. Have you been once again with your doctor and was she satisfied with you, dear Musch? How are Auntie Else and Uncle Manfred and the other aunties? (The following is deleted in the draft) As for me I wrote already earlier that my present life runs very monotonous and the days are exactly alike. For the last half-year I have only been engaged with office work and I am doing a lot of daily typewriting. Except that I have to do my own washing and mending. As I have had very little physical exercise during the year past I have grown bigger and when my weight was taken some time ago it showed an increase of about 20 pounds.) Some friends of mine and a number of other people are now holding their own daily divine services where the prayers are recited according to our customs and I have been entrusted with the same office during prayers as you were, dear Peter. I am also sometimes conducting the prayers.

X I passed the holidays as it was possible under prevailing circumstances. On the High Festivals we had good readers in our service and I got well over the Fast. We had also a big Tabernacle and the weather was fine all the days. **X**

Now my dear ones keep well, hoping to hear about you shortly. I am for to-day, with hearty kisses and much love

Yours Siegfried

[62]

See headnote to No. 55. This letter may have come by the same route.
This is the last letter Siegfried received from his parents [Fig. 6.2]; less
than a month later the United States declared war on Germany.

Hamburg 10.11.41

My Dear Siegfried

By a letter of Mr Sally Cohn to his father we got to know that you had received our letter of 27.4, and we are very sad up to today we have not received a reply from you. You can surely well imagine with how much longing we wait for a sign of life from you. We hope that you are well and we too thank G-d are the same, for that we must thank g-d. In the meantime we have had sadness and joy. Sadness through the death of dear Uncle Elkan, of which you have no doubt heard from his children. We all miss him very much, but for him it is well, because at the end he had to suffer much pain. Joy because of dear Papa's 80th birthday. The pleasure on this otherwise nice day was naturally disturbed, first by the mentioned sad event, but mainly that you, beloved child, could not be with us, may the Alm'ghty give that we may see each other again, our longing is great. We pray for you daily but do the same for us.

Now for today I wish you everything good, remain really well and write to us again immediately. Have a thousand affectionate greetings and kisses

From your very much loving

Mother

My Dear Siegfried!

After we heard that you were very pleased with our letter, I would ask you from my heart also to please us with a letter. As dear mother has already written, we are thank G-d well, but the longing for you is great. I hope also you are well. For today also affectionate greetings and kisses.

Your loving

Papa

6.2 Letter [No. 62] dated 10 November 1941 received by Siegfried from his parents. It is the last he received from them.

[63]
The first of a number of short messages that may have been sent via the
International Red Cross Prisoner of War Mail.

5 January 1942

Pincus & Adele Hirsch
Hamburg 13
Kielortallee 16
Germany

Siegfried Hirsch
Internment Camp No. 4, Section C
Tatura, Victoria, Australia

My Dear Ones

Long not heard from you hope you are well. Only April letter received
write more often. Affectionate kisses

Your Siegfried

---

[64]
The paragraph marked X – X in the draft was probably omitted from the
letter as sent.

4/2/42

My Dear Parents

I have unfortunately not heard from you and wait from delivery to delivery
once again to receive a letter from you. Many people here regularly
receive post from their parents. ?.....? by contrast there is never a letter
amongst them for me. Receipt of your dear letter at the end of July is
confirmed and request that you write more often, possibly by Air Mail
because this is sometimes quicker. The son of my earlier colleague Aron,
dear Papa, has recently received postcards and letters from his parents.
Above all I hope confidently that both of you are well. Thank G-d I can
report the same of me.

X My life at present is very monotonous, as you can imagine, and one day
is like another. Apart from the work I do in the camp for the community,
I have to attend to my own matters, washing, sewing and darning. Apart
from that there is opportunity to read and study and daily ?...? in the ?...?

to take instruction in the ?...?school. The food that consists of three meals a day and is cooked by our people is good and plentiful.

At present, as you will know, it is summer here, which in this part of the world is much hotter than in Europe. By contrast it is cool in the evenings (.....) and sometimes the nights are really cold. Nevertheless one gets used to the temperature differences if one lives in the climate for a longer period. Naturally I must put on something warm in the evening, if during the day as a consequence of the heat I have worn only a shirt and short trousers, however sometimes the nights are very warm and then all windows and doors are left open. **X**

I was very sad about David's report of the demise of Uncle Elkan. I hoped all the time that I knew of his illness that it would be possible to cure the same. It is good that he himself did not know that he was so seriously ill. As I heard he was buried at Selma's side and that Dr Carlebach, who had lost a true and upright friend, gave the eulogy. To dear Aunt Dora and you all I want to send my heartfelt condolences. I hope that the aunts as well as Uncle Manfred and Aunt Else are well. Further I hope that the wishes for your birthday dear Papa will in due course have reached you at the right time. About the day I heard some time ago from Leo. Have you recently again been to see your doctor and was he satisfied with dear Mother? I hope above all to hear from you both. I will write to you again shortly during which time I expect that post to me will be on its way and that I will soon receive a letter, because it will take a long time before there is an answer to these lines. For today I am with hearty kisses and affectionate greeting and tender love Your Siegfried

---

[65]
Probably the acknowledgement of Adele and Pincus's letter of 10 November 1941 (No. 62).

12/2/42

My Beloved Parents

You can perhaps imagine how indescribable my joy was when two days ago there wa a letter in the post from you ---- after I had waited an endlessly long time for one. I am therefore hurrying immediately to confirm receipt of your dear air mail lines of 10.11and hope that it will take very long before this letter reaches you. Just last week I wrote to you how very much I wait for lines from you and I hope that you will soon receive the lines of the 4th of this month. I (….) you your (?...?) letter of 27/4 which I received at the end of July and confirmed receipt immediately and asked that you write more often. I also hope that you will not wait for the arrival of these lines before you reply, rather also write between times, so that I receive a letter from you very soon. Above all (?...?) I* was very thankful to see from your lines that you are thank G-d well and I hope confidently is so now and when this letter arrives. I can also thank G-d report the same of myself only the longing for you is great. I ask only one thing of you, do everything to remain healthy so that we can see each other in good health. I pray every day (?...?) for you, as I know you pray for me daily and there is no minute when I do not think of you. That on the day of your 80th birthday, dear Papa, I was with you in my thoughts you can well imagine and how heavy my heart was spend it with you. My prayer to the Almighty was that you will experience this day for a long time. For today I still wish you both all the best. Have a thousand affectionate greetings and kisses from your affectionately loving

Siegfried

---

[66]
A short message of 25 February 1942 has been omitted. See footnote to No. 63.

---

[67]
The airmail letter of 10 November referred to in this draft is No. 62.

11/3/42

My Dear Parents

I hope that you have in the meantime received my two letters of 4 and 12 February. Your dear airmail letter of 10/11, which I received with such great joy, I have already confirmed. I hope that you are also well and I wait impatiently to receive a further letter from you – Also my health is good only the longing for you is great and I think continuously of you irrespective of what I am doing at the time as you can imagine my life at present is monotonous and one day is like another. Apart from the work one does for the community, one has only to look after one's own affairs like washing ones clothes, sewing and darning. Apart from that there is the opportunity to read and study and to take instruction in the camp school. The food that consists of three meals is good and is cooked by our own people. At present as you will know it is summer, though it is towards its end. In this part of the world this is much hotter than in Europe. In the evening, however, it often cools down a lot and sometimes the nights are really cold. At the beginning these unusual temperature differences are very unpleasant but this becomes less if one lives in this climate. One has to put on warmer clothes in the evening particularly if during the day because of the heat one has worn only a shirt and short trousers. Sometimes, however, the nights are also very warm and then one leaves all windows and doors open.

I hope shortly to hear from you again. For today I wish you both all the best from my heart. With a thousand affectionate kisses I am your most loving Siegfried

---

[68]
This short message of 25 March 1942 has been omitted. See headnote to No. 63.

---

[69]

5/4.42

My Dear Parents

Since almost two months have passed again since I received your dear letter of November and I answered you immediately, I hope the more shortly to have lines from you. I hope that you are not waiting with you next letter until my lines have arrived, since in this case because then it would take a long time before I hear from you. I hope confidently in the meantime that my two letters of February and my lines of March will in the meantime reach you and that you are both well. I too am thank G-d in good health. However, longing and worry accompany me perpetually. While writing these lines it is just Easter week and I need not tell you where my thoughts were on the Easter evenings, when we sat together and said the usual festival prayers. Apart from that we were able to celebrate the festival days as usual and as in previous years took account of all the requirements. Until I receive your Easter lines sadly a considerable time will elapse. Summer here is now at an end and the days are somewhat cooler, while the sun is so powerful that on clear days during the midday hours it radiates a pleasant warmth. Altogether the days here with a clear blue sky also in winter are more numerous than in Europe.

How is Aunt Dora, is she now calmer about the loss she suffered by the loss of dear Uncle Elkan: and how are the other aunts?

Have you recently been to the doctor, dear mother, and what did he say to you, do you still have continuous treatment? And how is it with problems with walking, dear Papa

For today take a thousand regards and kisses with great love from your

Siegfried

Regards for Hanna,

How is she

---

[70]
This short message of 24 April 1942 has been omitted. See headnote to No. 63.

---

[71]

28 April 1942

Dear Parents

I confidently hope that my lines of last month have reached you and that my last letter of 5 April will soon reach you. I too constantly wait for the next letter from you and impatiently expect that the same will arrive very soon. I hope that you are both well, which thank G-d I can report of myself. I hope that ion the meantime you have written somewhat more often and in shorter intervals, so that I do not have to wait so long until I hear from you again, since the post usually arrives irregularly, sometimes at shorter intervals and then again – much longer ones.

In the last letter I wrote about the Easter week. As last year we were able to spend Easter in the usual way. On both evenings we sat together for the customary festival prayers, but all the time I was with you in my thoughts.

In my last letter I asked you whether you had recently again been to your doctor and what he told you. Do you still have your usual treatment dear Mother, and how is it with your walking troubles dear Papa? How is Aunt Dora and the other aunts? Some time ago I had a letter from Uncle Max and Aunt Hedwig. They write that they are satisfied and have, as you know, arrived well. Have you heard from them recently?

At present it is much warmer here, the autumn days here are sometimes as warm as the summer nights in Europe.

My days are filled as before with the same activities. Cleaning, ?---?, sowing as well as reading, study, writing. For today I close wishing you all the best, with a thousand affectionate kisses with love

Your Siegfried

---

[72]
Draft of No. 73. Words in brackets were omitted from the letter that was finally sent.

24 Mai 1942

My Dear Beloved Parents

I assume with certainty that in the meantime my earlier letters have reached you and hope that also my lines of 5 and 29 April will reach you soon. Unfortunately in the last weeks I have not received a further letter from you and with every post I wait to hear from you, since this is such a long time ago. Above all I confidently hope that you are both well. Health-wise I too am well and I imagine what it will be like when I can be with my loved ones again. In the meantime the Whitsun holidays have passed, so one month goes after the other. On the first evening we sat together with a number of friends and studied in the customary manner. We decorated our evening and morning service with green branches. Naturally, the green here is quite different from that in Europe, namely mainly with rubber and eucalyptus trees that grow everywhere here. During the last fourteen days it has rained rather a lot here in contrast to the previous summer half year, a sign of the beginning of the winter months. It is overcast and the sun rarely shines through the clouds, while the temperature now frequently changes from cold to warm. The temperature differences are still marked at this time of year.

(While it was still cold and damp yesterday and the days before it is at present again mild in spite of the absence of sun. Last week I was surprised by a letter from Arthur Rubin, from who I had not heard for years. He visited Leo and Martha and got to know my address there. After a nine-year marriage he had a daughter who is now 2 years old.)

I confidently hope that next time I will be able to confirm receipt of a letter and in this expectation, I am for today with kisses and fondest love your

Siegfried

---

[73]
This letter dated 24 May 1942 by Siegfried appears to have left four days later after examination by an Australian censor and reached Hamburg by an unknown route. The outside shows that it was sent by Prisoner of War mail and that it was opened by the Wehrmacht censor in Hamburg. It was marked 'unbekannt' on 2 September and returned on 9 September 1942 with a sticker saying, "Abgereist ohne Angabe der Adresse" (Left without leaving an address). In Australia, on its return, or in the United Kingdom, it was once again subject to a censor. By this time Siegfried was back in Britain and the letter was returned to him at the address of his aunt, Mrs Henny Landau, 38 Northolme Road, London N5; this was the address Siegfried had given at the time of his internment in Australia [Fig. 5.3].

24 May 1942

My Dear good Parents

I assume with certainty that in the meantime my earlier letters have reached you and hope that also my lines of 5 and 29 April will reach you soon. Unfortunately in the last weeks I have not received a further letter from you and with every post I wait to hear from you, since this is such a long time ago. Above all I confidently hope that you are both well. Health-wise I too am well and I imagine what it will be like when I can be with my loved ones again. In the meantime the Whitsun holidays have passed, so one month goes after the other. On the first evening we sat together with a number of friends and studied in the customary manner. We decorated our evening and morning service with green branches. Naturally, the green here is quite different from that in Europe, namely mainly with rubber and eucalyptus trees that grow everywhere here. During the last fourteen days it has rained rather a lot here in contrast to the previous summer half year, a sign of the beginning of the winter months. It is overcast and the sun rarely shines through the clouds, while the temperature now frequently changes from cold to more warm. The temperature differences are still marked at5 this time of year and are typical for the climate. - I confidently hope that next time I will be able to confirm receipt of a letter and in this expectation, I am for today with kisses and fondest love your

Siegfried

---

[74]
A short message of 26 May 1942 has been omitted. See headnote to No. 63.

---

[75]

At this time Jews were being compelled to live in Judenhäuser ('Jew houses'). David Hirsch's mother, Dora Hirsch, had informed him that she was now living in the Altersheim (the Jewish Home for the Aged) in Sedanstrasse, Hamburg, while Siegfied's parents were living in the Jewish Orphanage. Emil and Bella Badrian, were about to move to the Hamburg Jewish Boys Orphanage at 3 Papendam. The rabbi referred to is Joseph Carlebach. The Peter referred to in this letter is probably the person to who Siegfried wrote in earlier letters from Australia [e.g. Nos. 49, 51 etc.]

From David Hirsch

> 75 Washington Ave
> New York City
> May 28, 1942

My dear Siegfried

I'm glad to tell you that I had a letter from my mother reporting that your dear parents are living now in the same building and on the same floor with her. Badrians are going to live in the orphanage Papendam. My mother wrote I should tell you that Peter is longing for some lines from you. Uncle Julius celebrates his 80th birthday. Almost all our family is now in the home for aged people.

Your questions about dates when letters has been sent by or received me I cannot answer. Life here is very quite. I cannot hold my letters longer than I have answered them.

I wrote you almost from the beginning that I was not optimistic about the conditions to enter this country. I did not yet change my opinion. You know that I didn't succeed in bringing out my folks.

Should I advise you I would try to volunteer there in defense work or civil *service*. I cannot agree with sailing over the ocean in this time.

Our Rabbi is now in Riga. Benny Meyer's widow got married to the old Mr Offenberg.

Else wrote that your things are standing with Dr Levy. Lazar Lanzkron has a job somewhere in the country, as it seems to me. He is now father of boy-twins.

Adolf asked this week for your address. He will send you a little money-order. Sulzbacher told in London from you. You did not change yet your nature. Why not?

I had to register. I don't care about exemption. We all have changed our nature.

There is no way to bring people here from oversea. Should I not succeed in bringing my family to this country during the war, I would rather prefer to go back to England.

Elkeles' father-in-law arrived here recently. I did not see him yet. In the course of time you get indifferent to all the former friends.

Keep well, good luck. I wish you a little more courage and resoluteness

Regards and love, Yours David

---

[76]
Other German Jewish internees in Australia appear to have received post from Germany, which is referred to in this letter as 'dort' ('there'). Similarly to Letter 73, this was marked 'unknown' on 22 October and returned to Siegfried four days later. On the way it passed censors in in Australia and Germany

16 June 1942

My Dear Good parents

Though in the last week much post has arrived from there, in part, already from the end of March, and unfortunately there was nothing amongst it for me and I wait daily to have post from you. I trust that in the meantime you have received my letters and that you both feel well. I can also thank G-d report that I am well. It struck me that for your birthdays I should already have written in my previous letter of 24.5, since this letter will not arrive in time. Nevertheless, I want to this today and wish you dear Papa and dear Muttchen all the best from all my heart. May the benevolent G-d give good health in the co0mming year, and may he give that we will see each other again. I pray daily to G-d and this prayer gives me strength. I think of you so much and then my happiest childhood years come to mind, which I spent under your protection and guidance. Then I think of the wonderful adolescence and later years which I was allowed to spend in my parental home in which I could sun myself in your love, your understanding, your parental companionship. All this is constantly lively before my eyes and fills me with infinite, deep gratitude to you. Also, I have not forgotten the worries and distressful hours that I caused you in my life, and only the regret reduces the consciousness that the child and young person does not understand how wrong it is to give parents worry and the hope still to put everything right. For today be affectionately greeted and kissed by

Your loving Siegfried

---

[77]

Siegfried wrote this letter [Fig. 6.3] to his parents on 26 June 1942. It is the last of which we have both the draft and the original letter. The various stamps on the outside [Fig. 6.4], show that it was sent by prisoner of war mail, that it passed three censors, presumably in Australia, Germany and on its return to Britain. It was identified in Hamburg on 23 October 1942 as undeliverable and entered the return postal system on 26 October. It bears a label, 'Abgereist ohne angabe der Adresse' (Left without leaving an address).

26 June 1942

My dear Parents

Again this week post arrived without anything for me from you. I trust that in the meantime you have received my letters and that the last of May and June arrive soon. I also hope that both of you are well and I can report of myself that I am thank G-d well. I wrote in my previous letter that for your birthdays I should have written one post earlier so that my wishes arrive in time. I would like in any case to repeat these again and wish you beloved Papa and beloved Muttchen all the best from my heart. May the dear G-d keep you well in the coming year and may he give that we see each other again. I pray for this daily and know that in prayer we are united, that gives me strength. When I think of you, and that is almost always, I remember the happy years of my youth that I spent under your parental guidance. Then I think of the so nice later years, which I was allowed to spent so happily in my parental home, and your love and understanding. Your fatherly and motherly comradeship is before my eyes and fills me with unending gratitude to you. I also know that through me you were not spared worries and distressing hours, but I got to know that parents immediately forgive, knowing that the young person does not yet sense that parents are something other than just friends. I confidently hope still to be able to express gratitude for everything. I hope soon to see your lines and in this expectation I am with affectionate regards and kisses your loving

Siegfried

6.3 Siegfried's letter [No. 77] to his parents, dated 26 June 1942, was returned to him from Germany [see Fig. 6.4].

6.4 The outside of the returned letter [No. 77] dated 26 June 1942, which was returned from Hamburg on 26 October 1942. Note the German and British censors' stamps and the label that reads "Left without leaving an address"

[78]

This is the draft of the final letter Siegfried wrote to his parents. The passage between X –X in this daft was probably omitted from the letter as sent. At the time there had already been five deportations from Hamburg. Pincus and Adele Hirsch were on the sixth transport which went to Theresienstadt on 15 July 1942, seven days after this draft was written. As Jews were limited to Judenhäuser and were progressively being deported, their mail was probably of little concern to the postal authorities, possibly unlike Nos. 73, 76 and 77. This letter was not returned.

8 July 1942

My Dear Parents

I hope that in the meantime you have received my earlier letters and that my lines of May and June will reach you soon, the latter with my birthday wishes. I hope confidently that you feel well health wise and I can also thank G-d report the same of myself. – Last week it was a year since Uncle Elkan [uncertain meaning] and I think of you dear Papa, Aunt Dora on account of this day. Also to David I have ?----? written, and would also like to bring my thoughts to the attention of Siegmund. Though the days and weeks here pass in so similar a way and one month passes like the other, the year also passes quickly, in any case it seems like that if one looks back at it. I only hope that soon years will come when one is no longer has to live separated from ones dear ones and everything difficult will have passed. – Recently from the son of your past colleague I received regards from you with which I was very pleased. Unfortunately the letter, which he had received from his father, was from the end of last year, {three words). As I* wrote to you last time I hope ?---/ soon to have new post from you. Recently I was surprised by a letter from Arthur Rubin from who I had not heard for a long time. He visited Leo and Martha and learned my address there. After nine years he had a daughter who is now 2 years old. X I hope that the old aunts and also Aunt Dora are well. Have you had post from Uncle Manfred and Aunt Else Harriet, I hope they are well. – I must close for today and am beloved Papa & beloved M other with a thousand greetings and kisses with much love Your Siegfried

X I also I had a letter from Ernst this week in response to my lines on the death of his mother. **X**

6.5a First page of the last draft letter [No. 78], dated 8 July 1942 that Siegfried wrote to his parents.

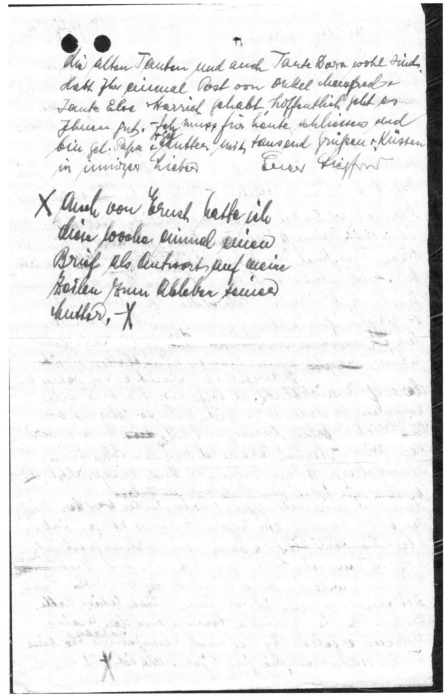

6.5b Draft of the second page of letter No. 78, dated 8 July 1942.

[79]
According to a note added at the bottom of this letter, it arrived in March 1943, when Siegfried was again living in London.

David Hirsch
75 Fort Washington Ave
New York City
August 28, 1942

Dear Siegfried!

Your letters of June 3 and July 10 I received with the same delivery of post. You are impatient to hear from your parents. So was I up to now. On the 13th of August I received a letter from the Red Cross that reads as follows: *Lieber David, hoffen Dich und Siegfried gesund, sind in Sorge. Wir sind wohlauf, wohnen Sedanstrasse. Innige Gruesse Dir und Siegfried, hoffen baldigst Nachricht. Pinkus Adele.*[1] Immediately after receipt I answered on the same way: My Dears, Siegfried quite well. He hopes to return to Else. Only then he can write to you by Red Cross. His return still undecided. David. I took my information about a prospective return to England from newspaper reports that our friends in England sent me. If it will come true, I do not now, of course. But it may be a little heartening for your parents to live in this belief. Anyway, I wish this letter should not reach you anymore in Australia but in England. Haven't you an opportunity to write your parents by the way of the Red Cross?

It is very easy to blame me for not writing you often. But believe me, it is not so comfortable for me either to live here alone. Sometimes you lose all the courage to go on. Unfortunately, I had no opportunity to write you important news. Things you wanted to know never came up in the meantime. I do my work only and do not care about anything else. Would you be in this country, you might understand me better

My family lives now together with family Sussmann. They rented a furnished house in Queen Elizabeth Walk and seem to feel quite comfortably. There are always problems as to the education of the children and as to providing facilities for a job for Joseph and a good school for Gotthelf. Hans is working at Dr Bondy's[2]. In his trade he could not find a position.

Of course, I registered for the army. Whether they will grant me exemption as minister, I do not know yet. Whatever will come, we have to take it. I had several times Red Cross letters from my mother. Naturally she can't write much.

I am anxious to get my family over. The necessary documents are now in Washington. The proceedings will take about a year. Even then there is the question how to accommodate a passage.

I do not understand what you have written about pending decisions you will have to take. Do you mean joining the army or returning to England? An emigration to the U.S.A. seems to be possible again. However I do not know whether I shall advise you to do so. It seems to me more reasonable, for the time being, when you will return to England.

Wishing you a better and more prosperous New Year than the last one.

Yours

David

---

[1] Dear David, Hope you and Siegfried well, are worried. We are well, live Sedanstrasse. Affectionate regards for you and Siegfried, hope news soonest. Pinkus Adele

[2] Dr Jonas Bondi, a German Jewish émigré chemist was the proprietor of a company that produced 'Vesop', a concentrated liquid yeast extract and 'Passop' a similar product of purely vegetable origin, suitable for Passover use.

Chapter 7

END NOTE

On *Yom Kippur*, 21 September 1942, a transport left Theresienstadt for Treblinka, north east of Warsaw, with Pincus and Adele and many other Hamburg Jews on board. The journey probably took about two days and on arrival they were all murdered. Siegfried was on the high seas on his way back from Australia to England.

By a decision of the Amtsgericht Hamburg (County Court, Hamburg) on 11 January 1951, File number 54 II 1307-1308/50, Pincus Hirsch and his wife Adele née Nussbaum were declared dead as of 8 May 1945.

At the end of November 2010 *Stolpertsteine* (Stumble stones) in memory of Pincus and Adele Hirsch were embedded in the pavement outside Kielortallee 16, their erstwhile Hamburg home.

Appendix 1

THE GERMAN TEXTS OF THE LETTERS

This Appendix the German text of the Hamburg letters of 1939 (Nos. 1 to 48) are reproduce, with the Hebrew salutations, abbreviations and phrases as in the original letters. These were kindly transcribed by Astrid Louven of Hamburg from the original texts handwritten in „deutsche Schrift". The German text of the Australia letters of 1941 and 1942 (Nos. 49 to 79), also reproduced in this chapter, have in part been redacted for the reason given at the beginning of Chapter 6.

The Hamburg Letters

[1] Hamburg, d. 31/3 39

Mein geliebtes Kind. לא״ט

Ich habe mich unendlich gefreut, dass Du abends noch angerufen hast, dadurch habe ich doch ziemlich gut geschlafen, auch Deine heutige Karte hat mich sehr beruhigt, weil ich daraus ersah, dass Du den gewünschten Aufenthalt bewilligt bekommen hast und dass Du sehr gut gereist bist. Häufig hat man vor dem Reisen Angst und man übersteht es dann doch besser, wie man denkt. Uns geht es G.s.D. gut; es ist sehr gut, dass ich diese Tage noch allerhand zu tun habe, dadurch komme ich nicht viel zum Nachdenken. Heut Morgen hat Bella Petrower sich telephonisch verabschiedet. Sie fährt noch heute mit dem Schiff, du wirst sie also schon am Sonntag dort sprechen. Beim Juwelier war ein besonders netter Herr, ein Herr Walter, der uns bedient hat, die Taxe kostete 8 M. und das Nachschätzen der Uhr noch einmal 3 M., es kam übrigens gestern wie wir gedacht haben ablehnende Antwort. Bei W. war schon alles überfüllt, nur in Anbetracht, dass Papa ein alter Kollege ist, haben sie es noch angenommen, die Herren haben sich alle sehr mit Papa gefreut. Preis 10.50 für Depot, die Sachen müssen bis zum 31. Oktober in Devisen eingelöst sein, wieviel werden sie uns zur Zeit mitteilen. Soeben kommen Deine herrlichen Blumen, tausend Dank, geliebtes Kind, ich habe mich unendlich gefreut auch über Deine lieben Zeilen. Ich werde sie immer wieder durchlesen und ganz ruhig sein und zum Allmächtigen beten, dass er unsere Wünsche in Erfüllung gehen lässt und uns recht bald wieder zusammen führt.

Hanna Hirsch ist nun bei uns, sie hat sich das Zimmer sehr nett eingerichtet, sie hat mir gestern und heute schon viele Wege abgenommen, was mir viel wert war. Die Päckchen von Tante Gella sind angekommen, ich kann ihr heute nicht mehr schreiben. Grüß sie herzlich, ich lasse tausend mal danken. Grüße auch Siegmund u. Josi die Kinder und auch Elkeles und Frau, hast Du mit letzterem gesprochen, war er zugänglich. Dass Nati nicht dort ist, ist sehr schade, deine Post ist eingesteckt worden. Sonst wäre nichts weiter zu berichten. Fräulein war noch nicht wieder hier.

Nun, mein geliebter Junge, wünsche ich Dir einen recht guten 31.3.39, eine recht gute Weiterreise. Schreibe möglichst bald nach Deiner Ankunft damit wir hören, wie die Überfahrt und Ankunft war. Tausend innige Grüße und Küsse von Deinem dich liebenden Muttchen.

(Kreissymbol) ein Kuss

(Die beiden Hannas grüßen herzlich.)

Hamburg, d. 31. März 1939

Lieber Siegfried! לאי״ט

Es herrschte gestern Abend, wie Du Dir wohl denken kannst, im Hirschlager großer Jubel, als Dein Anruf kam. Mama war so freudig erregt, dass sie gar nicht daran dachte, mich ans Telefon zu rufen. Ich kann Dir gar nicht sagen, wie sehr ich mich freute + Du hast eine große Mizwoh getan, dass Du angerufen hast. Es ist doch sehr schön, dass Du die Erlaubnis bekommen hast, bis morgen Abend in Amsterdam zu bleiben + wird der Allmächtige also auch (unles.) beistehen und Dir הצלחה u. ברכה geben. Auch noch besten Dank für die schönen Blumen, die wir soeben erhielten. Ich wünsche dir keine Gelegenheit zum Giavor. Vergiss nicht Montag einen halben Tag zu fasten. Ich wünsche Josi + (unles.), auch (unles.) Elkeles recht guten שבת und verbleibe mit Gruß und Kuss dein dich liebender Vater.

Grüße alle Lieben Siegmund und Frau. Bestelle Tante Gella unseren besten Dank.

[2] ב״ה
Hamburg d. 3/4 39

Mein Geliebtes לאי״ט

Ich bin froh, dass Du glücklich gelandet bist, möge der Allmächt'ge Dir nun beistehen, dass Du bald etwas Dich Befriedigendes findest. Du warst doch etwa nicht böse, dass wir anriefen, ich hätte es bis Dienstag nicht ausgehalten, ich freue mich nun schon auf Deinen Brief, der uns wohl Näheres wissen lässt. Es geht uns G.s.D gut, wenn nur nicht die Sehnsucht mich manchmal überfallen würde, ich bezwinge mich aber, denn ich habe Dir versprochen, mich gesund zu erhalten. Die Mostpralinen haben schon sehr abgenommen, wenn ich einen esse, denke ich an Dich und, da ich dies sehr oft am Tage tue kannst Du Dir denken, dass sie sehr bald alle sein werden. Gestern haben wir den neuen Gasherd eingeweiht, er backt und kocht wunderbar, auch Else hat einen Kuchen hier gebacken, so waren wir mit 4 Personen in der Küche, das war etwas für deine Mutter.

Wann soll ich eigentlich bei Mühlenbrock und bei Nelki anrufen, teile mir dies gelegentlich mit. Ich hoffe in Deinem Brief schon mehr über Schrank und Bett zu erfahren, ich kann wahrscheinlich eine eiserne Bettstelle bekommen. Wie ich höre ist James Wigderowitsch auch dort, wohnt derselbe auch bei Sterns? Ich wollte Dir noch mitteilen, dass die Herren bei M.M.W. uns sagten, Du solltest Dich doch einmal an Herrn Siegmund W. wenden, der auch im Lande lebt, ebenso an Herrn Minden, aber das überlasse ich Dir. Dass Dir der Aufschnitt in A. gut geschmeckt hat, kann ich mir denken, wir sollten auch etwas haben, aber Frau Freundlich hat alles für sich behalten. Heute kam ein Brief von Dr. Baer, den ich Dir zugehen lasse. Heute Abend sind nun Else, Liesel und Gotthelf bei uns, morgen Mittag Tante Harriet, es gab allerhand zu tun, aber Hanna Hirsch hat mir ja geholfen, allein hätte ich es nicht geschafft.

Nun mein Geliebtes muss ich für heute schließen, nächstens mehr, ich hoffe dann einen Antwortschein einlegen zu können. Grüße Sterns und Lanzkrons, auch David und Adolf herzlich von mir. Verlebe einen recht guten Jontef und nimm innige Grüße und Küsse von Deinem Muttchen.

Lieber Siegfried

Ich war wirklich glücklich zu hören, dass Du gottlob gut gereist bist und nicht seekrank geworden bist. Der liebe G'tt wird Dir auch ferner beistehen, auch Dich bald zu .....? kommen lassen. Ich war gestern in der Synagoge Beneckestraße, Carlebach konnte nachmittags nicht sprechen, da er sehr heiser ist, er wird schon den siebenten Tag פסח sprechen.

Ich wünsche noch gesegneten י"ט, grüße Sterns, Lanzkrons, David, Adolf und alle Lieben von mir. Halt Dich ferner recht wohl + munter + sei gegrüßt und geküsst von Deinem Dich liebenden Vater.

Guten יום טוב

Die beiden Hannas lassen grüßen.

[3] Hamburg d. 6. April

Mein gel. Junge לאי״ט

Deinen l. Brief erhielten wir kurz vor Jontef, der kam ja sehr schnell, im Gegenteil zu Deiner Schabboskarte, die erst am Sonntag Morgen eintraf. Ich habe mich unendlich gefreut, noch bevor wir uns zum Seder setzten, von Dir gehört zu haben. Wie hast Du, mein Liebling die ersten Jom-Touw Tage verbracht? Wir sind, dadurch dass der liebe kleine Gotthelf mit am Seder war, durch seine Lebhaftigkeit etwas über Dein Fernsein hinweggekommen. Er hat auch bei uns geschlafen und war auch der Kaffeetisch morgens dadurch ziemlich lebhaft. Am ersten Mittag war Tante Harriet bei uns und auch sonst hatten wir ziemlich viel Besuch. Heut Mittag hat Frau Oppenheimer bei uns gegessen, sie brachte uns einen sehr lieben Brief von Herm und auch sonst allerlei aus seiner Sendung. Wie ist es nun mit Deinem Zimmer. David schrieb an Else er hätte den ganzen Tag mit Dir gesucht. Habt Ihr etwas Passendes gefunden? Hoffentlich ist es sauber, das ist meine größte Sorge. Hast Du Dich schon um Dein Gepäck kümmern können, hoffentlich ist alles gut angekommen. Wenn Du mit Adolf ein eigenes Zimmer hast, musst Du doch wahrscheinlich allerhand von Deinen Sachen gebrauchen. Ich bin sehr gespannt auf Deinen nächsten Brief, ich denke doch, dass Du uns schon etwas Näheres darüber, wie sich Dein Leben in der nächsten Zeit abspielen wird, mitteilen kannst. Bei Elsa habe heute angerufen, die Auktion findet erst nächste Woche nach Ostern statt, ich bekomme dann Bescheid, auch bei Wissel habe angefragt, sobald er Bescheid hat, schickt er es uns zu. Ich hätte Dir gern einen Antwortschein beigelegt, dieselben sind aber nur am Mittwoch zu haben. Schreibe doch etwas über E. Nun Mein Liebling muss ich wohl schließen, da Papa auch noch schreiben will. Verlebe Jom-Touw weiter gut, grüße Sterns auch Lanzkrons, auch Tante Henny, David und die Kinder, wenn Du sie sprichst, nimm tausend innige Grüße und Küsse von

Deinem Dich liebenden Muttchen

Mein lieber Siegfried! לאי״ט

Hoffentlich hast Du die ט״י gut verlebt. Bin neugierig von Dir darüber

Näheres zu hören, auch hätte ich gern gehört, ob St. etwas über die andere Sache verlauten lassen hat.

Manfred + Else haben uns ט״יbesucht, am ט״יhast du David wohl gesprochen. Hast Du die englische Predigt verstanden? Du kannst Dir wohl denken, dass ich sehr neugierig bin von Dir zu hören. Von Heckscher erhielt ich heute einen netten Brief. Wie geht es Dir, lieber Junge, schmecken die englischen Mazzot gut? Es ist schade, dass man nicht jeden Abend telefonieren kann Wir müssen uns mit den schriftlichen Berichten zufrieden geben. Hoffentlich fallen diese immer gut aus. Weiter guten ט״י! Mit Gruß und Kuss Dein Dich liebender Vater

Lieber Siegfried!

Wie in wachen Träumen schwebt Dein Bild mir vor!...

Taucht aus tiefstem Dunkel heller nur hervor!

Schlaf in Deinem Zimmer ach so wunderbar,

morgens vor dem Fenster zwitschern Fink + Star

und um sieben Uhr wohl klappt Papa die Tür,

faul in meinem Bette komm ich mir dann für.

Milch- + Brotmann rennen durch das Treppenhaus.

Ja, da denk ich immer: Ziehste wieder aus?

Sonnenschein und vieles mich entschädigt zwar,

gütig ist gesonnen mir dein Elternpaar!

Deiner Abschiedsworte eingedenk mit vielen Wünschen und Grüßen Hanna H.

Lieber Siegfried, leider bin ich nicht wie meine Kusine an Dichteritis erkrankt; daher sende ich Dir heute nur herzliche Grüße, in der Hoffnung, dass es Dir so gut geht wie uns. Deine Hanna.

Die Blumen haben sich wunderbar gehalten. (Handschrift von Adele)

[4] PK
ב״ה
Hamburg d. 9.4. 39

Mein l. Siegfried לאי״ט

Vielen Dank für Deinen l. Brief, den wir heute früh erhielten und den ich nach Jontef ausführlich beantworten werde. Hoffentlich hast du auch unseren Schabbosbrief erhalten. Uns geht es gut, ich hoffe ein Gleiches von dir. Hast du den Brief von Dr. B. erhalten, antwortest du von dort oder soll ich ein solches von hier tun. Die Legung einer Dose des Telefons ins Schlafzimmer soll 17-18 M. kosten, ich wüsste gern deine Ansicht, ob ich es machen lassen soll, du musst mir aber gleich in deinem nächsten Schreiben darauf antworten, da ich Bescheid geben muss.

Nun für heute mein l. Kind gut Jontef, grüß Sterns und auch Fr. Lanzkron herzlich von mir und nimm auch du innige Grüße und Küsse von deiner Mutter.

Viele Grüße von den Hannahs und Else, die wieder einen Kuchen hier gebacken hat.

Mein lieber Siegfried

Ich will dir doch schnell einen Jontef-Gruß senden. Verlebe die Tage recht gut und sei bestens gegrüßt u. geküsst von deinem Vater

beantwort. 14/4/39

Herrn Siegfried Hirsch c/o Stern, London N. 4, Queens Road 87

[5] Hamburg 12/4 39

Mein Geliebtes

Ich hoffe unsere kurze Karte in Deinem Besitz und hoffe auch, dass Du die letzten Jaum Touw-Tage gleich uns gut verbracht hast. Wir hatten wieder sehr viel Besuch, ich denke, diese Nachricht wird Dir Freude machen. Deinen l. Brief habe ich mit einem weinenden Auge gelesen. Wie kann es nur möglich sein, dass der Transport und Zoll so viel Geld kostet, wer hat Dir dieses nun gegeben. Willi oder Addie teile mir dieses doch bitte mit. Es wäre doch vielleicht richtiger gewesen, wir hätten die Kisten vorläufig im Freihafen gelagert, aber das lässt sich ja nun nicht mehr ändern. Hoffentlich kostet nun die weitere Aufbewahrung nicht mehr so furchtbar viel Geld. Dass die Zimmer dort so unsauber sind, hatte ich schon gehört und mir darüber schon viel Sorgen gemacht. Kannst Du wenigstens Deine Koffer in Deine Wohnung nehmen oder wie hast Du dies eingerichtet? Wie ist es mit Deiner Wäsche und dem Strümpfe stopfen, ich wollte, ich wäre bei Dir, um das alles für Dich machen zu können.

Wie ist es, hast Du schon mit W. über Geschäftliches gesprochen oder seid Ihr durch Jaumtouw nicht dazu gekommen. Teile uns doch bitte immer alles mit, ob Erfreuliches oder umgekehrt, wir möchten alles mit Dir tragen. Heute kam beiliegendes Schreiben vom Verband, soll ich nun die Abmeldung an die Gewerbepolizei abschicken und was soll ich dem Verband mitteilen? Wenn Du wieder schreibst nimm meine Briefe zur Hand, damit Du alle Fragen beantworten kannst. Heute war Frl. Gerson hier, sie konnte nicht früher kommen, da ihr Vater sehr krank war. Sie hat uns alle Platten auf den Boden gebracht und auch einiges besorgt. Das Paket zu Poulson hat sie mitgenommen, sie lässt Dich vielmals grüßen, zum 15 hat sie eine Stellung im Haushalt angenommen. Vorgestern kam eine Karte von Rita Nachum, es geht ihr sehr gut, ich schreibe ihr Deine Adresse. Dann kann sie Dich, wenn sie in London ist, einmal anrufen. In 8 Tagen verlässt uns ja nun auch Else, ich freue mich für David, auch für Dich, hast Du dann doch noch jemand zum Aussprechen. Wir allerdings werden immer einsamer. Wie ist das Wetter drüben, hier ist es augenblicklich sommerlich warm, für die Jahreszeit ganz unnormal, wenn es bei Euch auch so ist, brauchst du wenigsten nicht zu frieren. Über Tante Lina haben wir herzlich gelacht. Adolf hatte auch schon darüber geschrieben. Wie ist es nun mit Schrank und Bett, ich hoffe auch darüber von Dir zu hören. Eben fällt mir ein, dass auch Kugelmans heute reisen, Du wirst ihn nun wohl bald einmal drüben sprechen. Auch Berta Polack will mir die Adresse von Henry aufgeben, der augenblicklich in London ist, Sie hat sehr bedauert, Dich nicht mehr gesprochen zu haben. Dass Onkel Emil heute 80 Jahre wurde, wusstest Du wohl durch David. Wir haben 5 M. an die Gemeinde abgelöst. Du wirst auch denken, was quasselt das Muttchen alles durcheinander, aber ich schreibe so, wie es mir gerade einfällt.

Nun mein geliebter Herzensjunge muss ich Schluss machen, unser Päppchen will die letzte Seite für sich haben. Falls ich vor Schabbos nicht noch einmal zum Schreiben komme, sende ich Dir schon heute meine herzlichsten Schabbosgrüße. Auch Grüße für alle dort und innige Küsse von Deinem Muttchen.

Heißt es eigentlich Queens Road oder Drive?

Mein lieber Siegfried לאי"ט

Nun ist ט"י aus und es beginnt die Zeit der Arbeit, wenn man die Erlaubnis dazu erhält. Hoffen wir das Beste, dass sich das Bimharo Bjomenu in jeder Weise erfüllt. Du hast mir doch wahrscheinlich viel für mich ....

zu erzählen und ich bin auf Deine nächsten Berichte wirklich neugierig. Wer ist denn Dein Cassierer, an den Du Dich vorläufig zu halten hast. Vorläufig ist ja der Besuch der Synagogen ziemlich*. Hoffentlich geht es Dir lieber Junge recht gut, auch hast die Jomtouwtage recht gut verlebt. Wie Mama Dir schon geschrieben hat, ist Onkel Emil heute 80 Jahre alt geworden. Schreib ihm ein paar gute Worte, er wird sich damit sehr freuen. In Erwartung deines J.t. Berichtes verbleibe ich mit Gruß + Kuss. Dein Papa

* (Wort fehlt im Original.)

[6] PK
Hamburg d. 16.4.39

Mein l. Siegfried

Dein l. Brief traf gestern Sonnabend 6 ½ Uhr nachmittags bei uns ein, wir haben uns riesig damit gefreut und haben wir mit dem Lesen desselben uns noch gut die Zeit vertreiben können. Solange es deine Zeit erlaubt, schreibe uns doch bitte immer so ausführlich, du kannst dir denken, wie uns jede Kleinigkeit interessiert, wie sehr wir uns nach deinen Briefen sehnen. Uns geht es gut, ich hoffe ein Gleiches von dir. Das Wetter ist auch hier wieder umgeschlagen, das war ja vorauszusehen. Eben waren Onkel Manfred und Tante Else hier, es ist glaube ich in der Sache wenig zu machen. Du schriebst uns, dass es in deinem Zimmer so kalt ist, kannst du nicht deine schöne Kamelhaardecke und deinen Pullunder zum Wärmen nehmen. Hoffentlich wird es bald ständig warm, dann fällt ja diese Sorge fort. Nun heißt es für heute wieder Schluss machen, nächstens wieder ausführlicher. Grüße alle herzlich und nimm auch du innige Grüße von deiner Mutter.

Lieber Siegfried לאי״ט

wir haben uns riesig gefreut, dass die Karte noch vor Nacht eingetroffen ist. Gruß und Kuss Papa

(Queens Road 87)

[7] Hamburg d. 18/4 39

Mein geliebter Siegfried לאי״ט

Ich hoffe unsere Karte vom Sonntag in Deinem Besitz und will ich nun

Deinen l. Brief etwas ausführlicher beantworten. Ich hoffe Dich bei guter Gesundheit was ich auch von uns berichten kann. Deine Beschreibung von London hat uns sehr interessiert, ich habe schon immer über den kolossalen Verkehr dort gelesen. Gerade jetzt habe ich wieder ein Buch, aus dem man viel ....des über England lesen kann. Dass Dich so friert, mein Liebling tut mir unendlich leid, könnte ich Dir doch etwas von der schönen Wärme unserer Wohnung schicken. Mit dem Nachsenden Deines warmen Hausmantels wird es nicht klappen, das schrieb ich Dir schon, vielleicht geht dies mit dem alten Regenmantel, den Else leider nicht mehr mitnehmen konnte, das Wörterbuch habe ich ihr mitgegeben, ebenso tausend innige Grüße für Dich. Jetzt ist sie wohl gerade auf dem Schiff, ich habe sie nur noch telefonisch gestern abend gesprochen, der Abschied tat mir wieder sehr weh, so geht ein lieber Mensch nach dem anderen, und man bleibt einsam zurück. Hoffentlich hast Du nun endlich Deine Sachen bekommen, dann hast Du doch auch Deinen schönen warmen Lodenmantel. Ich muss viel über Dein Wohnen und Wirtschaften nachdenken, es ist sicher eine große Umstellung für Dich, das müssen ja nun leider so viele durchmachen, lass Dir dies ein Trost sein und nimm es nicht allzu schwer. Dumm ist nur, dass Du mit der Sprache so zurück bist, aber mit etwas Energie wirst Du es schon bald meistern. Hast Du eigentlich schon einige von den vielen Hamburgern dort gesprochen, und teile uns doch bitte mit, ob noch irgend eine Aussicht auf den zuerst durch St. angeregten Plan besteht, es wird wohl nichts sein, sonst hättest Du wohl schon eine Andeutung gemacht. Mit Mühlenbruck habe ich telefoniert, ich soll am Freitag vorschicken, bei Nelki will ich noch heute Abend anrufen. Herr Grunert von Elsass sagte mir die Auktion sei verschoben, ich will nächste Woche wieder anrufen, Herr Wissel wartet noch auf Bescheid der Devisenstelle, dann bekommen wir es per Postanweisung zugeschickt. Heut bekommen wir die erste verkürzte Gehaltauszahlung, es macht RM 28 im Monat weniger, nett nicht wahr? Die Wirtschaftskammer hat angerufen, ob Deine Firma schon liquidiert sei, was wir bejahten. Heute kam durch Mühlenbruch eine Rechnung von Sallinger über RM 3,80 von November und Januar, das kann doch sicher nicht stimmen, das hättest Du doch beim Abschluss Deiner Bücher bestimmt gesehen. Ich schrieb an Mühlenbruck, dass Du nicht mehr hier seiest, dass wohl ein Irrtum vorliegen müsse. Es kommen noch täglich Prospekte und Empfehlungen, soll ich dieselben aufbewahren oder können sie gleich fort. Papa bittet schon wieder, dass ich Platz lassen soll, so muss ich für heute wieder

Schluss machen. Übrigens kam der Brief vom Karfreitag am Sonntag Vormittag hier an. Also nun noch viele, viele herzliche Grüße und Küsse von deinem Muttchen.

Lieber Siegfried!

Es freut mich zu hören, dass es Dir gottlob gut geht. Ich hörte heute, dass Herr Iska Emanuel auch nach dort abgereist ist. Es wäre sehr schön, wenn Du später bei demselben solange er nicht zu entfernt wohnt, lernen könntest. Er lernt sehr gut, auch war ....? sehr deutlich. Lieber Siegfried, ich möchte Dich sogar bitten, dass ich Dir schon gesagt habe, alles gleich zu besorgen und nichts aufzuschieben, sei es geschäftlich oder eine Mizwoh, denn wisse für jede Mizwoh, die der Mensch ausübt, wird ein Engel geschaffen, der dem Menschen zur Seite steht und ihn beschützt. Ich hoffe immer günstige Berichte von Dir zu erhalten und verbleibe mit Gruß und Kuss Papa.

Guten Schabbos.

Lieber Siegfried!

S.G.w. verging der ט״י für diese ......nisreiche Zeit. Meine Gedanken begleiten Dich wirklich immer und ich hoffe, dass Du tapfer alle Krisen überwindest, dann wird ה״י auch mit Dir sein. Dank meiner angenehmen Gegenwart befinden sich Deine lb. Eltern sehr munter, ist Mama auch sehr tapfer. Ich fühle mich wohl hier, es beruhigt mich auch, Deinen Eltern zur Seite zu sein.

Mit vielen Wünschen Hanna H.

[8] PK
Hamburg d. 21.4.39

Mein l. Siegfried

deine l. Karte erhielten wir heute Freitag Morgen, da gestern nur eine Post ausgetragen worden ist. Inzwischen hoffe ich Else gut dort angekommen und wirst du ja nun mündlich über unser Wohlbefinden gehört haben. Die Briefe sind gleich heute von Hanna geschrieben worden und werden zusammen mit dieser Karte befördert werden. Die Sache von Wissel ist heut erledigt, wegen M. Eppendorfer Baum schreibe nächstens. Ich hoffe in deinem morgigen Brief ausführlicher zu hören, wie du deine Tage verbringst und womit du deine Zeit ausfüllst. Ich wüsste für heute nichts weiter mitzuteilen. Ich wünsche dir einen recht guten Schabbos, grüße Sterns, Fr. Lanzkron, David u. Else und sei auch du innigst gegrüßt und geküsst von deiner Mutter.

Ich freue mich, dass das Wetter besser ist, auch hier ist es so.

Lieber Siegfried לא״יט

ich bestätige dein l. Schreiben von vorgestern u. hoffe, dass diese Zeilen dich beim besten Wohlsein antreffen. Ich weiß nicht bestimmt, ob mir Kugelmann deine Adresse aufgegeben haben. Ich glaube, er war gerade י״ט hier. Ich freue mich auf den ausführlichen שבת Brief, wünsche für heute recht guten שבת und verbleibe mit Gruß und Kuss Papa

beantw. 25.4.39

(Queens Drive 87)

[9] Hamburg d. 27.4.39

Mein Geliebtes. לא״יט

Gestern abends 6 Uhr Mittwoch traf Dein lieber ausführlicher Brief ein, herzlichen Dank. Da Du in Deiner Schabboskarte schreibst, Du würdest vielleicht am Sonntag schreiben, hat Papa sich schon am Dienstag furchtbar aufgeregt, dass noch kein Brief von Dir hier war. Du kennst doch unser Päppchen, sich etwas einreden, wird bei ihm groß geschrieben. Der so prompt bei Dir eingetroffene Brief wurde Mittwoch morgens 8 Uhr in den Kasten gesteckt. Man muss nämlich um einen Antwortschein zu bekommen, schon vor 8 Uhr nur mittwochs an der Post in der Hansastraße sein, es ist ein kolossaler Andrang dort. Um 8 ½ Uhr sind schon alle ausverkauft. Diese Woche hat es nicht geklappt, da wir mit dem Schreiben warten wollten, bis Dein Brief hier war. Die gewünschte kleine Sendung geht heute an Dich ab. Tante Else besorgt es. Das andere war nicht zu machen, ich konnte sie ja nicht zwingen, vielleicht klappt es demnächst mit dem alten Regenmantel, wozu brauchst du den eigentlich? Ich freue mich sehr, dass Du unberufen so guten Appetit hast und es Dir so gut schmeckt, schade ist es nur, dass Du mittags wenn Du unterwegs bist, nicht etwas Warmes zu Dir nehmen kannst, hoffentlich kannst Du es mit der Zeit einrichten.

Wie fühlst Du Dich sonst, schläfst Du gut und ist sonst alles in Ordnung. Ach mein Liebling, wie gern würde ich wieder für Dich sorgen, die

Sehnsucht überfällt mich manchmal mit Macht, aber ich sage mir immer, Kopf oben behalten. Was Deine Mitteilungen über die betreffende Sache betrifft, so wollen wir es dem Allmächt'gen überlassen, er wird schon das Richtige für Dich bestimmen. Ist die Korrespondenz, die Du zu erledigen hast, geschäftlich oder alles privat?

Von A. Eppendorfer Baum haben wir vorige Woche RM 20 erhalten, ich weiß gar nicht genau, wie viel er uns noch schuldig ist. Es ist nur eine Aufstellung über RM 25, 80 und 100 zu finden. Hat er Dir bei Deinem letzten Besuch noch etwas für uns gegeben. Wenn nicht, hat er uns also bisher mit den letzten RM 20, RM 225 gezahlt, wären also noch RM 93 zu zahlen.

N. Oberaltenallee habe ich angerufen, er versprach zu schicken, hat dies aber nicht getan, ich werde ganz energisch mit ihm sprechen. Auch Elsass macht Ausreden, es wäre noch nichts wieder verkauft. Ich werde nächste Woche einmal persönlich hingehen. Ich kann übrigens kein Verzeichnis finden, was noch zu verkaufen ist. Weißt Du vielleicht, wo ich dieses finde, auch wüsste ich gern, wo die Kaakstwiete ist, wo er wohnt. Die Sache mit Deinem Gepäck ist haarsträubend, ich werde, wo ich nur kann, von Gärtner abraten, es ist unerhört, dass er mit solchen minderwertigen Firmen in Verbindung steht. Meinst Du übrigens, dass ich Sterns einmal persönlich schreiben soll und ihnen meinen Dank aussprechen, hast Du von Addie noch vor seiner Abreise etwas bekommen? Am 15. Mai fährt nun auch Elsa Hirsch mit der Manhattan und Anfang nächster Woche ist Rudolf Glückstadt mit Familie in London. Er hat sich gestern von mir verabschiedet, ich habe ihm auch Grüße für Dich mitgegeben. Onkel Elkan und Tante Dora kommen öfters abends zu uns, Tante Dora hat uns Elses Brief vorgelesen. Grüße David und Else herzlich von mir, auch Sterns und Frau Lanzkron, Petrowers und auch Adolf. Papa möchte auf meinem Bogen noch etwas schreiben, daher will ich nun schließen. Ich freue mich schon auf Deine nächste Nachricht, das Schönste für mich, wenn ich nur schon Deine Handschrift sehe. Also leb wohl für heute mein Geliebtes, nimm tausend Grüße und Küsse von Deinem Muttchen.

Hamburg d 27/4. 39

Mein lieber Siegfried לאי״ט

Dein l. Brief hat mir gestern besonders große Freude bereitet, da Du denselben schon für Anfang der Woche avisiert hast + denselben erst

Mittwochabend eintraf + kannst Du Dir denken, wie ich mich freute, als er gestern Abend eintraf. Diese Woche war Onkel Erich ..., erzählte wie großartig er gefeiert wurde, erst in der Synagoge des Waisenhauses, Festgottesdienst mit Predigten von Carlebach + dann alle möglichen schriftlichen + persönlichen Gratulationen u.a. hat Max Warburg einen sehr schönen Brief geschrieben + Dr. Fritz Warburg Wein geschickt. Du hast doch auch geschrieben, er hatte sich schon gewundert, dass Deine Gratulation noch gefehlt hat. Wie war es mit dem *aumern* dieses Jahr, hast Du in London auch so häufig vergessen wie in Hamburg, oder ging es besser. Wenn die liebe Mama an Dich denkt, muss ich ihr immer etwas aus dem schönen Kasten geben, und da sie, wie Du dir denken kannst, ja sehr häufig an Dich denkt, hat der Kasten schon große Lücken bekommen. Wie alle guten Gedanken durch eine Tat bekräftigt werden müssen, so ist es auch hiermit. Onkel Emil gab mir auch die Adresse von Max Warburg auf + teile ich sie Dir mit, vielleicht kannst Du davon Gebrauch machen.

Die Adresse lautet: M.M. Warburg
London E.C. 2 Gresham House
24 Old Broad Street

Deine Zeit füllst Du wohl hauptsächlich mit Sprachübungen aus oder was treibst Du sonst noch? (Fortsetzung auf einliegendem Bogen.)

Lieber Siegfrid

Hast Du vielleicht bei Deinen Büchern den Zionswächter mitbekommen. Herr Kahn wollte ihn gern geliehen haben, ich konnte ihn nicht finden. Du schreibst, Du hättest uns viel mitzuteilen, dass Du nicht weißt, wo Du anfangen sollst. Wir haben also noch die Hoffnung, viel Gutes und Interessantes von Dir zu hören. Hast Du auf dem Programm Deiner Zukunftsprojekte noch das Dentalgeschäft oder ist dasselbe ausgeschaltet? Also lieber Junge, sei recht präcise mit dem Schreiben, sei bestens gegrüßt + geküsst von Deinem Papa.

Guten שבת

[10] PK
Hamburg d. 30.4.39

Mein l. Siegfried

Deine leider nur so kurze Karte erhielten wir gestern Nachmittag, hoffentlich geht es dir gut. Du schreibst nichts darüber. Wir sind G.s.d.

wohl, nur sind wir, da auch hier das Wetter kalt und regnerisch war, nicht viel fort gewesen. Heute ist es wärmer, Papa hat eben einen schönen Spaziergang gemacht. Ich hoffe, dass du nicht allzu sehr frierst, ich hätte dir gern etwas Warmes geschickt, weiß aber nicht, wie ich dies bewerkstelligen soll. Wie Else schreibt, wohnt sie in einem unheizbaren Zimmer, dies ist doch mit den kleinen Kindern sehr hart. Wie ist es mit deinen Sachen, sind sie noch in einem einigermaßen brauchbaren Zustand, ich hoffe in deinem Brief Näheres darüber zu hören. Auch wüsste ich gern einmal wie du dir deine Zeit einteilst, und wie es mit deinen Fortschritten in der Sprache ist. Hast du das Päckchen von Tante Else nicht erhalten, ich hoffe all meine Fragen in deinem nächsten Brief beantwortet zu bekommen. Ich muss allerdings meinen Brief schon am Dienstag schreiben, da ich wie ich dir schon schrieben, nur am Mittwoch einen Antwortschein bekomme, der dann gleich in den Brief hineingesteckt werden muss. Also für heute wieder Schluss. Viele, viele herzliche Grüße und Küsse von deiner Mutter

Schick deinen Brief rechtzeitig ab.

Gruß und Kuss Papa

(Queens Drive 87)

[11] ב"ה
Hamburg d. 2/5 39

Mein Geliebtes. Es ist jetzt 6 ½ Uhr, ich dachte, dass heute vielleicht Post von Dir käme, die ich dann gleich beantworten könnte, ich will aber mein Schreiben nicht aufschieben, weil ich gleich morgen früh zur Hansastraße will, um einen Antwortschein zu bekommen. Wie geht es Dir mein Liebling. Deine letzte Karte hat mich nicht befriedigt, hattest Du Ärger mit Deinen Sachen? Ich hoffe in Deinem nächsten Schreiben drüber zu hören. Wie ist es eigentlich mit der Aussicht auf Arbeiterlaubnis, besteht irgendeine Möglichkeit? Wie Du schreibst, musst Du soviel unterwegs sein und hast viel Korrespondenz zu erledigen, ist diese alles in geschäftlichen Angelegenheiten, interessieren *St.* sich noch dafür. Ich hätte auch gern einmal etwas über Deine Wirtin gehört, ist sie eine einigermaßen nette und saubere Frau. Es ist kaum zu glauben, dass in einer so großen Stadt wie London die Einrichtungen für Heizen und warmes Wasser noch so primitiv sind. Ist dies nur in Eurem Stadtteil so oder auch in den besseren. Wie bekommst Du überhaupt das Geschirr mit kaltem Wasser sauber.

Hast Du wenigstens Aufwaschtücher und Handtücher. Jetzt wenn Du Deine eigenen Sachen hast, findest Du ja alles vor, ich habe Dir alles mitgegeben. Sorgen macht es mir auch, dass Du Deinen Appetit nicht so befriedigen kannst, wie Du möchtest, könntest Du Dir nicht morgens noch etwas zurechtmachen, dass Du isst, bevor Du fortgehst, oder bekommt Ihr nicht so viel Brot. Wenn ich Dir doch nur etwas schicken könnte, ich mag mich oft nicht satt essen, wenn ich an Dich denke. Ich bin wirklich gespannt, ob Du das Päckchen von Tante Else bekommen hast, wie letztere mir sagte, ist für Adolf auch nicht alles angekommen. Gehe am Freitagnachmittag einmal zu Bella, vielleicht hat dieselbe etwas für Dich. Du solltest mir noch einmal schreiben, wie es mit Deiner Wäsche und den Strümpfen ist, ob Du jemand zum Stopfen gefunden hast. Hast Du eigentlich schon etwas außer der City von London gesehen oder hast Du keine Zeit und Lust hierzu. Am Schabbos wird Tante Hedchen 70 Jahre alt, wenn Du Porto übrig hast, schreibe ihr ein Kärtchen, sonst richte ich Glückwünsche von Dir aus. Siegfried Nussbaum hat ja nun am Freitag sein Visum bekommen, er hat gleich bei uns angerufen, er fährt am 15. mit der Manhattan. Petrowers folgen ja auch wohl schon am 2. Juni, könntest Du nicht etwas von seinen Vertretungen bekommen, oder ist nicht viel damit los? Frau O. hätte gern Dein Zimmer gehabt, sie war sehr enttäuscht, als sie hörte, dass es schon besetzt sei, mir ist es lieber so.

Für heute mein liebes Kind, muss ich Schluss machen, ich hoffe bestimmt morgen von Dir zu hören. Grüße alle und nimm auch Du tausend innige Küsse von Deinem Muttchen.

Morgen sind es schon 5 Wochen, dass Du fort bist.

Lieber Siegfried לאי״ט

Ich habe Dir vorige Woche die Adresse von Max aufgegeben. Ich wollte Dir nur mitteilen, dass ich gehört habe, dass vor der Wohnung von *Max* mehrere Lifts nach New York gestanden haben, auch ist wohl anzunehmen, dass er seinen dauernden Aufenthalt in NY nimmt. Näheres weiß ich darüber nicht. Ich will Dir auch noch sagen, dass was Mama Dir auch schon geschrieben hat, dass Du morgens ein Stück Brot zu Dir stecken sollst, damit Du nicht flau wirst, wenn Du in die City gehst. Ich bin neugierig, von Dir etwas Näheres über Deine Beschäftigung zu hören. Ich verbleibe für heute mit Gruß + Kuss. Papa

[12] PK
Hamburg d. 5.5.39

Mein l. Siegfried

Deine sehr ausführliche Karte vom 2. Mai erhielten wir, da ich zu einer ausführlichen Antwort erst deinen ausführlichen Brief abwarten will, für heute nur, dass es uns G.s.d. gut geht, und hoffe ich, dass dieses auch bei dir der Fall ist. Ist Addie1 noch in London, dann grüße ihn von mir, desgleichen alle l. Bekannte und Verwandte. Ich hoffe also bestimmt morgen von dir zu hören, ich wünsche dir einen recht guten Schabbos und sende dir innige Grüße und Küsse. Deine Mutter

Henry P. ist nicht mehr dort, er kommt aber noch einmal, seine Mutter will mir dann seine Adresse mitteilen.

Lieber Siegfried! לאי״ט

Ich wünsche dir einen recht guten שבת Kuss Papa

(Queens Drive 87)

[13] ב״ה
Hamburg d. 9/5 39

Mein geliebter Siegfried לאי״ט

Deinen l. Brief vom 5.5. erhielten wir am Schabbos Nachmittag, herzlichen Dank. Ich hoffe, dass auch Du unsere Schabboskarte sowie ein Packchen erhalten hast, teile uns dieses bitte mit. Ich hoffe, dass es Dir gut geht, auch wir sind G.s.D. wohl, nur mein Arm macht mir noch immer zu schaffen, daher auch die schlechte Schrift, morgen gehe ich nach langer Zeit einmal wieder zu Frau Battenfeld, vielleicht gibt sie mir wieder etwas dafür. Ich war natürlich entsetzt, dass Du so bestohlen worden bist, ich glaube bestimmt, dass dieses beim Spediteur geschehen ist, es ist ja eigentlich unerhört, dass so etwas geschehen kann, wenn man einer Firma auf Treu und Glauben seine Schlüssel aushändigt. Teile uns bitte sofort mit, wie sich die Versicherung dazu stellt. Es freut mich sehr, dass Du Dir morgens eine Speise machst, ich habe auch neulich einmal im Reformhaus so eine Probetüte bekommen und sie mir zurecht gemacht, es hat ausgezeichnet geschmeckt, und besonders ist es sehr nahrhaft. Dass Adolf so schnell einen Arbeitsplatz gefunden hat, ist ja großartig, er schreibt ganz begeistert nach Hause. Du hast wohl schon gehört, dass wir vielleicht in absehbarer Zeit ausziehen müssen, Du kannst Dir denken wie schrecklich der Gedanke für mich ist, wenn ich die ganze Umstellung und Unruhe nun schon hier durchmachen muss, zumal ja dann alles Disponieren und alle Arbeit auf mir allein ruht, da Papa mir ja in dieser Hinsicht wenig helfen kann. Nun hoffentlich kommt es noch nicht so bald. Heute habe ich einen schönen warmen Hausmantel gekauft, den ich Papa zum Geburtstag schenken will, ich denke er wird ihm gefallen und er wird sich damit freuen. Es war allerdings keine große Auswahl jetzt da, dieselben gehen mehr zum Winter. Am Sonntag gehe ich mit Tante Else ins Kino, zum ersten Mal seit du fort bist, es wird Bel Ami gegeben. Hanna H. gab einen kleinen Abschiedskaffee für Elsa, beiliegende Karte von den Teilnehmerinnen desselben. Nun verlassen John und Bella wohl auch bald England um weiterzuwandern, vielleicht kann John Dir etwas Warmes dort lassen. Du kannst ja einmal fragen. Wie ist es mit Deinen Fortschritten in der Sprache, schreibst Du uns bald einen englischen Brief. Onkel Manfred und Tante Else nehmen ja ein Intensivkursus, besonders Tante Else scheint schon sehr weit zu sein. Heute hat Oberaltenallee die ersten RM 5 geschickt, nachdem ich zweimal angerufen habe, über meine Anfragen über M. und Elsas hoffe ich im nächsten Brief zu hören auch über Deine Aussichten dort. Wir wollten ja eigentlich über Schwuaus nach Wilhelminenhöhe, es ist uns aber noch zu kalt, wir haben noch immer etwas geheizt, ich wollte uns nun für Mitte Juni auf 14 Tage anmelden, wie denkst Du darüber? Ist Max W. noch dort, willst Du ehe er fort geht noch mit ihm sprechen, oder ihm später schreiben, es kommt ja natürlich in erster Linie darauf an, wie Deine Aussichten sind. Wie ich hier hörte, ziehen viele Hamburger nach Cardiff, das Leben soll dort viel billiger sein. Hast Du Kugelmann schon gesprochen? Eben ruft Tante Harriet an, sie lässt Dich grüßen und fragen, ob Du ihr Päckchen bekommen hast.

Du hast nun wieder viele Fragen zu beantworten. Stoff für den nächsten Brief.

Also mein geliebter Junge, leb wohl für heute. Nimm viele innige Grüße und Küsse von Deinem Muttchen

Viele Grüße für alle dort. Unsere Nachbarin grüßt Dich herzlich.

Hbg. d. 9/5 39

Mein lieber Siegfried לאי״ט

Das ist ja eine nette Bescherung mit der *Genäwe* Deiner Sachen, hoffentlich bekommst Du dieselbe ersetzt.

Ich bin neugierig auf Deinen nächsten Brief, da ich hoffe, etwas über Deine geschäftlichen Aussichten zu erfahren. Hat David etwas in Aussicht? Wenn Du nicht selbst zu *Max* gehen willst, kannst Du doch Minden einmal fragen, ob er weiß, ob *M.* in London bleibt oder ob er nach Amerika geht. Ich wundere mich, dass Kugelman noch gar nicht bei Dir war. Ich weiß allerdings nicht, ob er Deine Adresse weiß. Hast Du einmal mit jemand gesprochen wegen eines zustehenden Schiur?

Es ist schon 10 ¼ Uhr, also für heute Gruß + Kuss Papa

[14] PK
Hbg. d. 12.5.39

Mein l. Siegfried. Es ist jetzt 6 ½ Uhr, bis jetzt ist der in Deiner gestrigen Karte avisierte Brief nicht eingetroffen. Ich kann nun nicht länger warten und will Dir nur in Kürze meine herzlichsten Schabbosgrüße senden. Es geht uns G.s.d. gut, ich hoffe ein Gleiches von Dir. Frau Battenfeld war mit meinem Herzen g.l. und unberufen zufrieden auch mit Papa. Da sie für 5 Wochen verreist hat sie uns für fast 13 Mark Sachen verschrieben ganz nett, nicht wahr, es soll für den Atem bei mir sein, bei Papa für seine Sachen, die er immer hat, na, die Hauptsache, dass es hilft. Hanna Hirsch schreibt gerade an David, dass einer von Euch sich um Elsa kümmert, die am Mittwoch abend von Southampton kommt und nach Manchester weiterfährt, Hanna lässt Dich grüßen. Ich hoffe nun morgen bestimmt ausführlich von Dir zu hören, auf all meine Fragen Antwort zu bekommen. Du musst wohl sehr viel zu tun haben, dass Du das Schreiben immer so aufschiebst. Also für heute nochmals innige Grüße und Küsse von Deiner Mutter.

Viele Grüße an Sterns u. Fr. Lanzkron

Lieber Siegfried

Ich hätte viel zu fragen. Ich will aber Deinen morgigen Brief abwarten und sende für heute innigsten Schabbos Gruß Papa

(beantwortet) 17.5.39

(Queens Drive 87)

[15]

ב״ה

Hamburg d. 15/5 39.

Mein lieber Siegfried! לא״יט

Ich schreibe Dir früher außer dem Schabbosbrief, den die liebe Mama noch schreiben wird, einen Extrabrief, da ich Dir verschiedene Fragen vorlegen möchte, um deren Beantwortung ich Dich bitte. Deinen lieben Schabbosbrief habe ich mit Vergnügen gelesen, das aus demselben ersah, dass Du gottlob wohl bist, was ja die Hauptsache ist. Nun kommt die geschäftliche Seite, worüber Du in sieben Sprachen schweigst. Es ist ja sehr schön, dass Du das Sprichwort Schweigen ist Gold beherzigst, aber den Eltern gegenüber muss es seine Grenzen haben. Ich weiß, dass es in England mit der Arbeitserlaubnis sehr schwer ist + muss man sich daher mit dem Gedanken vertraut machen, dass Du vorläufig noch nichts verdienen kannst. Ich habe doch von anderer Seite gehört, dass man mit auswärtigen Vertretungen etwas beginnen kann. Du hast auch nichts darüber geschrieben, ob die andere Sache irgend eine Aussicht hat. Lieber Siegried, Du darfst mich nicht missverstehen, es ist durchaus keine unangebrachte Neugierde von mir, sondern nur ein Ausdruck des väterlichen Interesses. Hast Du übrigens erfahren, wie die Aussichten mit den gestohlenen Sachen sind.

Siegfried Nussbaum reist auch morgen ab. War Herr Joseph Kugelmann schon bei dir? Es hat mich gefreut zu hören, dass Du bei Herrn Dr. Spitzer zum Schiur warst. Es wäre sehr schön, wenn Du bei ihm einen dauernden Schiur bekommen könntest, einen besseren Lehrer kannst Du gar nicht erhalten. Ich würde sehen, einen Schiur in Schulchan Aruch oder Tenach zu nehmen. Hast Du mit Petrowa wegen seiner Vertretungen gesprochen?

Ich möchte Dich bitten, lieber Siegfried, über diejenigen Sachen von den vorbenannten, über die Du Auskunft geben kannst, etwas zu schreiben, ich wäre Dir dafür sehr dankbar.

Ich verbleibe für heute mit innigstem Gruß + Kuss. Dein Papa

Mein geliebter Siegfried. Ich wollte Dir eigentlich auch heute ausführlich schreiben, aber Leo war bei uns und kam ich nicht dazu, da der Brief nun des Antwortscheines wegen morgen früh fort muss, muss ich mich kurz fassen, zu Schabbos s.G.w. mehr. Hoffentlich bist Du wohl und munter auch wir sind G.s.D. gesund. Papa ist natürlich ungeduldig, er möchte

Näheres über Deine Aussichten hören, dass dies nicht so schnell geht, und wohl überhaupt sehr schwierig ist, lässt er sich nicht ausreden, ich habe ihn deshalb schreiben lassen, Du wirst ja selbst am besten wissen, was Du mitteilen kannst. Ich hoffe morgen wieder von Dir zu hören, hoffentlich recht bald wieder ausführlich, es ist das Schönste für mich, wenn so ein recht langer Brief, wie der letzte, kommt. Heute ging wieder eine Feodora an Dich ab, direkt vom Geschäft, auch Elsa wird vielleicht eine Tafel für Dich haben, schreibe mir dann, wenn Dein Vorrat alle ist, sie wird ja sonst zu alt.

Es ist 10 Uhr und gleich Schlafenszeit, deshalb für heute noch die innigsten Grüße und Küsse von Deinem Muttchen

[16] Hamburg d. 19.5.39

Mein geliebter Junge. לא״יט Soeben Freitag 10 Uhr kam Deine l. Karte, dieselbe ist wohl des Feiertags halber erst heute ausgetragen worden, ich hoffe, dass Du inzwischen auch unseren Brief mit Antwortschein erhalten hat. Dein letzter ausführlicher Brief kam noch am Schabbos 6 ½ Uhr mit der letzten Post, wir hoffen, dass wir auch morgen wieder ausführlich von Dir hören werden. Ich hoffe, dass es Dir gut geht, auch wir sind G.s.D. wohl und munter. Mein Arm hat sich unberufen gebessert, diese Woche war ich nun Professor Hansen wegen meiner Augen. Er sagte, dass dieselben G.s.D. gut seien, ich habe nur einen starken Bindehautkatarr, wofür ich Tropfen bekam, außerdem sind meine Gläser nicht mehr scharf genug. Ich habe mir nun eine hochmoderne Brille mit sehr guten Zeisgläsern gekauft, wenn Du mich damit sehen könntest, würde ich Dir sicher gefallen, ich sehe einer englischen Lady bestimmt ähnlich. Hoffentlich werde ich noch einmal eine solche werden. Halte uns jedenfalls auf dem laufenden, ob in absehbarer Zeit eine Aussicht für uns besteht. Ich freue mich sehr, dass Du Dich ehrenamtlich beschäftigen kannst, das gibt Dir doch sicher Befriedung, hoffentlich ist bald Aussicht auf andere Beschäftigung. Wie ist es nun mit der Versicherung geworden, bekommst Du alles ersetzt, schreibe mir noch mal wie es mit den Taschentüchern ist, Tante Dora ist ja augenblicklich nicht hier, wenn Du es ersetzt bekommst, würde ich mir drüben welche kaufen. Die sind doch bestimmt besser als Deine alten hier. Wie ist es mit Deiner Schreibmaschine, ist mit derselben auch etwas nicht in Ordnung, mir war so, als ob Tante Else eine Bemerkung darüber machte. Das mit der Wäsche ist ja wirklich katastrophal, es wäre ja ein Jammer, wenn Deine guten Sachen so schnell ruinieren würden, hier wäre

Muttchen mal wieder am Platz. Wie ist es mit der Sprache, machst Du schon Fortschritte? Ich fand es nett, dass Du schon einen kleinen Ausflug machtest, waren es Deutsche oder Engländer, mit denen Du zusammen warst? Dass Addie Dir so beisteht, freut mich von ganzem Herzen. Er ist doch wirklich ein aufrichtiger Freund. Du wolltest mir einmal mitteilen, ob ich an Sterns direkt schreiben und mich bedanken soll. Am Sonntag nach Mittag waren wir bei Onkel Max zum Kaffe um noch einmal mit Siegfried zusammen zu sein, letzterer ist ziemlich vergnügt fortgegangen. Onkel Max wird übrigens am Dienstag 60 Jahre alt, wenn es Dir möglich ist, schicke ihm ein Kärtchen, es müsste dann allerdings schon Dienstag früh hier sein, da sie, wie auch Onkel Manfred und Tante Else über Schwuaus nach Wilhelminenhöhe fahren. Wenn Onkel Elkan und Tante Dora nicht bis dahin von Leipzig zurückkommen, sind wir Jontef ganz allein. Wie ich Dir schon schrieb, war ich mit Tante Else im Film, Bel Ami, er war ganz reizend und haben wir uns während der paar Stunden prachtvoll amüsiert. Es kommen ja leider auch wieder Augenblicke, wo man sehr traurig und niedergeschlagen ist, wenn man so im Sommer auf der Straße ist, so erging es mir diese Woche, als ich an Davids früherer Wohnung vorbeiging und links ein großes Brettergerüst sah. Auch geht mir so mancherlei durch den Kopf, ach mein Geliebtes, Du fehlst mir auf Schritt und Tritt. Bist Du in den letzten Tagen bei Bella gewesen, sonst gehe einmal hin und frage, ob sie etwas für Dich hat. Teile mir gleich etwas darüber mit. Grüße von den beiden Hannas. Einliegenden Brief brachte gestern Tante Bella. Papa erzählte heute, dass der Vater von Max Levin plötzlich gestorben ist, ich nehme an, dass er es weiß, kümmere Dich jedenfalls mal um ihn. Ich habe mir diese Woche einen netten blauen Hut und einen türkischen Schal gekauft, ich hatte beides sehr nötig. Ich hoffe mir morgen wieder ausführlich von Dir zu hören und verschiedene Anfragen beantwortet zu erhalten. Da Papa noch auch schreiben will, muss ich heute schließen, über Wäschepreise Elsass etc. im nächsten Brief. Also recht guten Schabbos und tausend innige Küsse von Deinem Muttchen.

Lieber Siegfried!

Liebes Muttchen hat heute schon alles geschrieben, auch sende ich also nur noch innigsten Schabbos-Gruß + Kuss. Papa

[17] ב"ה
Hamburg, d. 22.5.39

Mein Geliebtes לאי"ט

Deinen l. Brief erhielten wir noch am Schabbos-Nachmittag, ich hoffe, dass auch unser Schabbos Brief rechtzeitig in Deinem Besitz war. Was nun Papas Anfragen betrifft, so schrieb ich dir ja schon, dass dieselben nicht in meinem Sinn waren, denn ich wusste ja, dass Du uns nichts verschweigst und wie Du es ja auch schon hier getan, uns alles mitteilen wirst. Ich war ja, wie Du Dir denken kannst, über den Inhalt Deiner Zeilen ziemlich niedergeschlagen, denn wenn ich auch schon hier gehört habe, dass für garantierte Personen die Arbeitserlaubnis sehr schwer zu erhalten sei, so dachte ich doch, dass es vielleicht durch Willi St. Beziehungen eher möglich wäre, eine solche für Dich zu erreichen. Im Übrigen hast du recht, Du musst erst ordentlich die Sprache können, und dann wollen wir den Mut nicht verlieren, auf G'tt vertrauen, der Allmächt'ge wird Dir schon beistehen und Dich das Richtige finden lassen. Die Hauptsache ist vor allen Dingen, dass Du gesund bist und bleibst, ich bin, wie ich Dir schon schrieb froh, dass Du Dich ehrenamtlich beschäftigen kannst. Uns geht es G.s.D. gut, ich freue mich, wenn ich ordentlich Beschäftigung habe, damit die Gedanken nicht so viel spazieren gehen können. Vorige Woche bekamen wir von Tante Gella wieder 3 Päckchen mit Butter und Käse, es ist wirklich großartig von ihr und denk dir am Freitagmorgen kam von ihr an die Adresse von Hanna Hirsch ein Päckchen mit dem Inhalt, den Du immer .....(unleserl.) am Freitagabend bekommst. Wir haben es gleich Freitagmittag mit schönen Schwenkkartoffeln und Gurke verzehrt, Du kannst Dir denken, wie wir uns daran gelabt haben. Hast Du eigentlich schon einmal etwas von Lotte Solling gehört, und bist Du schon mal bei Professor Türkheim gewesen, hat Herr Kugelmann schon etwas von sich hören lassen? Heut Abend ist Frau Oppenheimer bei uns und am 2ten Tag mittags Martha Wittmund. Onkel Max haben wir per Telefon gratuliert, er ist bis heute Nachmittag im Geschäft und fährt dann nach Wilhelminenhöhe. Wir haben ihm 6 leinene Taschentücher geschenkt, viel zu nobel, nicht wahr? Hast Du ihm geschrieben? Er sagte mir am Telefon, dass er eine Karte von Adolf in einem fabelhaften Englisch bekommen hätte, sprichst Du nicht manchmal mit ihm Englisch. Hast Du eigentlich die Handarbeiten abgeliefert, passen die Sachen den Kindern.

Bei Elsass habe ich vorige Woche angerufen, er hat noch für ungefähr 19M für uns verkauft, nach den Feiertagen will ich persönlich hingehen, um einmal zu vergleichen, was noch offen steht. Nun will ich Dir noch die gewünschten Wäschepreise mitteilen, sofern ich sie augenblicklich selbst weiß.

Oberhemd weiß 45 (Pfennig?), weißer Kragen 10, steifer Kragen 15, Schlafanzug 60, Taschentuch 5, 17 Socken 10, Bezug 40, Betttuch 30, Kaffeedecke 45, nach Woll und Netz?unterwäsche, Kissenbezug muss ich mich erst erkundigen, teile ich dann später einmal mit.

Heute ist hier herrliches Wetter, hoffentlich bleibt es in den nächsten Tagen so. Nach den Feiertagen verabreden wir einmal einen Telefonanruf, ich muss deine Stimme mal wieder hören.

Für heute mein gel. Junge muss ich schließen. Verlebe einen recht, recht guten Jontef und nimm tausend innige Küsse von Deinem Muttchen.

Die beiden Hanna's lassen grüßen.

Lieber Siegfried! לאי״ט

Ich danke dir noch für die Beantwortung meiner Anfragen. Es tut mir leid, dass Mama nicht damit zufrieden war, aber ich musste von Dir darüber hören. Ich wünsche Dir nun recht guten ט״י auch. Wenn es dort Käskuchen giebt, lass ihn Dir recht gut schmecken, iss aber nicht zuviel davon. Ich hoffe morgen s.G.w. von Dir zu hören.

Für heute herzlichsten Gruß + ט״יKuss Papa.

[18] PK
Hamburg d. 26.5.39

Mein geliebtes Kind. לאי״ט Deine beiden lieben Karten erhielten wir, und hoffe ich auch unseren Brief und den an Sterns rechtzeitig dort eingetroffen, letzterer war bereits fort, als Deine Karte mit dem Hinweis auf diesen, ankam. Wir haben Jaumtauw gut verbracht und sind auch heute G.s.d. wohlauf. Heute Morgen habe ich mich allerdings ziemlich aufgeregt. Tante Else erzählte mir am Telefon, Hr. Adolf habe geschrieben, Ihr würdet jetzt in der Volksküche essen. Wie ist dieses denn gekommen, haben Sterns das von Euch verlangt. Ich bin natürlich in großer Sorge, ob das Essen Dir auch genügt, ob Du dabei auch Deine Kräfte behältst, denn man weiß ja gar nicht, ob Du überhaupt dort etwas verdienen kannst und wie lange es also dauern wird, bis Du Dir selbst anderes Essen leisten kannst. Auch schrieb er, dass Ihr augenblicklich wieder zusammen schlafen müsst, und dass Ihr Mäuse hättet. Ach, es ist ein Trauerspiel mit Euch dort, man mag sich hier überhaupt nichts gönnen, wenn man an

Euch da draußen denkt. Ist Max W. noch dort, könntest Du nicht einmal Deinetwegen mit ihm sprechen. Schreibe mir bitte ausführlich, wie es Dir geht, ob Du auch satt wirst und Dich kräftig fühlst. Demnächst kommt Liesel ... (unles.) von David und Else nach dort. Wenn es geht, gebe ich ihr wieder etwas für Dich mit. Am Dienstag s.G.w. schicke ich Dir wieder etwas zum Naschen, ist das vom Geschäft jetzt angekommen. Ich erwarte also baldigst Deinen ausführlichen Bescheid, gut Schabbos und tausend Küsse von Deinem sich um Dich sorgenden Muttchen

Lieber Siegfried לאי״ט

Mir ist die Sache auch unverständlich. Wie hängt es zusammen? Für heute Gruß und Kuss Papa.

Guten שבת

(keine Adresse)

[19] Hamburg d. 30.5.39

Mein geliebter Siegfried לאי״ט

Herzlichen Dank für Deinen l. Schabbosbrief, der wie immer mit der letzten Post hier eintraf. Ich hoffe auch unser Schreiben in Deinem Besitz und erwarte ich mit Spannung Deine Antwort auf denselben, ebenso hoffe ich auf meine sonstigen Anfragen Bescheid zu erhalten, ich möchte mir doch gern ein Bild von Deinem dortigen Leben machen, auch habe ich, wie ich mich erinnere, Verschiedenes von hier angefragt. Also mein Geliebtes, nimm Dir einmal Zeit und schreibe uns über alles was wir wissen möchten. Wie ich Dir schon schrieb haben wir Jaumtouw gut verlebt, ich hatte schöne Blumen wie Flieder, Maiglöckchen und Tulpen, auch hatte ich einen sehr schönen Käsekuchen gebacken, von dem ich Dir gern ein Stück geschickt hätte, es war ebenso in dieser Beziehung wie sonst und so war es ja auch in Deinem Sinn, nicht wahr? Am ersten Tag waren wir bei *Dr.* Carlebach, am zweiten in der Parkallee, und so war es uns, da wir ja auch ....(unleserl. ??Tisch) besuch hatten nicht gar so einsam. Schreib auch Du mir, wie Du die Tage verbracht hast, ob Du eingeladen warst u.s.w.

Nun zu dem Inhalt Deines letzten Schreibens. Die ablehnende Antwort von Dr. W. habe ich ja eigentlich erwartet, wenn ja auch noch immer ein kleiner Hoffnungsschimmer auf das Gegenteil war. Ich verstehe nur nicht, wenn er Aussicht auf eventuelle Garantie für ein Heim mit Pfund 12 im

Monat gemacht hat, könnte er die Summe (die ich im Übrigen für ein Heim enorm hoch finde, da man hier doch schon dafür eine Privatpension bekommt) doch auch so geben. Man kann von hier aus natürlich absolut nicht darüber urteilen, und wie Du ja auch schon schreibst, sind das Ganze ja vorläufig noch Pläne, Du wirst uns wohl auf dem Laufenden halten und kann man ja erst, wenn so etwas spruchreif ist über Näheres korrespondieren. Unendlich würde ich mich freuen, wenn Du für Dich selbst irgendetwas Günstiges erreichen könntest, ich bitte täglich zum Allmächt'gen, dass er Dir beisteht.

Heute früh hat Liesel sich von uns verabschiedet, sie reist morgen, vielleicht kannst Du sie sprechen, ich gab ihr etwas zum Naschen für Dich mit, ich selbst schicke ebenfalls heute etwas für Dich ab. Warst Du einmal wieder bei Bella, frage doch nach, ob sie etwas für Dich hat. An Max Levin haben wir geschrieben, hoffentlich ist die Karte angekommen, ebenso der Brief an Sterns. Jetzt 5 Uhr schreibe ich den Brief weiter. Ich war inzwischen mit Papa bei Warburg, wir hatten telefonischen Bescheid bekommen, aber sollten die Tage von Juwelier Hintze für Einlösung durch Devisen abholen. Es ist alles zusammen auf 385 Mark taxiert worden, es müssen bis zum 31. Oktober also ca. Pfund 20 geschickt werden, ich weiß nicht genau wie es gerechnet wird, jedenfalls ist dieses ja nicht möglich, und wird es dann doch verkauft, nur mit dem Unterschied, dass wir inzwischen RM 60 Spesen hatten. Wenn wir gewusst hätten, dass die Einlösung schon so bald sein muss, hättest Du wohl auch nicht zu dem Depot geraten. Nun geschehene Dinge lassen sich ja nicht ändern. Bei Elsass bin ich auch gewesen, habe die RM 19.40 ausgezahlt bekommen. Herr Grunert sagte mir, dass er für die Restsachen ein Pauschalangebot von RM 25 vorliegen hätte, er riet mir sehr,darauf einzugehen, da er die Sachen einzeln nicht loswerden kann, dieselben würden ja durch das lange Herumstehen auch nicht besser, ich bin also darauf eingegangen. Schrank und Bettstelle etc. werden nächste Woche abgeholt. Ich schick den Brief schon heute fort, da ich ihn gern selbst schließen möchte, für den Antwortschein muss man ihn ja offen zur Post schicken. Papa schreibt Dir extra ein paar Zeilen, da wollen wir dann den Schein hineinlegen. Nun, mein lieber Junge, sind die 4 Seiten bald wieder voll, daher für heute Schluss. Ich erwarte also Deine baldige Nachricht und sende Dir tausend Küsse Dein Muttchen

Hamburg 30/5 39

Mein lieber Siegfried! לאי״ט

Für Deinen l. Brief herzlichen Dank, ich freue mich, dass es Dir gottlob gut geht, und dass Du Jaumtouw gut verbracht hast. Die l. Mama schrieb Dir ja schon, dass es uns auch G.s.D. gut geht, und dass wir die Tage gottl. gut verlebt haben. Auch über die Sache mit M.W. hat Mama Dir ja schon geschrieben, ebenso, dass wir uns bald einen ausführlichen Brief über unsere diversen Anfragen erwarten. Sieh doch mal die bis jetzt von uns erhaltenen Briefe durch, und wirst Du Dich dann erinnern welche Anfragen Du noch zu beantworten hast. Meine goldene Uhr ist mit RM 100 taxiert worden, ich würde sie ja sehr gern einlösen, aber es wird sich noch nicht machen lassen. Der רב hat Jaumtauw sehr gut über מגלת רות gesprochen, wir haben auch am 2ten Tag bei ihm besucht. Ich sehe also Deinem ausführlichen Brief mit Vergnügen entgegen, und verbleibe mit Gruß + Kuss Dein Dich liebender Vater

Ich wünsche recht guten שבת

[20] PK
Hamburg d. 2.6.39

Mein gel. Siegfried לאי״ט

Deine l. Karte erhielten wir gestern Donnerstag Nachmittag und beruhigte mich der Inhalt etwas. Ich erwarte ja doch Näheres in Deinem uns zugesagten ausführlichen Brief. Ich wollte Dich noch bitten, Deine Karte immer am Dienstag zu schreiben, damit wir sie am Mittwoch hier haben. Papa stellt immer so an, wenn am Mittwoch Nachmittag keine Post hier ist, Du kennst doch Dein Päppchen. Auch könntest Du doch Deinen Schabbosbrief schon am Donnerstag anfangen, dann hast Du doch mehr Zeit zum ausführlichen Schreiben. Du kannst Dir doch denken, dass wir gern alles beantwortet haben möchten. Uns geht es G.s.d. gut, das Wetter ist auch hier herrlich. Hoffentlich bleibt es so, wenn wir nach der nächsten Woche nach Wilhelminenhöhe gehen. Während Jaumtauw war das Essen dort einfach fabelhaft, die Leute waren alle begeistert. Onkel David u. Tante Else sind heute wieder zum Helfen nach dort. Diese Woche hatten wir eine Karte von Else, es hat uns gewundert, dass David gar nicht reingeschrieben hat. Bist Du schon bei Bella gewesen und hast Du Dich gefreut. Lade ist gestern abgegangen, auch Liesel hat wohl welche mitgebracht, ebenso hatte Bella welche, lass sie Dir gut schmecken. Ich wünsche Dir einen recht guten Schabbos und sende Dir innige Grüße und

Küsse Mama

Ich wünsche einen recht guten Schabbos.

Gruß und Kuss Papa

beantw. 6.6.39

(Queens Drive 87)

[21] PK
Hamburg d. 9/6 39

Mein l. Siegfried. לא״ט Deine l. Karte ist gestern Donnerstag Morgen bei uns eingetroffen, ich hoffe auch unseren Brief vom Mittwoch in Deinem Besitz. Es geht uns g.s.d. gut, nur bin ich mal wieder ein Pechvogel, ich habe eine Wurzelentzündung bin bei Dr. Streim (von dem ich Dich herzlich grüßen soll) in Behandlung. Ich habe ziemlich viel Schmerzen. Wir wollen doch am Mittwoch nach Wilhelminenhöhe, ich werde aber wohl noch nicht fahren können. Dr. Streim meint, dass es bis dahin noch nicht besser sein wird. Das nennt man doch wirklich Pech. Ich werde Dir noch am Montag schreiben, wohin die nächste Post soll. Es freut mich, dass Du von Bella so schön beschenkt worden bist. Sie wollte Dir aber doch noch von sich einen alten schwarzen Regenmantel und eine gestückte Fries?unterlage geben, frage sie doch einmal, wie es damit ist. Dass Du die Schokolade bekommen hast ist gut, vielleicht bekommst Du diese Woche wieder welche. Wir haben Onkel Elkan einen schönen Korb mit Cigarillos, sonst Cognac, Schokolade, diverse Fischkonserven etc. geschenkt. Hanna Hirsch hat ihn sehr hübsch mit Krepppapier garniert. Dass Du wieder Tennis gespielt hast, freut mich sehr. Wenn es Deine Zeit erlaubt, tue es nur öfter. Morgen hoffe ich von Dir zu hören. Für heute wünsche ich Dir gut Schabbos und sende innige Grüße und Küsse Deine Mutter

Lieber Siegfried

Ich wünsche Dir recht guten שבת

Innigen Gruß und Kuss Papa

(Queens Drive 87)

[22] PK
Hamburg d. 12/6 39

Mein l. Siegfried לאי״ט

Deinen l. Brief erhielten wir wie immer, herzlichen Dank, ich habe mich sehr gefreut, dass meine Befürchtungen unbegründet waren. Zweck unserer heutigen Karte ist, Dir mitzuteilen, dass wir leider erst am Donnerstag fahren können. Dr. Streim hofft bis dahin die provisorische Füllung machen zu können. Ich habe seit Schabbos wenigstens keine Schmerzen mehr. Aber ein Pech ist es ja doch, denn Kosten werden wir auch wahrscheinlich haben, weil große Nachfrage nach Zimmern draußen ist und wir Herrn Frank wohl etwas vergüten müssen, das lässt sich ja nun eben nicht ändern. Dr. Streim war am Sonnabend zweimal hier, um sich nach mir umzusehen. Ich fand es einfach großartig. Übrigens waren wir gerade bei Onkel Elkan zum Gratulieren, darauf kam er nachmittags noch einmal. Seit gestern ist das Wetter umgeschlagen, es ist kühl und regnerisch, bei Euch ist es wohl ebenso. Deine letzte Karte traf auch erst am Donnerstag morgens ein, Du wolltest es ja gern wissen. Morgen s.G.w. schreibe ich wieder, also für heute noch innige Grüße und Küsse von Deiner Mutter.

(über der Anrede umgekehrt geschrieben):

Frau Oppenheimer ruft Mittwoch 7 ½ Uhr hiesige Zeit bei John an von uns aus, wenn möglich sei Du dort.

Lieber Siegfried!

Ich bin froh, dass die Schmerzen bei der l. Mama aufgehört haben.

Gruß u. Kuss Papa

(Queens Drive 87)

[23] Hamburg d. 13. Juni 39

Mein Geliebter Siegfried. לאי״ט Meine gestrige Karte hoffe ich in Deinem Besitz gelangt, und kann ich Dir auch G.l. heute berichten, dass die Besserung in meinen Zähnen bis jetzt unberufen angehalten hat, hoffentlich bleibt es so, dass wir am Donnerstag fahren können, dann können wir das Zimmer noch gerade 14 Tage behalten, ab. 29. ist es wieder besetzt. Die verschiedenen Mitteilungen in deinem letzten Brief haben mich sehr interessiert und erwarte ich mit Spannung weitere Nachricht über Deine Unternehmungen. Teile mir doch in Deinen nächsten Zeilen einmal mit, wie es mit der Versicherung geworden ist, ob Du alles vergütet bekommen hast, und ob Du Dir etwas wieder gekauft hast. Auch wüsste ich gern einmal, wie Du eigentlich Deine Anzüge untergebracht hast, ob sie auch nicht so kraus werden. War der Ausflug am Sonntag schön, bist Du auch schon einmal im Hyde-Park gewesen? Dann wüsste ich gern, wie es mit deiner Gesundheit ist, ob alles, Verdauung usw. in Ordnung ist. Nun hat das neugierige Muttchen schon wieder so viel Fragen gestellt, wie sollen die nun alle wieder beantwortet werden. Halt, es kommt noch eine, wie geht es mit der Sprache, kannst Du Dich schon besser verständigen? Eben war Leo bei uns, er und Martha haben für den 10.

Juli Vorladung für Visum-Erteilung, da heißt es auch von diesen beiden bald Abschied nehmen. Ich hoffe, dass Du es Dir einrichten kannst, morgen Abend bei John zu sein, dann werden wir uns ja, wenn Du diesen Brief erhältst, persönlich gesprochen haben. Tut es dir leid, dass die beiden fortgehen, oder bist Du nicht viel mit ihnen zusammen gewesen, ich hoffe von Dir etwas über sein Abschiedsgeschenk zu hören. Wir haben vorige Woche für Päppchen ein schönes Lüsterjacket gekauft, desgleichen haben wir Stiefel für ihn vermessen lassen. Herr Falke, unser Fußdoktor, hat uns einen Schumacher empfohlen. Das Geburtstagsabendessen für Onkel Elkan war ganz nett, wir hatten gebratene Schollen mit gemischtem Salat, Butterbrot und Käse und Zitronenpudding mit Erdbeeren. In 14 Tagen kommt wohl auch James Mathiason nach dort, ich sprach ihn immer beim Zahnarzt. Hast Du Dr. Nathan zufällig gesprochen, er hat einen Kindertransport nach drüben gebracht. Wir quatschen hier jetzt sehr viel Englisch, da Hanna H. sich in der Sprache üben will, und wir machen mit. Das Wetter ist auch wohl bei Euch wieder anders geworden, gewöhnlich ist es ja dort wie bei uns. Bei Onkel Elkan war am Schabbos sehr viel Besuch, das war so recht etwas für Deinen Onkel, weniger für Deine Tante, ich habe letzterer übrigens etwas gegeben. Wie ist Davids Wohnung geworden, hat er die Möbel ziemlich zusammenbekommen, grüße die beiden von mir. Diese Woche bekamen wir einen Brief von Frau Simreich zu lesen, dieselbe schreibt nicht sehr begeistert, das Verdienen ist auch dort sehr schwer, sie erkundigt sich nach uns und nach Dir. Grüßen soll ich Dich von Frau Markus, Alice Mutter und von den Nachbarn von unserer Etage, die sich ständig nach Dir erkundigen, ebenso von der Dame über uns. So, nun ist der Stoff für heute wieder alle, etwas Platz muss ja auch für Päppchen bleiben. Lass es Dir weiter gut gehen und nimm innige Grüße und Küsse von Deinem Muttchen. (Wenn Du nichts anderes hörst, schreib den nächsten Brief nach Wilhelminenhöhe, Rissener Landstr. 127.)

Geliebter Siegfried! לאי״ט

Außer den schon mitgeteilten Sachen, habe ich auch für einen Überzieher Maß nehmen lassen und werde denselben, wenn wir s.G.w. von Wilhelminenhöhe zurückkommen, anfertigen lassen. Was wird bei Dr. Spitzer gelernt? Schreibe mir mal darüber. Hast Du den Rabbi nun schon mal sprechen hören und hast Du etwas davon verstanden? Ist in London Minhag Aschkenas oder Minhag Paulin?

Es war hier heute ziemlich kühl + muss man sich wohl für Wilhelminenhöhe mit Winterzeug versehen. Es grüßt und küsst Dich Dein Papa

Schabbos + Sonntag ist Rausch Chaudesch. Vergiss nicht Hallel zu oren.

Ich wünsche rechten guten Schabbos.

[24] PK
Blankenese d. 16.6.39

Mein l. Siegfried לאי״ט

Das war eine große Freude, als ich Deine Stimme endlich einmal wieder hörte, wenn es nicht so teuer wäre, würde ich öfter telefonieren. Seit gestern nachmittag sind wir nun hier in Wilhelminenhöhe. Wir haben ein schönes sonniges Zimmer, die erste Nacht habe ich natürlich kaum geschlafen. Dafür aber heute morgen über 3 Stunden im Liegstuhl unter Tannen gelegen, es war einfach herrlich. Es ist sehr besucht hier, sehr viel Bekannte, vorstellen ist kaum nötig. Kaum hatten wir am Mittwoch abend das Telefongespräch beendet, kamen Onkel Elkan und Tante Dora und berichteten uns von David, wir hatten einen großen Schrecken. Hoffentlich geht es ihm zufriedenstellend. Gerade als wir am Schabbos gemütlich beim Abendbrot saßen, wurde er operiert. Grüße die beiden herzlich. Ich wünsche gute Besserung, ich werde nächste Woche selbst schreiben. Hoffentlich erhalten wir statt der ausgefallenen Karte nun einen ausführlichen Brief von Dir, allerdings wird derselbe hier wohl erst am Sonntag eintreffen. Sind Petrowers gut weggekommen. Frau Oppenheimer war sehr aufgeregt. Nun mein Guter wünsche ich Dir einen guten Schabbos und sende Dir innige Küsse Deine Mutter

Mein lieber Siegfried!

Du kannst Dir denken, dass auch ich mich sehr erschrocken habe, als ich von der Operation von David hörte. Ich bin nun Kurgast in Wilhelminenhöhe. Hoffentlich bleibt das Wetter gut. Ich wünsche recht guten שבת Mit innigem Gruß + Kuss Papa

(Queens Drive 87)

[25] Blankenese, 20.6.39

Mein geliebter Siegfried לא״יט

Deinen l. Brief erhielten wir gleichzeitig mit Deiner Karte am Sonntag früh, herzlichen Dank für Deine l. Zeilen. Hoffentlich hast Du unsere Karte von hier erhalten ebenso unseren letzten Brief mit Antwortschein von vorigem Dienstag. Du erwähntest nichts davon. Wir fühlen uns G.s.D. hier sehr wohl, die Verpflegung ist sehr gut und reichlich und wir halten uns fast den ganzen Tag im freien auf, meistens liegen wir in unseren Stühlen und gucken in die Luft, für mich ist das ein Ideal. Morgens zum ersten Frühstück bekommen wir 2 Brötchen, Fein- und Schwarzbrot soviel wir wollen, Butter und Marmelade, Cacao oder Kaffee und jeden Tag Obst, Apfel, Banane oder Apfelsine, mittags gibt es drei Gänge, nachmittags Tee und Kuchen und abends immer sehr reichhaltig Belag, Bratkartoffel, Gemüsesalat etc. du siehst also, dass man es hier gut aushalten kann. Wegen der Wartenummer, habe ich gleich an Tante Else telefoniert, habe aber bis heute noch keine Formulare erhalten. Wenn ich daran denke, dass wir uns nicht wiedersehen sollen, bis Du uns einmal von Amerika anfordern kannst, könnte ich verzweifeln, hoffentlich glückt es auf andere Weise.

An David haben wir gestern geschrieben, ich hoffe doch, dass es ihm weiter gut geht. Von Tante Henny ist es sehr nett, dass sie Dich öfter zum Essen einladet, Rosalind ist gewiss ein nettes Mädchen geworden. Hast Du jemand sonst aus der Familie Landau kennen gelernt? oder kommst Du nicht viel zum Besuche machen. Dass Gertrud W. drüben ist, hatte ich schon gehört, sie hat Glück gehabt, in Antwerpen durfte sie doch nicht arbeiten. Mein Liebling, Du bist mir nicht böse, wenn ich heute nicht mehr schreibe, es ist bald Kaffeezeit, und ich muss vorher noch Papa's Bart abnehmen. Ich hoffe, bald wieder von Dir zu hören, nimm für heute innige Küsse von Deinem Muttchen.

Mein lieber Siegfried! לא"ט

Es hat mich sehr gefreut zu hören, dass Gerhard W. zu Minden gekommen ist; man sieht da wieder was Protection ausmacht, da so viele andere es nicht erreichen können, Arbeitserlaubnis zu bekommen. Ich habe die Hoffnung noch nicht aufgegeben dass Du es auch noch einmal erreichst. Also weiter auf Gott vertrauen.

Es gefällt uns hier sehr gut in Wilhelminenhöhe. Hoffentlich ist der Aufenthalt für die l. Mama von gutem Erfolg.

Innigsten Gruß und Kuss Papa

[26] ב"ה
Blankenese, d. 23.6.39

Mein gel. Siegfried לא"ט

Deine l. Karte erhielten wir gestern und hoffe ich auch unseren Brief in Deinem Besitz. Es geht uns G.s.D. sehr gut, wir erholen uns unberufen glänzend hier, wir sind den ganzen Tag im Freien im Liegestuhl (mein Ideal), essen gut, haben nette Gesellschaft, also was wollen wir mehr. Deinem Wunsch gemäß bleiben wir noch ein paar Tage länger, also bis Sonntag in 8 Tagen, ab Montag ist das Zimmer besetzt, es ist große Nachfrage, es sind sogar verschiedene Leute aus Berlin hier, hoffentlich bleibt das Wetter weiter so herrlich, dass wir es noch weiter ausnutzen können. Soeben war Dr. Plaut hier, er erzählte uns, dass er Dich drüben gesprochen hat, dass er Dich G.s.D. gut aussehend findet, worüber wir uns natürlich sehr gefreut haben. Tante Harriet ist sehr froh, dass sich auf ihre Annonce etwas gemeldet hat, sie hat durch Tante Else gleich beides erledigen lassen, sie dankt Dir herzlich und schreibt Dir nächste Woche, ich würde mich ja sehr freuen, wenn sie Erfolg hätte. Man weiß ja nicht, wie lange es hier noch dauern wird, es wäre jammerschade, wenn es aufhören würde. Dass bei Herm nun ein Junge angekommen ist, hast Du wohl auch gehört. Frau Oppenheimer schrieb es mir aus Frankfurt, ich will heute noch beiden gratulieren. Das Formular an das Konsulat ist abgeschickt, die Nummer wird ja nicht gerade sehr niedrig sein. Ich glaube, sie sind schon bei 19.000. Heute hatten wir eine Karte von David, hast Du dieselbe gelesen, wir haben uns köstlich amüsiert. G.s.D. dass er seinen Humor nicht verliert, grüße ihn auch Else herzlich von mir und sage ihm, dass wir uns sehr gefreut hätten. Es ist schön, dass Du Dich mit den Sachen von John gefreut hast, schade ist es, dass Dir die Taschentücher nicht so gefallen, er konnte sie wohl nicht anders bekommen, es ist ja dumm, dass er für die Sachen von seinem Schwager so viel Zoll hat zahlen müssen. Diese Woche sind in Hamburg als Liebesgabe von Herrn Bialoglowski Hühner? verteilt worden, wir hatten auch Benachrichtigung, mussten ja darauf verzichten. Am Montag kommen hier die ersten Ferienkinder an, 80 an der Zahl, da wird es wohl etwas lebhaft werden.

Hoffentlich erhalten wir nun morgen den versprochenen ausführlichen Brief, der uns auf all unsere Fragen Antwort gibt. Was ich auch noch sehr gern wissen möchte ist, ob Du noch in irgend einer Verbindung mit der betreffenden Familie stehst, Du weißt ja, was ich meine, schreibe doch bitte einmal darüber. Päppchen macht gerade ein wunderhübsches Schnarchkonzert, das kann er hier besonders gut, ich stehe manchmal des Nachts 3 mal auf, um ihn anzustoßen, unsere Betten stehen nicht zusammen.

Ich wünsche Dir nun noch einen recht guten Schabbos und sende Dir viele, viele innige Küsse Dein Muttchen

Mein lieber Siegfried! לאי"ט

Es sind hier augenblicklich so viele Herren, dass wir jeden Tag mit Minjan oren können, was mich, wie Du Dir denken kannst, sehr freut + ist auch für Herrn Frank sehr angenehm, da derselbe wieder אבלist + dadurch Gelegenheit hat vorzuoren. Über den Bericht von Dr. Plaut von dem Dir die l. Mama schon schrieb, habe ich mich selbstredend sehr gefreut + hoffe ich, dass auch Dein Befinden dem Aussehen entsprechend ist. Wirklichen Naches habe ich von der Karte von David gehabt, man sieht daraus, dass er sich trotz aller Unannehmlichkeiten seinen Humor + seinen חןbewahrt hat.

Ich muss auch noch für שבת umziehen, sende deshalb nur noch die innigsten Schabbos Grüße + verbleibe mit Gruß +Kuss Papa

Massel Tauw zur Geburt des kleinen Oppenheimer

bald bei Dir אמן.

ב"ה [27]
Blankenese d. 27.6.39

Mein gel. Siegfried לאי"ט

Deinen dieswöchentlichen Schabbosbrief erhielten wir bereits am Schabbosmorgen, was uns natürlich große Freude bereitete, ich hoffe, dass Du auch unseren Brief bei gutem Wohlergehen erhalten hast. Auch uns geht es G.s.D. nach wie vor unberufen gut, alle finden uns G.s.D. glänzend aussehend. Das Wetter war bis Schabbos einfach herrlich, es ist jetzt kühler, nichtsdestoweniger haben wir trotzdem gut eingewickelt stets fast 4 Stunden in unseren Liegestühlen gelegen. Heute Vormittag haben wir mit Herrn und Frau Adolf Warisch und Frau Bundheim einen wunderschönen Spaziergang nach Sonneneck durch lauter Tannenwald gemacht. Wir hatten von dort aus einen prachtvollen Ausblick auf die Elbe. Ich habe gar nicht gewusst, dass hier eine so schöne Gegend ist, es ist manchmal direkt wie im Harz. Seit gestern sind 80 Ferienkinder hier, es ist natürlich dadurch lauter, aber auch daran gewöhnt man sich. Wir fahren nun s.G.w. am Sonntag Abend nach Hause, wir nehmen mit Herrn und Frau Willi Sänger, die schon einige Wochen hier sind, zusammen ein Auto, das uns dann von hier aus mit unserem Gepäck direkt nach Hause bringt. Hierher hatten wir einen von Herrn Frank empfohlenen Spediteur für unser Gepäck, wir fuhren mit Straßenbahn, Hochbahn und Auto, was uns sogar noch mehr kostete. Es sind außer den schon genannten Gästen noch Herr Siegmund Cahn und Frau, jetziger Oberkantor, Herr Aron, verschiedene junge Mädchen aus Hamburg und Gäste aus Berlin und Frankfurt hier. Morgen kommt Tante Hedwigs Schwester Toni mit ihren beiden Kindern, sie waren gestern hier um zu mieten. Wie kommt es, dass Du noch nichts von der Versicherung gehört hast, vielleicht kann Elkeles, der doch wie ich von Frl. Rosskamm hier hörte, wieder in Amsterdam ist, etwas in der Sache unternehmen. Von der Gewerbepolizei war ein sehr netter Herr persönlich bei uns, derselbe wollte Dein Büro sehen, ob nicht mehr darin ist, als er es als Schlafzimmer eingerichtet sah, lachte er und war beruhigt. Als ich ihn wegen der Bestätigung für den Verband fragte, sagte er mir, das ginge von ihnen direkt aus. Übrigens stand auch Deine Firma bereits von Amtswegen gelöscht in der Zeitung. Von Berta Polack habe lange nichts gehört, als ich einmal bei ihr anfragte, sagte sie mir, Henry sei in Amerika, käme aber noch einmal nach Europa. Dass ich für unseren Verbrauch etwas von den Reserven nehmen muss, ist ja natürlich, denn so viel, wie es monatlich ausmacht, kann ich mit dem besten Willen nicht einsparen, nun vorläufig reicht es ja G.l. noch. Die Firma Sallinger hat sich vielmals entschuldigt, es lag ein Irrtum ihrerseits vor. An M. Eppendorfer Baum hatte ich wieder telefoniert, er wollte dieser Tage etwas schicken, ich weiß nicht, ob er es inzwischen getan hat, ebenso N. Oberaltenallee. Die Aufstellungen etc. habe ich inzwischen alle gefunden und bin ich über alles im Bilde. Mit Elsass konnte ich nichts weiter machen, es stimmt genau mit Deinem Verzeichnis, ich hätte ja ablehnen können, aber es wäre wohl nicht viel anderes dabei rausgekommen, wenn ich zurück bin, will ich wieder anrufen. Der Bericht über Deine Wirtin ist ja nicht gerade begeisternd, aber Du musst es ja vorläufig so hinnehmen.

Nun mein Geliebtes muss ich für heute Schluss machen, der Briefträger kommt gleich, der nimmt die Post mit. Also nimm für heute innige Grüße und Küsse von Deinem sehr an Dich denkenden Muttchen.

Lieber Siegfried!

Ich kann Dir heute nur herzlichsten Gruß senden, da doch Mama drängt, dass der Brief weg kommt.

Also Gruß + Kuss Papa

[28] ב״ה
Blankenese d. 29.6.39

Mein Geliebtes לאי״ט

Deinen l. ausführlichen Brief erhielten wir gestern Mittwoch früh, eine Dame brachte ihn uns als wir schon auf unseren Liegestühlen lagen, und hatten wir dann so eine schöne Beschäftigung, ihn zu lesen. Es hat mich natürlich alles sehr interessiert, ich kann mir doch nun schon ein besseres Bild über Dein Leben dort machen. Freut mich, dass Du Dir besseres Essen und auch mal ein Ei leisten kannst. Da wirst Du doch wenigstens nicht von Kräften kommen. Über die Erdbeerpreise kann ich Dir noch nichts mitteilen, da hier ja keine Geschäfte sind und ich so nichts erfahre. Wie gern möchte ich auch einmal wieder Knackwürste essen, Fleisch haben wir hier am vergangenen Schabbos gehabt, jeder eine schöne Scheibe, sehr wohlschmeckend, das erste Mal seit dem Barmitzwoh-Schabbos von Josef. Ich glaube, ich habe sehr zugenommen, ich esse und trinke ja viel mehr als zu Hause, vor allen Dingen jeden Nachmittag Tee und Kuchen. Wir müssen täglich für uns beide 9 Mark bezahlen, wir wollen deshalb jetzt lieber Schluss machen, dafür vielleicht s.G.w. zu Sukkaus wieder hergehen. Ich weiß auch nicht, ob die Füllung in meinem Zahn länger liegen kann, derselbe macht sich schon hin und wieder bemerkbar. Seit gestern nun Toni und Kinder hier, der Junge kommt nächste Woche nach Schweden auf eine Hascharah. Toni bringt ihn nächste Woche nach Berlin, er ist ein lieber Junge, du kennst ihn ja auch von Hamburg her. Hast Du übrigens gehört, dass mit Siegfried Nussbaums Stellung Essig war, als er ankam, hatte Herr Stern gerade 15 Leute entlassen müssen und konnte ihn daher nicht einstellen. Er hat jetzt etwas bekommen, ich glaube in einem Hotel, ich werde aus Tonis Erzählung nicht recht klug. Du schreibst bei der Antwort über Deine Anzüge, dass ich an alles denke, Du ahnst ja nicht, mein geliebtes Kind, wie oft und wie sehr ich immer an Dich denke; möge der Allmächt'ge geben, dass wie Du ja auch schreibst, unsere Trennung nicht allzulange dauert. Ich vergaß übrigens Dir im vorigen Brief mitzuteilen, dass wir schon vom amerikanischen Konsulat Antwort bekommen und zwar die Nummern 17.333 und 34 und dass wir in unabsehbarer Zeit an die Reihe kämen, mit G'ttes Hilfe werden wir hoffentlich nicht unabsehbar auf ein Wiedersehen warten müssen.

Wie geht es David, ist er schon wieder zu Hause und was haben sie beim Konsulat für einen Bescheid bekommen? So sehr es mich für ihn freuen würde, wenn Else David bald folgen könnte, so sehr würde es mir für Dich leid tun. Es ist zu schön, dass Du hin und wieder bei ihr essen kannst, sie kocht doch so gut, auch dass sie Deine Wäsche und Strümpfe stopfen besorgt, es ist für mich überhaupt eine Beruhigung, dass Du eine Häuslichkeit bei ihnen hast. Hans und Erna kommen wohl auch bald nach dort, wir hatten eine Karte von ihnen als Antwort auf unsere Geburtstagsglückwünsche. Warum hast Du Onkel Elkan noch nicht geschrieben, ich glaube, er ist sehr beleidigt, wenn Du es noch nicht getan hast, hole es bitte sofort nach. Dass es mit der Sprache noch nicht so klappt, tut mir leid, du begreifst doch sonst so leicht. Die Hemmungen beim Sprechen musst Du ablegen, immer darauf losquatschen, so lernst Du es am leichtesten, es schadet nichts, wenn Du auch mal ausgelacht wirst. Hier lernt auch alles Englisch, jeder spricht von Auswanderungsmöglichkeiten, das Publikum wechselt sehr, da viele Leute nur 8-10 Tage hier bleiben, Heut kommt auch Dr. Carlebach mit einigen Kindern, hast Du Frau Dr. dort einmal gesprochen. Um auf Deine Mitteilung über den Lunch zurückzukommen, so finde ich einfach fabelhaft, was es dort für 2 penny alles gibt, ich würde Dir raten, wenn es Deine Zeit und Dein Geld erlauben doch immer hinzugehen, ich bemerke nochmals, dass es die Hauptsache erst einmal ist, dass Du Dich weiter gesund erhältst. Es ist dumm, dass Deine Wirtin keinen großen Wert auf Sauberkeit legt, immerhin ist es schon etwas, dass sie wenigstens mit

der Bettwäsche nicht so spart. Ich hoffe nun morgen wieder von dir zu
hören, die nächste Nachricht gibst du dann wieder nach Hause. Wenn es
Dir möglich ist, schreib immer recht ausführlich, mich interessiert jede
Kleinigkeit, es ist meine größte Freude, Deine Briefe und Karten immer
und immer wieder zu lesen. Also für heute Schluss. Recht guten Schabbos
und innige Grüße und Küsse von Deinem Muttchen.

Wie Du Dir denken kannst, sind die Pralinen natürlich längst alle, ich
habe aber inzwischen schon andere gehabt, sie schmeckten aber nicht so
gut wie die von Dir gespendeten.

Lieber Siegfried! לאי"ט

Wir haben heute eine Karte von Onkel Elkan erhalten, worin er schreibt,
Siegfried scheint uns ganz vergessen zu haben. Schreibe ihm also gleich
Sonntag. Du weißt, dass er großen Wert auf solche Sachen legt. Ich muss
mich noch שבת anziehen, also für heute nur noch die herzlichsten Grüße
+ Küsse von Papa.

Mit dem Zions Wächter habe ich mich geirrt, die Zeitung heißt der Orient,
welche ich inzwischen gefunden habe. Guten שבת

[29] ב"ה
Hamburg, 4. Juli 39

Mein lieber Siegfried לאי"ט

Wir sind seit Sonntag Abend wieder in unserem Heim. Es war in
Wilhelminenhöhe sehr schön. Verpflegung ausgezeichnet, und hatten wir
auch bis auf einige kühle Tage gutes Wetter. Am letzten Schabbos hatten
wir die Ehre Herrn Oberrabbiner Doctor Carlebach bei uns zu sehen, und
hat er uns auch mit einer Predigt erfreut, und zwar in Veranlassung der
Bar Mizwah des Sohnes von Johannan Levisohn in Antwerpen. Die Eltern
waren in Wilhelminenhöhe. Auch bei Tisch hat der רב gesprochen und
der Schabbos hat dadurch eine besondere Weihe erhalten. Nachmittags
ging der Raw mit unseren Herren nach Hamburg zum Auneg Schabbos,
und am Sonntag Abend um 6 Uhr war eine Trauung in der Synagoge,
auch musste der בר wieder zurückfahren. Wir sind dann auch mit Herrn
und Frau Sänger um 9 Uhr in einem Auto nach Hamburg zurückgefahren.
Es war sehr bequem + waren wir 9 ½ Uhr wieder zu Haus. Den Stoff
zum Überzieher haben wir noch nicht besorgt, wollen dies aber in den
nächsten Tagen tun, ich lasse ihn bei Rappaport arbeiten, er hat Erlaubnis

bekommen für einen arischen Schneider zu arbeiten. Es ist 12 Uhr bis jetzt geht es mit dem Fasten gut, ich denke, dass ich ausfasten kann.

Für heute verbleibe ich mit Gruß + Kuss Papa

Mein Geliebtes. Deinen l. Brief erhielten wir auch diesmal wieder am Schabbos früh, herzlichen Dank. Nun sind wir wieder zu Hause und denke ich gern an die schönen Tage in Wilhelminenhöhe zurück. Es war ja zu schön, dass wir so vom Wetter begünstigt waren, selbst wenn es etwas kühler war, habe ich eingepackt im Liegestuhl gelegen. Am letzten Schabbos hat Papa Dir ja schon geschrieben, nach Nacht haben wir mit vielen anderen Gästen noch bis gegen 12 Uhr um Dr. C. herum gesessen, er hat Döntjes und wahre Witze, die ihm passiert waren, erzählt, wir haben alle herzhaft gelacht. Am Schabbos waren mit Personal 55 Erwachsene und 70 Kinder zu verpflegen. Tante Harriet ist vollkommen erledigt, sie hat nicht die richtige Hilfe, es wird Zeit, dass sie mal etwas anderes bekommt, leider hat sie bisher keine Antwort auf ihre Bewerbungsschreiben erhalten. Toni ist gestern mit Hans und Tante Hedwig nach Berlin gefahren, morgen fährt der Junge nach Schweden und kommt Tante Hedwig dann noch einige Tage mit nach Wilhelminenhöhe. Was Du über die Angelegenheit mit der betreffenden Familie schreibst, so möchte ich Dich bitten, auf gar keinen Fall Dich durch irgendwelche Bedenken auch unseretwegen bestimmen zu lassen, auf die Sache einzugehen, wenn sie Dir nicht zusagt. Es hinge viel zu viel davon ab, wenn man sich für's Leben bindet. und nicht restlos befriedigt ist, also keine voreiligen Entschlüsse, Du hast schon recht, es kommt alles so, wie es von G'tt bestimmt ist. Dass drüben so große Brände sind ist ja furchtbar, Du hast wohl nichts davon gesehen, ich nehme an, dass es weit von Dir entfernt ist. Am Donnerstag kommt Erna nach hier, Hans ist inzwischen zu seiner Mutter nach Wien, wenn es klappt, werden sie ja noch am 12ten nach dort fahren. Sprichst Du Siegmund Hannover manchmal und hast Du Onkel Elkan schon geschrieben? Dass es mit der Bürgschaft für Hanna Hirsch nicht geklappt hat, schrieb ich Dir glaube ich, schon, sie hat sich nun nochmals nach drüben an Frau Witter? gewandt, ob sie etwas erreicht, weiß sie nicht, es hat jeder seine Sorgen. Ich hoffe nun bald wieder von Dir zu hören. Grüße Sterns und alle Verwandten und Bekannte und nimm Du tausend innige Küsse von Deinem Muttchen.

Morgen geht ein Päckchen ab, schreibe bitte, ob es angekommen ist.

[30] PK
ב"ה
Hamburg d. 7/7. 39

Lieber Siegfried לאי"ט

Herzlichen Dank für Deine l. Karte. Es freut mich, dass Du G.l. gut gefasteti hast. L. Papa hat um 2 Uhr angebissen, Du weißt ja, dass Dr. Neufeld schon im vorigen Jahr nicht einen ganzen Tanis an diesem Tag erlaubt hat.

Unseren Brief hoffe ich in Deinem Besitz ebenso das Päckchen. Seit gestern abend ist Erna hier, sie schläft in Deinem Bett, auch Hans, der am Montag kommt, wird die eine Nacht bei uns wohnen, da sie ja schon am Dienstag fahren. Am Sonntag Mittag sind Onkel Elkan, Tante Dora und Tante Auguste bei uns zu Tisch, auch gestern abend waren Onkel E. u. Tante D. bei uns zum Abendbrot. Es herrscht augenblicklich großer Betrieb bei uns, außer dem Wohnzimmer waren heute sämtliche Räume mit Schlafenden belegt. Von Dr. Streim soll ich Dich herzlich grüßen, er ist leider in seiner Angelegenheit noch nicht weiter gekommen. Erna hat verschiedenes mitgebracht und so waren Hanna H. und ich den ganzen Vormittag beschäftigt, auch schon für Sonntag alles zu richten. Morgen hoffe ich wieder einen ausführlichen Brief zu bekommen. für heute gut Schabbos herzlichen Gruß und Kuss Mama

Adr. Fr. Oppenheimer Frft a/M. Gaustraße 16, Hamburg, Bornstr. 24 b. Schloss

Mein lieber Siegfried

Es hat mich sehr gefreut, dass Du diese Woche am Tanis für mich eintreten konntest, da ich nicht ausgefastet habe. Für heute herzlichen Gruß u. Kuss.

Guten שבת Papa

9/7. 39 (vermutlich beantwortet)

(Queens Drive 87)

[31] ב"ה
Hamburg d. 11/7 39

Mein geliebter Siegfried לאי"ט

für Deinen l. Schabbosbrief sowie für Deine l. Karte vom Sonntag herzlichen Dank, die letztere war eine besondere Freude, da wir ja heute Dienstag sonst nichts von Dir bekommen. Uns geht es G.s.D. gut, ich hoffe, dass dies auch bei Dir der Fall ist. Wir waren gestern bei Fr. Battenfeld sie war mit uns beiden zufrieden, sie fand auch, dass wir uns gut erholt hätten, nichtsdestoweniger haben wir wieder für RM10 Medikamente bekommen, aber das sind wir ja nun gewohnt. Wir fuhren dann gleich zur Stadt und haben Stoffe eingekauft, einen Überzieher eine gestreifte Hose und dann einen sehr schönen Stoff zum Anzug, den Du ja Papa zum Geburtstag schenken wolltest, Du weißt doch, dass derselbe am Sonntag ist. Eigenartig ist, dass der arische Schneider bei dem R. arbeiten darf, Herr Levien, Michaelisstraße ist. Ich habe dann gleich noch einige Einkäufe für Hans erledigt, ich hoffe, dass dieselben seinen Beifall haben, die Verkäuferinnen in dem Geschäft halfen beim Aussuchen, sie sagten, als ich den Namen von Hans nannte, sie würden seinen Geschmack noch kennen. Es waren ein paar schöne Tage mit Erna, nun kommt heute Mittag wieder der bittere Abschied. Das Wetter ist sehr stürmisch, hoffentlich hat E. nicht so sehr unterwegs zu leiden. Die beiden sind guten Mutes, haben ihren Humor nicht verloren, sind natürlich glücklich über das Wiedersehen mit Mäxchen. Onkel Elkan und Tante Dora sind natürlich sehr traurig, dass nun auch ihre letzten Kinder sie verlassen, aber es ist ja schließlich gleich, ob ein Kind oder 3 fortgehen, man bleibt allein und die einzige Hoffnung ist, dass man in nicht allzu langer Zeit wieder zusammenkommt. Hanna H. hat noch nichts wieder gehört, Marta und Leo können sich am Freitag ihr Visum holen, die Untersuchung war in Ordnung, sie fahren nach Chikago. Eben kam eine Karte von Max und Hanne Dörte Levien, sie schreiben, dass sie auch viel Schwierigkeiten haben. Zu unserer Freude teilen sie uns mit, dass Du G.s.D. und unberufen gut und frisch aussiehst, ich wünsche und hoffe von ganzem Herzen, dass es weiter so bleibt. Du wolltest uns doch einmal etwas über Deine Unterhaltungen mit Kezi und Mrs. Graham mitteilen, oder ist nichts Positives dabei herausgekommen. M. Eppendorfer Baum hat uns wieder RM 20 geschickt, N. hat noch nichts wieder (trotz Versprechens) von sich höeren lassen. Henry Polack ist noch in New York, seine Mutter lässt es mich wissen, wann er wieder in London ist. Von Dr. Streim soll ich Dich wieder grüßen, er ist in seiner Sache noch nicht weiter gekommen, ich muss heute, hoffentlich zum letzten Mal, wieder zu ihm. Die Sache mit Elsass hat sich wieder zerschlagen, ich soll in den nächsten Tagen wieder

Bescheid von ihm haben und teile Dir dann darüber mit. David bekommt ja jetzt immer das Nachrichtenblatt, ich nehme an, dass auch Du dasselbe liest. Im Kulturbund bin ich noch nicht wieder gewesen, nach den 3 Wochen werde ich s.G.w. wieder einmal hingehen, es werden hier jetzt nur Filme gegeben. Was Deine Reise zu Siegmund betrifft, möchte ich Dir eigentlich abraten, ich glaube, es ist besser, wenn Du dort bleibst, Ihr könnt Euch ja schließlich auch schriftlich beraten, also lass es lieber. Erna wird Dir auch meine Besorgnisse sagen,dieselbe kann Dir auch über unser schönes Essen am Sonntag berichten.

Nun ist der Stoff für heute wieder beendet, der Brief muss auch gleich des Antwortscheins wegen zur Post. Mit den 2 Tafeln hattest Du übrigens Recht, Du wirst sie wohl Ende der Woche erhalten.

Nun leb wohl für heute mein Geliebtes, nimm innige Grüße und Küsse von Deinem Muttchen. Grüße für alle, auch Tante Henny, ebenso an Leviens. Vergiss nicht Papas Geburtstag.

Hbg d. 11/7 39

ב"ה

Lieber Siegfried לאי"ט

Wir sind nun wieder von unserem Sommerurlaub in unser Heim zurückgekehrt.

Am מוצא שבת war es in Wilhelminenhöhe noch recht gemütlich. Wir saßen nach הבדלה

im Speisesaal + Dr. Carlebach erzählte verschiedene Döntjes, worüber wir uns köstlich amüsierten. Unter anderem erzählte er, im vorigen Jahre hatte er die Tochter von Hermann Bacharach getraut. Auf einem Nebenbalcon stand ein Herr und Dr. Carlebach hörte, als er sagte, der Pollack da nebenan sieht aus wie Dr. Carlebach. Du kannst Dir denken wie wir gelacht haben. Auch wir haben seit ihrer Ausreise noch gar nichts von Kugelmann gehört, was uns sehr wundert. Es bestätigt sich da wieder die Wahrheit des Sprichworts, aus dem Auge, aus dem Sinn. Übermorgen s.G.w. wirst Du ja Erna und Hans sprechen, sie werden heute Abend abreisen.

Für heute Gruß und Kuss von Papa

[32] PK
Hamburg d. 14/7. 39

Mein l. Siegfried לאי"ט

Unseren Brief von Dienstag hoffe in Deinen Besitz gelangt, inzwischen hast Du wohl von Erna und Hans mündlich über unser Wohlbefinden gehört. Ich hoffe, dass die beiden gut gereist sind. Groß war gewiss die Freude beim Wiedersehen mit Mäxchen. Ich war mit in der Ferdinandstraße, es war ein kolossaler Betrieb dort, es war ziemlich aufregend für mich. Am Dienstag abend ist Frau Oppenheimer zurück gekommen, sie war am Mittwoch bei uns und erzählte sie mir, dass sie von einer Cousine von Spiers erfahren hätte, dass dieselben auch in London seien, Betty hätte sich dort als Ärztin niedergelassen und die Eltern seien bei ihr. Sie bat die Cousine, sich doch die Adresse zu verschaffen, sobald wir dieselbe erfahren haben, teile ich sie Dir mit. Vielleicht kannst Du dieselbe aber schon dort erfahren, da Betty als Ärztin doch sicher registriert ist. Am 17. August fahren Leo und Martha mit der New York, auf der anderen Linie war für August und September bereits alles besetzt, und sie wollten nicht länger warten. Martha wird das Fortgehen ganz besonders schwer, sie wäre, glaube ich, froh gewesen, wenn noch nicht alles geklappt hätte. Gestern war Berta Polack hier, sie erwarte(t) in nächster Zeit ihr Permit für Afrika, dann ist wieder eine gute Freundin fort. Henry bleibt noch längere Zeit in Europa. Er kommt auch noch einmal nach dort, sie teilt mir dann seine Adresse mit.

Für heute wünsche ich Dir noch einen recht guten Schabbos und sende Dir innige Grüße und Küsse Mama

(Seite 1 oben umgekehrt): Liebe Grüße für alle

Mein lieber Siegfried לאי"ט

Ich hoffe Hans + Erna dort gut angelangt. Prima (?) Nun ist der Verwandtenkreis in London bald größer als hier. Innigsten Gruß und Kuss Papa

Guten שבת

Queens Drive 87

ב"ה [33]
18/7/39

Mein lieber Siegfried! לאי"ט

Ich bestätige den Empfang Deines l. Briefes vom 14. Juli, und will Dir heute einen Bericht geben über die Feier meines Geburtstages, und wie schön ich beschenkt wurde. Vor allem sage ich Dir meinen herzlichsten Dank für den schönen Anzugstoff, den wir in Deinem Auftrage gekauft haben. Die l. Mama hat mir Taschentücher, Cigarettenspitze, Cigarillos, Cigaretten etc. Blumen, Schirm, 3 Schlipse, Kuchen geschenkt. Auch von den anderen Familienmitgliedern war ich mit Cigarren, Chokolade etc. beschenkt. Hanna Hirsch hat mir sogar ein englisches Gedicht verehrt, was wirklich bewundernswert ist; außerdem haben mir die beiden Hannas 2 Bücher über Spracheigenheiten der englischen Sprache von M. Bergmann geschenkt. Gestern Abend waren Onkel Elkan, Tante Dora, (unleserl.), Tante Else, Frau Oppenheim bei uns, es war sehr gemütlich. Nun hätte ich gern noch eine fromme, nette Schwiegertochter bei den Geschenken aufgezählt, aber damit muss ich mich wohl noch etwas gedulden, hoffentlich nicht zu lang. Bei der Schwierigkeit, mit der es in England verbindet, ist Arbeitserlaubnis zu erhalten, ist es vielleicht der einzige Weg durch Einheirat in ein schon bestehendes Geschäft dieses schneller zu erreichen. Diesen Schabbos hat Dr. Carlebach im Altenheim gesprochen, Mama war gestern bei Frau Dr. Carlebach + hat sich die wiederbeauftragten Grüße für uns abgeholt. Anbei schicken wir Dir ein Exemplar von dem von Hanna Hirsch verfassten Gedicht. Nun habe ich Dir, wie ich glaube, alles erzählt + verbleibe mit Gruß + Kuss Dein Papa

Wir haben uns sehr mit den verschiedenen englischen Grüßen auch von Rosalind gefreut, mir scheint Du machst doch schon Fortschritte, es brauchte ja nicht so viel von R. geändert werden.

Mein gel. Siegfried לאי"ט

Auch Deine l. englische Karte von Eurem Ausflug erhielten wir, es freut mich sehr, dass Du Deine freie Zeit benutzt, um Dich im Freien aufzuhalten. Wir sind jetzt nur auf unseren Balkon angewiesen, es war gut, dass wir in Wilhelminenhöhe soviel in der Luft sein konnten. Von seinem Geburtstag hat Papa Dir ja schon geschrieben, wir hatten den ganzen Tag Besuch, abends waren wir gemütlich zusammen, es gab dann Bickbeerenkuchen, Zuckerkuchen und meinen schönen Kuchen mit

Corinthen und Rosinen, nur eins hat mir gefehlt, dass Du mein Liebes nicht dabei warst. Über Erna und Hans verfrühte Ankunft haben wir von verschiedenen Seiten gehört, sie schreiben ja begeistert über ihre Reise, wie schön, dass Ihr nun alle dort zusammen seid. Ihr könnt Euch doch nun gegenseitig beraten. David hat wieder sehr ulkig an Papa geschrieben, er meint, wenn auch wir einmal in der Nacht ankämen, bräuchten wir nur Aslo Geresch zu pfeifen, dann bekämen wir ein mehr oder minder hartes Nachtlager. Isidor Isaak und Frau haben nun auch ihr Certifikat bekommen und werden uns demnächst verlassen, er war übrigens einige Tage sehr krank, es geht ihm aber G.s.D. wieder besser. Papa hat ihn gestern besucht. Auch Frau Markus Möller, Hermans Mutter kommt demnächst zu Euch, um dort auf ihre Einreise nach Palästina zu warten. Dass Bob de Jong am 15. August geheiratet hast Du wohl schon gehört, vergiss nur nicht, ihm zu gratulieren. Bei Dr. Neufeld ist am Schabbos Nachmu Barmitzwoh, wir werden ihm dieser Tage schreiben. Vorige Woche hat Frl. Gerson wieder bei uns angerufen und sich nach unserem und Deinem Befinden erkundigt, sie ist immer noch anhänglich. Schreibe ihr doch einmal ein paar Zeilen. Johns Schwiegermutter erzählte mir von den Sachen, die er Dir zum Abschied schenkte, es wären Kuchen, Cakes, Marmelade, Fischkonserven und außerdem 4711 und Cigaretten gewesen, schreibe mir doch einmal ob dies wirklich der Fall war.

Hast Du auch schon etwas von ihm aus New York gehört, sie haben schöne Bilder vom Schiff geschickt. Gestern sind endlich die Kartons vom Boden abgeholt worden ich habe noch etwas darauf zahlen müssen, um sie nur los zu werden. Wie Dir Adolf, mit dessen englischer Karte wir uns sehr freuten, vielleicht erzählte, gibt es die Antwortscheine jetzt am Dienstag Mittag und schreibe ich dafür jetzt gleich nach dem Kaffee. Nun will ich in die Küche und rote Grütze kochen, hast Du drüben auch schon welche gegessen. Es ist schade, dass ich Dir keine schicken kann. Ich hoffe dieser Tage wieder von Dir zu hören, grüße alle Lieben und nimm auch Du wieder viele, viele Grüße und Küsse von Deinem Muttchen.

Schreibe mal eine Karte nach Parkallee.

[34] PK
Hamburg 22.7.39

Mein l. Siegfried לאי״ט

Deine l. Karte erhielten wir gestern Nachmittag und hoffe ich auch unseren Dienstag Brief in Deinem Besitz. Es geht uns G.s.D. gut, ich hoffe ein Gleiches von Dir. Tante Harriet hat leider keine Antwort auf ihr Schreiben erhalten. Ich hätte es ihr so sehr gewünscht, da sie es hier so furchtbar schwer hat. Auch Hanna Hirsch hat heut ein Schreiben vom Konsulat erhalten, dass wohl ihr Avidavit jetzt genügt, dass sie aber noch einige Monate warten muss. Es ist wohl schon so, wie Du geschrieben hast, dass alle Nummern von den 4 Konsulaten hier zusammengeworfen werden, der eine dadurch früher, der andere später drankommt. Es ist natürlich für sie sehr bedauerlich, da sie ja keine rechte Existenz mehr hat. Unsere Gedanken treffen sich wirklich. Gerade heute wollte ich anfragen, ob Du schon einmal an Adolf nach Chikago geschrieben hast. Schiebe es bitte nicht mehr auf. Sobald ich Spiers Adresse habe, teile ich sie Dir natürlich mit. Fr. O. will diesbezüglich noch einmal in Frankfurt nachfragen. Hast Du augenblicklich gar keinen Englischunterricht. Es ist doch wichtig, dass Du weiter kommst. Kauders sind jetzt wohl auch drüben angekommen, der alte Herr Kugelmann fährt dieser Tage in seine Heimat. Er will auch sehen, ob er etwas über Spiers erfahren kann.

Für heute noch recht guten Schabbos und herzliche Küsse Mama.

Grüße auch Onkel Siegmund und Tante Tina einmal von mir.

(Seite 1 oben umgekehrt geschrieben): Faste gut

Lieber Siegfried לא״ט

Es freut mich, dass Ihr solch einen schönen Ausflug gemacht habt + Euch gut amüsiert habt. Ich wünsche ט״ב, recht gutes Fasten. Innigsten שבת-Gruß von Deinem Papa

(beantw. 26/7. 39)

(Queens Drive 87)

[35] Hamburg d. 25.7.39

Mein geliebter Siegfried

Deinen l. Brief erhielten wir wieder am Schabbos Nachmittag nur einmal, gerade in der Woche als Erna hier war, traf derselbe nicht am Sonntag morgen ein. Ich hoffe, dass Du auch unsere Schabboskarte erhalten hast, und auch die übrige Roswes(?)sendung, die wir losgelassen haben, bei allen prompt eingetroffen ist. Es ist erstaunlich, dass Du alle Neuigkeiten, die ich Dir mitteile schon weißt, ich glaube Hamburg und London sind schon eine Kille geworden. Das Allerneueste weißt Du aber wohl noch nicht, nämlich, dass Frau Oppenheimer am Freitag ihr Permit bekommen hat und uns wohl noch vor Jomtauw verlässt. Sie geht aber nicht nach London, sondern an einen kleinen Platz zu ihrem Neffen Julius Sickel, wie schon gesagt, unser Kreis wird immer kleiner. Hast Du noch gar nichts von der Versicherung gehört, es wäre doch ein Jammer, wenn Du für all die guten Sachen nichts ersetzt bekämst. Wie fandest Du denn die Handschuhe und die Krawatte, die Hans von Erna geschenkt bekam? Hast Du Dir inzwischen schon einmal rote Grütze bestellt, gute Erdbeeren waren übrigens auch hier nicht billig. Tante Else hat mir erzählt, dass Adolf schon zweimal bei einer Familie Bier zum Essen geladen war, ist das die betreffende Familie, Du weißt ja, was ich meine. Wieso kommt es, dass A. dort eingeladen wird. Hast Du nun schon einmal irgend etwas zwecks Arbeitserlaubnis unternommen. Schreibe doch bitte einmal darüber. Die Adresse von Dr. Neufeld ist Tel Aviv Frug Street 8 II., die Barmitzwoh ist schon diesen Schabbos, wir haben gestern einen Luftpostbrief geschrieben. Übrigens geht auch Dr. Wertheimer in allernächster Zeit fort. Können wir wieder einen anderen Arzt nehmen. Die Stoffe für Papa haben wir bei Siem u. Sievers gekauft, nächste Woche hoffe ich, dass Papa erst einmal den Überzieher bekommt. Hoffentlich hast Du beim Erhalt dieses Briefes die Tanis gut überstanden und auch gut *angebissen*. Der Brief muss fort, deshalb für heute tausend Küsse von Deinem Dich liebenden Muttchen.

Heute nur innigsten Gruß, da ich morgens nicht mehr schreibe.

Gruß + Kuss Papa

[36] PK
ב″ה
Hamburg, d. 28.7.39

Lieber Siegfried, לא″ט

Deine l. Karte erhielten wir gestern Donnerstag Nachmittag, besten Dank. Könntest Du nicht schon am Dienstag schreiben, dass wir Mittwoch Nachricht haben, die Woche ist so lang ohne Post von Dir. Ich hoffe, dass es Dir gut geht, ich habe mal wieder Schmerzen im rechten Knie, es hat sich scheinbar ein Nerv entzündet, ich habe schon heiß und kalt darauf versucht, bis jetzt hat noch nichts genützt. Hanna H. hat nun heute doch Vorladung zum 28. August bekommen, es ist ja gut für sie, da sie kaum noch Verdienst hat. Es hat ja kaum noch Zweck, dass ich Dir noch

Neuigkeiten von hier schreibe, da du alles genau so schnell dort erfährst. Heute war Dr. Liepmanson bei mir, er fährt Ende September nach Los Angeles, er wollte die Adresse von Fips (?) wissen zwecks Verkauf einiger Sachen, er lässt Dich grüßen.

Dass Herm. und John nichts von sich hören lassen, finde ich merkwürdig, ich werde Frau O. einmal fragen, was das bedeutet. Papa hat G.s.D. großartig gefastet, auch angebissen, er hat von 1-6 im Bett gelegen, was sehr gut für ihn war. Morgen hoffe ich mal wieder einen recht langen Brief von Dir lesen können.

Für heute gut Schabbos und viele, viele innige Küsse von Deiner Mutter.

Lieber Siegfried, לא״ט

hoffentlich ist auch dir der תענית gut bekommen. Ich wünsche Dir guten שבת

Grüße alle Lieben von mir.

Innigsten Gruß + Kuß.

Papa

Mr.Siegfried Hirsch c/o Stern – London N 4 – Queens Drive 87 - England

[37] ב״ה
Hamburg d. 31. 7. 39

Mein geliebter Siegfried לא״ט

für Deine l. Karte herzlichen Dank, Du hattest schon Recht, dass wir etwas enttäuscht waren, denn der Schabbos fängt erst an, schön für uns zu sein, wenn wir einen recht ausführlichen Brief von Dir haben. Du glaubst gar nicht, wie niedergeschlagen ich gerade an diesem Tage bin, wo ich nicht durch Arbeit von meinen Gedanken abgelenkt bin. Es ist ein Glück, dass Onkel Manfred und Tante Else noch hier sind, wenn die zu uns kommen, werde ich doch immer etwas aufgeheitert. Wir haben schon verabredet, dass wir Rausch-haschonoh s.G.w. zusammen sein wollen, vorausgesetzt, dass sie nicht in Wilhelminenhöhe zum Helfen angefordert werden, für Sukkaus haben wir uns schon draußen angemeldet. Mein Knie ist G.s.D. etwas besser, wenn es mich auch beim längeren Gehen noch schmerzt. Am Schabbos und auch Sonntag war hier eine enorme Hitze, heute ist es G.s.D. kühler. Lotte Solling hat sich wohl sehr gefreut, als sie Dich sprach, hat sie denn für September wieder eine andere Stellung, weil sie dann nach London kommt. Über Spier's Adresse konnte ich noch nichts erfahren, Du kennst ja Frau O. sie erzählt gern, ohne das manchmal etwas dahinter ist, trotzdem tut es mir sehr leid, dass sie nun fortgeht. Toni Singer, Tante Hedwigs Schwester will auch eine Haushaltstelle in England annehmen, der Junge ist ja in Schweden und die Tochter soll hier noch weiter angelernt werden, damit sie dann auch nach dort kann. Wie wir hörten, hat Gottfried Möller Arbeitserlaubnis bekommen, stimmt das? Es kommt also doch wohl einmal vor, hoffentlich wird auch Dir es gelingen, ich bete jeden Abend zum Allmächt'gen darum. Wegen Herm. und John habe ich mit Frau O. gesprochen, sie kann sich ihr Stillschweigen auch nicht erklären. Dr. Wertheimer habe ich heute gesprochen, ich habe ihm Grüße für Dich mitgegeben, er erzählte mir, dass er nicht in London bleibt, sondern an einen kleinen Platz an der See geht, er trennt sich sehr schwer von hier. Heute hat Papa seinen Überzieher anprobiert, hoffentlich wird er gut sitzen, man kann ja bei der ersten Anprobe nicht viel sehen. Eben hat Tante Else angerufen, ihr Abschiedsgespräch, ab morgen haben sie kein Telefon mehr, also auch das nette Klönen muss ich nun entbehren. Sie erzählte mir, dass Adolf geschrieben hätte, es wäre bei David und Else sehr gemütlich gewesen und es hätte auch sehr gut geschmeckt, ebenso dass Ihr Euch einen neuen Wohnpartner suchen müsst, hoffentlich findet Ihr einen netten Menschen.

Nun mein Geliebtes muss ich für heute wieder Schluss machen, wann werden wir wieder einmal ein mündliches Plauderstündchen miteinander haben. Schreib bald, nimm tausend innige Küsse von Deinem Muttchen.

Ein Päckchen geht dieser Tage ab, teile mir mit ob es angekommen ist.

Lieber Siegfried לאי״ט

Herr Boninger, der nach Chile geht, reist heute ab, da er über London kommt, habe ich ihm Deine Adresse aufgegeben und ihn ersucht bei Dir vorzusprechen, und Dir Grüße von uns zu bestellen, hoffentlich tut er es. Hast Du eigentlich viel die Recepte eingereicht, die Du mitgenommen hast, ob vielleicht Aussicht ist daraufhin Arbeitserlaubnis zu erhalten. Ich hätte darüber gern mal etwas gehört. Ich habe heute meine Arba Minim bestellt. Die Gemeinde hat eine Anzahl zur Verfügung. Wie geht es den anderen Familienmitgliedern David, Else, Hans Erna +Kindern. Grüß sie alle von mir und sei Du lieber Siegfried besonders gegrüßt +geküsst von Deinem Vater.

[38] ב״ה

Hamburg d. 4.8.39

Mein gel. Siegfried לאי״ט

Deinen l. Brief erhielten wir gestern, herzlichen Dank. Es geht uns G.s.D. gut, ich hoffe ein Gleiches von Dir. Was Du von der Versicherung schreibst ist sehr bedauerlich, Du hast schon Recht, wenn es ans Bezahlen geht, ist es überall das Gleiche. Hoffentlich erhältst Du doch noch etwas. Das die Heiratssache so ganz aussichtslos scheint, tut mir ja einerseits leid, Du hättest dadurch vielleicht eher festen Fuß fassen können, aber so eine Sache ist von G'tt bestimmt, da können wir Menschen wenig machen. Ein sehr harter Schlag ist es für mich, dass Onkel Manfred und Tante Else nun schon so bald fortgehen. Wie ich Dir schon schrieb, sind sie die einzigen mit denen ich mich noch über alles unterhalten konnte, und die mir Ablenkung brachten. Mit Onkel Elkan kann man nicht vernünftig reden, und Tante Dora ist durch den Verlust ihrer Existenz und ihren dadurch bedingten Aufenthalt im Altenhaus derartig runter, dass eine Unterhaltung mit ihr keinen Trost bringt. Ich freue mich natürlich trotzdem, dass Onkel Manfred und Tante Else nun wieder eine Existenz finden, und vor allen Dingen, dass sie wieder mit ihrem Jungen zusammen kommen; wann werden wir dieses Glück haben? Was nun einen anderen Arzt betrifft, den man zu allem Guten ja doch haben muss, bin ich mir völlig im Unklaren. Dr. W. empfiehlt Dr. Wolffsohn, ich weiß aber nicht, ob wir ihn nehmen, es könnte doch sein, dass wir dann in einiger Zeit wieder wechseln müssten, was meinst Du dazu, wenn wir Dr. Henneberg nehmen würden, schreibe uns einmal darüber. Ich habe mir im Ausverkauf einige Stoffe gekauft, gestern und vorgestern war die Schneiderin hier und hat mir 2 Kleider gemacht, ich habe 3 von meinen Kleidern als Hauskleider degradieren müssen, sie sind jetzt ungefähr 12 Jahre alt und sind mir viel zu eng geworden. Die beiden nun sind sehr hübsch geworden, kosten zusammen RM26. Es würde mich sehr interessieren, mit wem und worüber Du Gespräche und Korrespondenz zwecks Arbeitserlaubnis führst, Du wolltest doch einmal darüber schreiben. Nun wünsche ich Dir noch einen recht guten Schabbos und grüße und küsse Dich innigst Dein Muttchen

Mein lieber Siegfried לאי״ט

Auf die betreffende Sache, von der Du in Deinem l. Briefe schreibst möchte ich nochmals zurückkommen. Vor allem will ich bemerken, dass mir nichts ferner liegt, als Dich in dieser so wichtigen Sache zu beeinflussen.

Ich möchte nur von Dir wissen, ob Dir das Mädchen gefällt, und ob das Geschäft derart ist, dass es eventuell noch eine Familie ernähren kann. Den ersten Punkt kannst Du natürlich nur selbst entscheiden, über den zweiten Punkt müsste man Erkundigungen einziehen. Wenn Du nichts dagegen hast, würde ich Kern mal darüber schreiben. Wie ist es mit der religiösen Seite? Dass der Sohn nicht auf die Sache zurückgekommen ist, ist noch kein Beweis, dass er überhaupt auf die Sache nicht eingehen will. Mit der Sprache ist ja schließlich eine Sache, die sich mit der Zeit bessern wird. Also hoffen wir auf G'tt, wenn dieses nichts ist, dass sich etwas anderes finden wird. Lerne fleißig englisch, dass Du bald die Sprache gut beherrschen wirst. Ich wünsche recht guten שבת und verbleibe mit Gruß + Kuss Dein Papa

Was sagst Du denn zu Onkel Manfred und Tante Else? Ich wollte Dich noch erinnern, dass Montag in 8 Tagen s.G.w. der Geburtstag der lieben Mama ist.

Nochmals Gruß + Kuss Papa

Ich konnte Papa nicht verhindern nochmals über die Sache zu schreiben. Er lässt mir keine Ruhe, Du kennst ja Dein Päppchen, wenn es sich um eine Heirat handelt, lässt er sich nicht überzeugen, dass es nichts ist. Also nochmals innige Grüße Muttchen

[39] Hamburg d. 7.8.39

Mein Geliebtes

Herzlichen Dank für Deinen l. Brief, den wir diesmal wieder erst am Sonntag Morgen bekamen. Es tut mir sehr leid, dass Du über mein Schreiben niedergeschlagen warst, Du kennst mich doch, ich kann häufig nicht gegen meine Stimmung an und mit wem soll ich mich dann aussprechen, wenn nicht mit Dir. Du kannst es mir wohl nachfühlen, dass ich traurig bin, wenn nach Dir nun auch Geschwister und alle guten Freunde (auch Berta Polack hat ihr Permit), fortgehen, man wird so einsam und hat zu viel Zeit zum Nachdenken. Aber ich will mich zusammennehmen und immer daran denken, mich gesund zu erhalten und den Allmächt'gen bitten, dass er uns beisteht, und uns recht bald in Freuden wieder zusammenführt.

Berta Polack sagt mir heute am Telefon, dass Henry kürzlich hier war, er ist jetzt in Schweden, sie weiß nicht, ob er noch einmal nach London kommt, sie kommt am Donnerstag zu mir und will mir dann Näheres erzählen. Hast Du zufällig gehört, wo Bob's Hochzeit stattfindet, wir wollen telegrafieren, schreibe uns dann umgehend die Adresse, vergiss auch Du nicht zu gratulieren. Inzwischen hast Du wohl von Frau Oppenheimer Antwort erhalten, sie hat sich Deine Adresse geben lassen, Herms Junge heißt Lucien, Margot geht es jetzt wieder gut, sie sind augenblicklich in der Sommerfrische. John hat vorläufig Stellung als Schauför, das hast Du wohl schon von Eschwege's gehört. Ich wollte immer schon einmal anfragen, ob Du eigentlich etwas von Tante Lina und den Kindern hörst, teile mir doch gelegentlich darüber mit. Nun möchte ich noch gern Deinen Rat in folgender Sache haben. Unsere Bettumrandung im Schlafzimmer ist bald gänzlich hinüber. Ich bin mir vollständig uneinig, was ich machen soll. Ohne eine solche ist es mir für Papa zu gefährlich und ob es ratsam ist eine neue zu kaufen, der Preis ist wohl mindestens RM 50 weiß ich auch nicht, es ist ja nicht sicher, ob wir später eine solche gebrauchen können. Schreibe Du mir, wie Du darüber denkst. Ebenso weiß ich nicht recht, ob ich einen Koffer kaufen soll, hier haben wir keinen nötig und wenn wir wirklich noch einmal weggehen, müssen wir doch Kisten haben, ich weiß nicht recht, was ich machen soll. Das Wetter war hier in den letzten Tagen auch sehr schlecht, starke Gewitter mit sehr heftigen Regengüssen. Habt Ihr schon einen neuen Zimmergenossen oder bemüht Ihr Euch gar nicht, die Miete stellt sich dann doch gewiss teurer. Hat Hans schon irgendwelche Aussicht oder ist es für ihn ebenso schwer? Nun hast Du wieder einige Fragen zu beantworten, nimm Dir also beim Schreiben diesen Brief vor. Ist übrigens das Päckchen angekommen? Nun mein Geliebtes muss ich für heute wieder Schluss machen. Die beiden Hanna's lassen wieder grüßen. Von mir nimm innige Grüße und Küsse Dein Muttchen.

Mein lieber Siegfried לאי"ט

Es ist wichtig, dass Du einmal mit Gertrud gesprochen hast, wenn sie auch augenblicklich nicht viel dabei machen kann. Ich würde auch einmal eine Annonce wegen Einheirat in Jewish Chronicle machen, vielleicht kommt das Glück auch mal zu Dir. Wenn man hier die Annonce aufgeben kann, ist es vielleicht zu machen. Meinen Überzieher habe ich noch nicht der Schneider wollte heute zur zweiten Anprobe kommen.

Für heute innigsten Gruß + Kuss Papa

Guten שבת

[40] PK
Hamburg, 11.8.39

Lieber Siegfried, לא"ט

Deinen l. Brief erhielten wir erst heute Freitag morgen, besten Dank. Es geht uns G.s.D. gut, auch mein Knie ist G.l. in der Besserung. Ich habe einen Lichtkasten gekauft, was mir sehr gut getan hat. Hoffentlich bleibt es nun besser. Ich habe ziemlich viel Schmerzen ausgehalten. Fr. O. habe ich die ganze Woche nicht gesprochen. Die Dame ist eine angeheiratete Kusine von Herrn Spier. Fr. O. hat ihr nochmals wegen der Adresse geschrieben. Gestern war Berta P. bei uns, Henry war am Sonntag mit seiner jungen Frau hier, sie sind jetzt in Schweden, ob er noch einmal nach London kommt, ist fraglich. auch sie selbst kommt nicht nach dort. Ihr Permit ist noch unterwegs, es wird wohl noch einige Wochen dauern bis sie fährt. Am Sonntag sind Tante Auguste, Martha und Leo bei mir zum Mittagessen, da sie ja am Donnerstag reisen. Wir werden also unser Telegramm auch an Tante Gella's Adresse schicken. Wie mir Tante Dora erzählte, sind Ursel und Sulamith Brautjungfern. Am Freitag(?) ist ja Ernas und Hans Hochzeitstag gratuliere ihnen in unserem Namen, ich danke Erna für ihre Zeilen zu meinem Geburtstag.

Für heute nun noch gut Schabbos und innige Grüße und Küsse

Mama

Mein lieber Siegfried לא"ט

Ich wünsch einen recht guten שבת und verbleibe mit den innigsten Grüßen

Dein Papa

[41] ב"ה
Hamburg d. 15.8.39

Mein geliebtes, gutes Kind לא"ט

Das war gestern Abend die schönste Geburtstagsfreude, Deine l. Stimme wieder einmal zu hören. Innigen Dank auch für Deine lieben Zeilen, und für die schönen Pralinen, es hat mich tief gerührt, dass Du schon vor Deiner Abreise an meinen Geburtstag gedacht hast. Möge der Allmächt'ge geben, dass alles, was Du schreibst in Erfüllung geht, und wir s.G.w. im nächsten Jahr wieder zusammen sein werden.

Es war recht gemütlich gestern Abend, wenn ich selbst auch ziemlich wehmütig gestimmt war, denn die meisten der lieben Gäste sind ja bald nicht mehr hier, aber es ist ja nichts daran zu ändern. Auch am Sonntag Mittag war es recht nett, es hat allen vorzüglich geschmeckt. Wir hatten Spargel und Erbsen mit Kartoffelkroketts, dann russische Eier mit Lachsscheiben und Gewürzgurke garniert und Kartoffel und Mayonaisesauce und Apfelweinpudding mit Himbeersaft, ganz fein nicht wahr? Martha isst nicht gern Fisch und war sie begeistert dass ich auf ihren Geschmack Rücksicht genommen hatte. Das Abschiednehmen nachher war ja auch natürlich nicht leicht, aber was soll man machen. Um noch einmal auf meinen Geburtstag zurückzukommen, so bin ich sehr schön beschenkt worden. Tante Auguste hat mir ein sehr hübsches Taschentuch gearbeitet, von Leo und Tante Dora bekam ich Schokolade, die beiden Hannas gaben mir eine Gummitasche? so eine in blau, wie ich sie in braun eine von Dir bekam, dieselbe ist hinüber, mit einem sehr schönen Gedicht von Hanna Hirsch. Von Onkel Manfred und Tante Else bekam ich ein sehr schönes Tischtuch, von Berta Polack eine Wachstuchtasche mit Reißverschluss sehr geschmackvoll, auch in blau, von Fr. Oppenheimer 4711 Parfum und Seife und von der Parkallee Briefpapier. Zum Abend hatte ich meinen Rosinenkuchen und Blätterteig gebacken und hatte noch einen prachtvollen Kranzkuchen von Hellmann, so nun bist Du ganz im Bilde. Nicht zu vergessen ist, dass ich von allen Post hatte, auch von Siegmund und Josi Tante Henny Landau und von Eli und Goldine Leers aus Rotterdam. Nun auf einige Mitteilungen aus Deinem Brief. Dr. Wertheimer ist noch hier, er kommt am Donnerstag noch einmal zu uns, um sich mein Knie, das G.s.D. und unberufen fast besser ist noch einmal anzusehen, ich werde dann noch einmal wegen seines Nachfolgers mit ihm sprechen. Seine Sache dort ist wirklich fabelhaft, ich wünschte auch, dass es mit uns auch einmal so klappte. Deine Sachen hoffe ich in gewünschter Weise erledigen zu können. Was den Kauf eines Koffers für uns betrifft, so schreibe mir doch bitte noch einmal die Maße unseres alten, ich habe sie vergessen. Sage bitte Erna, dass ich das Gedicht von Blumberg längst Onkel Elkan gegeben habe, ich dachte sie hätte es längst bekommen. Ich wollte schon immer einmal anfragen, ob Nathi und Martha noch in Holland sind, auch ob und wie Du von Addie und Ernst etwas bekommst und in welcher Weise sie dies erledigen, ob sie Dich es in irgend einer Weise fühlen lassen. Schreibe doch bitte, wie es mit Betty St. geworden ist, ob sie schon operiert ist, und wie es ihr geht, ich möchte ihr dann doch einmal schreiben. Aus der Oberaltenallee kann ich trotz vielem telefonieren nichts bekommen. Ich kann da schwer etwas machen. Hast Du nun schon einmal an *Adolf* nach Chikago geschrieben, schiebe es bitte nicht länger auf. Ich will heute abend nach langer Pause wieder einmal ins Kino gehen, es ist bereits 6 ¼ Uhr und muss ich nun Schluss machen. Sei bitte nicht böse, dass heute kein Antwortschein dabei ist, ich konnte den Brief diesmal nicht zur rechten Zeit fertig haben. Also mein Inniggeliebter, nochmals herzlichen Dank und tausend innige Küsse von

Deinem Muttchen.

Mein lieber Siegfried לאי״ט

Ich habe (mich) sehr gefreut, gestern Abend am Telefon Deine Stimme zu hören, ich konnte aber nicht viel antworten, da ich zu aufgeregt war. Die Hauptsache ist, dass ich gehört habe, dass es Dir gottlob gut geht. Hoffentlich kannst Du uns auch bald mitteilen, dass Du Dich geschäftlich betätigen kannst. Diese Woche soll ich auch meinen

Überzieher + Hose bekommen, den Anzug wird Liselote arbeiten. Ich muss jetzt zu מנחה

gehen, füge noch die innigsten Grüße + verbleibe mit Papa

(folgende Zeilen in Adeles Handschrift):

Onkel Emil u. Tante Bella, die wir am Schabbos besuchten lassen herzlich grüßen, ebenso die beiden Hanna's.

[42] PK
Hamburg d. 18.8.39
ב״ה

Mein l. Siegfried לאי״ט

Deine l. Karte vom 16. bestätige ich, Dir herzlich dankend. Ich hoffe dass Du inzwischen unseren Brief, sowie den von Nick erhalten hast. Das war gestern ein schwerer Abschied, Hanna sieht noch heute ganz elend aus, Auch Dr. W. hat sich gestern von uns verabschiedet, er kommt aber nicht über London, hat sich aber doch Deine Adresse geben lassen. Am Dienstag fährt auch Fr. Markus, wenn ich irgend kann, will ich sie morgen noch einmal besuchen. Auch hier ist das Wetter augenblicklich sehr schön, hoffentlich bleibt es noch ein bißchen so. Der Film diese Woche „Frau am Steuer" mit Lilian Harvey und Willi Fritsch war ganz nett, es war nur nicht sehr voll, und das mag ich nicht gern. Die Pralinen sind dieselbe Sorte, sie sind nur jetzt in einer anderen Packung ½ Pfund, ... (gestrichen), also habe ich 2 Kartons, ich denk doch dass sie bis Rauschhaschonoh halten, wenn ich zuviel esse, werde ich zu dick. Tante Henny schrieb mir auch noch, auch Marcus. Sie sind jetzt wohl wieder zu Hause. Für heute sende Dir nun noch innige Grüße und Küsse und wünsche Dir einen recht guten Schabbos.

Mama..

Lieber Siegfried לאי״ט

Die l. Mama lässt mir keinen Stoff über zum Schreiben. Ich muss mich also darauf beschränken Dir die innigsten שבת Grüße zu senden. Mit Gruß + Kuss Papa.

(Queens Drive 87)

(beantw. 21/8. 39)

[43] ב״ה
Hamburg d. 21.8.39

Mein lieber Siegfried לאי״ט

Deine leider nur so kurze Karte erhielten wir diesmal wieder erst am Sonntag. Es geht uns G.s.D. gut, ich hoffe ein Gleiches von Dir. Hanna Hirsch bekam heute einen Brief von Selma aus Holland, dieselbe schrieb, dass es Tante Gella gar nicht gut geht, hast Du auch durch Siegmund etwas darüber gehört? Ich wollte schon immer einmal bei Dir anfragen, ob Du Dir eigentlich schon Deine Papiere vom hiesigen amerikanischen Konsulat noch dort hast schicken lassen, sonst müssen wir es beantragen, schreibe mir unbedingt im nächsten Brief darüber. Vorige Woche war ich bei Elsass, es ist wieder etwas verkauft worden, ist aber immer noch etwas da. Herr Grunert lässt Dich grüßen. Von Leo und Marta kam schon eine Karte vom Schiff, sie schrieben, sie ständen noch unter dem Eindruck des Abschieds, versuchen nun sich etwas einzuleben. Hast Du nun schon nach Chikago geschrieben, sonst tue es bald. Onkel Manfred und Tante Else sind eifrig mit Vorbereitungen beschäftigt, ich glaube auch, dass sie es nicht ganz leicht haben werden, wenn sie erst einmal dort sind, können sich ja immer etwas anderes suchen. Sie nehmen ihren Petroleumofen mit, derselbe ist überholt worden, es ist so einer wie wir hatten, glaubst Du, das Petroleum sich billiger stellt als Gas. Tante Else will mir ihre

Nähmaschine geben, dieselbe ist doch elektrisch und kann ich mir dann mal wieder selbst etwas nähen, ich brauche dann ja nicht zu treten. Heute hat Papa seinen Überzieher und die Hose bekommen, sitzt beides gut, den Anzug will der Meister selbst arbeiten, wir sollen dann aber beinah 20 Mk mehr Arbeitslohn geben, wie bei Sinnreich, das ist uns zu teuer, ich muss erst noch einmal mit ihm reden, und mich noch anderswo erkundigen. Sonst kann ich Dir für heute nichts mehr mitteilen. Ich hoffe, dass wir in den nächsten Tagen von Dir ausführlich hören. Lass es Dir weiter gut gehen, mein Liebstes und nimm innige Grüße und tausend Küsse von Deinem Muttchen.

Die Pralinen schmecken ausgezeichnet. Gruß an Stern, Frau Lanzkron und alle Verwandten.

Mein lieber Siegfried!

Wir mussten uns vorige Woche ja mit einer Karte begnügen + hoffen diese Woche wieder einen ausführlichen Brief zu erhalten. Hast Du Dich mal erkundigt wie es dort mit den Synagogenplätzen יום טוב ist, wirst Du für einen niedrigen Preis einen Platz haben können. Sprich doch mal mit Herrn Stern? darüber.

Ich glaube, ich habe schon einmal angefragt, ob Du mal mit Herrn Minden wegen der Arbeitserlaubnis gesprochen hast, man muss doch sehen, dass man durch Protection irgend etwas erreicht.

Mit innigstem Gruß + Kuss Papa

[44] PK
Hamburg d. 25.8.39
ב״ה

Mein lieber Siegfried לא״יט

Deinen l. Brief erhielten wir, herzlichen Dank, ich hoffe, auch unser Schreiben vom Dienstag in Deinem Besitz. Uns geht es G.s.D. gut, ich freue mich, das gleiche von Dir zu hören. Deine Wünsche werde ich soweit es möglich ist erfüllen. Ich war gerade ein paar Tage vorher bei Henkels, um mir ein Brotmesser zu kaufen. nun gehe ich nächste Woche noch einmal um mich nach dem Stecker zu erkundigen. Mit den Pralinen stimmt es, es sind 1200 gr. in 2 Packungen, ist auch dieselbe Qualität nur die damalige Aufmachung gibt es nicht. ¼ Teil ist bereits erledigt, du weißt ja, ich muss zu oft an dich denken. Herrn Kugelmann geht es einigermaßen, er soll nur im Krankenhaus keinen Besuch haben. Leider ist hier vorgestern ein sehr trauriger Fall passiert. Frau Klier, geb. Schlesinger ist nach kurzer schwerer Krankheit gestorben. Ich habe heute schon eine große Korrespondenz erledigt. Ich habe Siegm. und Josi geschrieben, da letztere gestern Geburtstag hatte, dann Adolf und Liesel nach Rio, Du hast wohl schon gehört, dass letztere auch die Papiere für ihre Eltern abgesandt hat. Nächste Woche s.G.w. schreibe ich mehr, für heute herzliche Schabbosgrüße und innige Küsse.

Mama. Ich hätte gern gewusst, ob der Brief von Nick eingetroffen ist.

Lieber Siegfried!

Gestern hat der רב einen הספד für Benny Meyer ז"ל gehalten. Ich war da und haben wir Elkan + ich nach מעריב קדיש gesagt, da wir heute Jahzeit von Mama ז"ל haben.

Mit herzlichem Schabbos-Gruß + Kuss Papa

Queens Drive 87

[45] ב"ה
Hamburg d. 28.8.39

Mein Geliebtes לא"ט

Deinen l. Brief erhielten wir gestern Sonntag Morgen und danke ich Dir herzlichst auch für das gesandte Photo mit dem ich mich unendlich freute. Wie mir vorkommt, bist Du etwas stärker geworden, oder irre ich mich? Ich schreibe Dir jetzt gleich Montag früh um Dir zu sagen, dass wir G.s.D. gesund sind, ich hoffe, dass dieses auch bei Dir der Fall ist, wenn irgend möglich antworte uns gleich. Heute ist es zum ersten Mal etwas kühler, die Hitze hat mich ziemlich belästigt. Ich werde mich heute wegen der Jod-Stifte erkundigen, wenn ich sie nicht bekomme, frage ich Dr. St. den ich doch wegen meines Zahnes wieder aufsuchen muss, ich gebe Dir dann, wenn möglich, Nachricht. Der Petroleumofen war doch immer vollständig dunstfrei, etwas Arbeit ist doch bei jedem, er muss gefüllt werden und der Docht geputzt werden, ich werde mich jedenfalls erkundigen, ob es noch etwas anderes gibt, ich glaube zwar nicht, da Petroleum ja heute überholt ist. Der Letzte brief neulich war abgeschickt, schade, dass Du ihn nicht bekommen hast. Schneider L. war vorige Woche hier, er lässt Dich vielmals grüßen, er kann den Anzug nicht unter RM 75 machen, ich habe mich noch bei einem anderen Schneider erkundigt, der verlangte sogar RM 85. Was Deine Mitteilung über Minden usw. anbelangt, so hätte ich gern einmal gewusst, ob sich Deine Mitteilung über die Herren auf Deine oder unsere Angelegenheitabout bezieht, ich verstehe es eher auf unsere. Schreibe doch umgehend darüber, Du kannst Dir denken, wie viel mir daran liegt, etwas darüber zu hören. Heute morgen ist Hanna H. zum Konsulat zur Untersuchung, wir warten gespannt auf das Resultat. Die Auktion bei Onkel M. sollte erst am 5 September sein, die beiden sind wie Du Dir denken kannst sehr niedergedrückt. Eppendorfer Baum lässt von sich auch nichts hören, ich muss immer erst telefonieren. Ich will erst abwarten, wie sich alles entwickelt, dann werde ich Oberaltenallee energisch auf den Leib rücken. Nun mein Liebes, Geliebtes will ich Schluss machen, ich möchte, dass der Brief bald fortgeht. Ich bitte ständig zum Allmächt'gen, dass alles gut geht, und wir weiter voneinander hören können. Alles Gute, mein Gold, bleib gesund, auch wir wollen stark bleiben. Tausend innige Grüße und Küsse

Dein Muttchen

Soeben telefoniert Hanna, dass alles in Ordnung ist, sie am 6. Sept. ihr Visum holen kann. Hoffentlich kann sie nun auch fahren.

Dass Betty noch nicht operiert werden braucht, freut mich, grüße sie und ich lasse ihr alles Gute wünschen.

Mein lieber Siegfried לאי״ט

Was Du von Minden schreibst, hat mich sehr überrascht, man sieht hier wieder die Wahrheit des Psalmistenwortes *Al tivtechu bin Divim*

Hoffen wir, dass sich noch alles zum Guten wendet.

Herzlichen Gruß + Kuss Papa

[46] ב״ה
Hamburg d. 29.8.39

Mein Geliebtes לאי״ט

Heute nur kurz ein paar Zeilen, dass es uns G.s.D. gut geht. Ich hoffe, dass Du unseren gestrigen Brief erhalten hast, auch die Musterprobe von Jodo-Muc. Möchte der l. G'tt nur geben, dass alles gut abläuft und wir weiter voneinander hören können, ich mag gar nicht daran denken, wenn es anders sein könnte, mir ist überhaupt alles noch zu lebhaft in

Erinnerung. Marta und Leo haben gestern telegrafiert, dass sie gut bei Adolf angekommen sind, ein großes Glück. Ich musste wieder zu Dr. Streim, vielleicht will er den Zahn ziehen, es ist ja auch besser, wenn er doch immer wieder schmerzt. Dass bei Hanna alles geklappt hat, schrieb ich ja schon, nun kommt es ja darauf an, dass sie fortkann, hoffentlich.

Mein Liebling, sollte G'tt es anders bestimmen, als wir hoffen und wünschen und ich Dir nicht schreiben kann, so sende ich Dir heute schon meine innigsten Wünsche zu Deinem Geburtstag. Mögen alle Deine Wünsche in Erfüllung gehen, dass Du recht, recht, recht bald an das gewünschte Ziel kommst, bleibe gesund und möge der Allmächt'ge uns ein recht baldiges Wiedersehen schenken. Ich hoffe aber immer noch zu G'tt, dass ich Dir doch zu dem Tag noch einmal? schreiben kann.

Für heute leb wohl, mein Liebling, tausend innige Grüße und Küsse

in Liebe Dein Muttchen

Lieber Siegfried לאי״ט

Auch ich will vorsorgen, und ich sende Dir daher schon heute zu Deinen Geburtstage (22. Elul), 6. Sept. die herzlichsten Glückwünsche.

Möge die Zukunft eine recht glückliche für Dich sein und sich auch zum Guten wenden. Gleichzeitig wünsche ich auch ein recht gutes gesundes + glückliches Jahr, falls wir uns vorher nicht mehr schreiben können.

Für heute innigsten Gruß + Kuss Papa

[47] ב״ה
Hamburg d. 31.8.39 Donnerstag

Mein gel. Siegfried לאי״ט

Soeben 6 ½ Uhr erhielten wir Deinen l. Brief, der ja sehr schnell hierher kam, innigen Dank. Hoffentlich hast Du auch inzwischen unseren Dienstags Brief sowie das Jodo-Muc bekommen. Ich schreibe gleich heute Abend wieder, vielleicht erhältst Du dann den Brief noch am Schabbos. Wir sind G.s.D. gesund, nur natürlich sehr unruhig, da man ja immer noch nicht weiß, wie alles verläuft. Möge doch nur der G'tt geben, dass alles noch gut geht, ich bitte stündlich darum. Was Du über unsere Sache schreibst, ist ja sehr, sehr bedauerlich, hältst Du es für richtig, dass Papa, wenn alles ruhig bleibt, einmal selbst an M.W. schreibt. Es kommen ja außer uns nur ganz verschwindend wenig Leute noch in Frage, da die meisten nicht mehr hier sind. Frau Oh.? war gestern hier, sie hat immer noch nicht die Adresse erfahren können. Wenn es möglich ist, will sie nächste Woche zu Herm fahren, dann nach dort, ich habe sie zu Schabbos Mittag noch zum Essen geladen. Onkel Manfred hat heute angerufen, wir wollen s.G.w. Rausch-haschonoh zusammen sein, da sie ja doch nun noch hier sind. Der Schneider war heute zur ersten Anprobe hier, ich war noch nicht mit dem Sitz zufrieden, hoffentlich wird er gut werden. Ist es bei Euch auch noch so warm, ich schwitze ganz kolossal. Vorige Woche hatten wir einen Brief von Herrn und Fr. Dr. Neufeld, sie bedanken sich für unsere Glückwünsche, lassen Dich herzlich grüßen, es geht Ihnen gut, aber sie haben noch wenig Parnohse. Es ist gleich 10 ½ Uhr, ich möchte dass Papa den Brief morgen früh gleich einsteckt. Also mein Geliebtes, alles Gute, hoffentlich hören wir in den nächsten Tagen von Dir. Gut Schabbos tausend innige Küsse von Deinem Dich liebenden Muttchen

Lieber Siegfried לא"ט

Wie steht es nun mit dem Englischen, verstehst Du die Leute schon besser, es wird hoffentlich bald kommen. Ich wünsche guten שבת + verbleibe mit innigstem Gruß + Kuss Papa

[48] Hamburg d. 6.9.39

Mein geliebter Siegfried לא"ט

Herzlichen Dank für Deinen l. Schabbosbrief, ich hoffe auch unsere Karte in Deinem Besitz. Ich bat Dich schon in meinem letzten Brief, doch etwas zeitiger mit dem Schreiben anzufangen, damit Du nun einmal auf all unsere Fragen antworten kannst, und Du auch auf unsere Mitteilungen, die wir Dir über uns schreiben, eingehen kannst. Ich habe so das Gefühl, mein Geliebter, als fehle Dir der Mut zum Schreiben, oder irre ich mich, es wäre natürlich nicht recht von Dir, Du musst den Kopf oben behalten und auf G'tt vertrauen, er wird Dir schon seine Hilfe zu teil werden lassen. Du weißt doch, dass meine Gedanken immer bei Dir sind und wie wir uns freuen, wenn wir an allem, was Dich angeht teilnehmen können, das geht aber nur, wenn du uns immer ausführlich schreibst. Und nun zu Deiner Mitteilung über das Essen. Ich war natürlich über Deinen Bericht auch vor den Kopf gestoßen, besonders über die Redewendung was andere können, musst du auch können, denn eigentlich muss man ja, wenn man etwas übernommen hat, diese Verpflichtung auch erfüllen. Man darf natürlich nicht einseitig urteilen, es ist ja wirklich für B. etwas viel, ständig zwei Gäste am Tisch zu haben, aber das haben sie ja vorher gewusst. Nichtsdestoweniger bist du ihnen ja doch zu Dank verpflichtet, denn ohne sie wärst Du wohl noch hier. Was das Finanzielle betrifft, glaube ich zwar nicht, dass sie alles allein tragen, oder ist es doch an dem. Mir ist natürlich die Hauptsache, dass Du nicht von Kräften kommst, wiege Dich bitte von Zeit zu Zeit, wenn Du abnimmst musst Du unbedingt nachhelfen. Du könntest doch vielleicht an den Tagen wo Adolf nicht in die Kantine geht im Restaurant essen, das würden Sterns dann doch nicht merken, oder bezahlen sie direkt in der Kantine, jedenfalls musst Du Dir das genau überlegen. denn Du darfst sie ja um G'tteswillen nicht vor den Kopf stoßen, schreibe mir jedenfalls noch über die Sache. Gestern war Frau Quandt hier und hat mir den schönen Mantel gemacht, den Stoff hast Du mir doch noch voriges Jahr geschenkt. Er sitzt sehr gut und heute habe ich mir im Ost-Indienhaus ein sehr feines Sommerkleid gekauft, dunkelblau mit kleinen weißen Tupfen, kleiner weißer Weste, hochgeschlossen mit Schoß und dunkelblauem Gürtel – 3/4 langem Ärmel, es steht mir sehr gut. Elsass hat gestern Schrank, Bettstelle, Fahrrad und Leitz-Ordner abholen lassen, ich bin neugierig, was da heraus kommt. Frl. Gerson schrieb uns beifolgenden Karte, wegen der Kapitalangelegenheit haben wir wirklich rechnen(?) müssen, Deine Adresse werde ich ihr mitteilen auch Lotte Solling schrieb mir eine Karte und bat um Deine Adresse, ich sollte ihr auch die ihrige mitteilen (umseitig). Teile mir doch bitte mit, ob Deine Schokolade angekommen ist, auch ob Du Dich mit Bellas Gabe gefreut hast. John wollte Dir vor seiner Abreise nach U S A noch etwas schenken, er wird Dir wohl telefonieren, ob Du nächste Woche hinkommen sollst, teile mir doch bitte mit, was er Dir gegeben hat, es interessiert mich. Die nächste Seite muss wieder für Päppchen bleiben, daher muss ich nun schließen. Ich hoffe, dass Du unsere Bitte um Ausführlichkeit erfüllst, nimm tausend Küsse von Deinen immer den Dich denkenden Muttchen.

Seite 3

Lotte Solling c/o Mrs Parkinmoore

Rosetrees Portinscale Keswick/Cumberland/England (das Wort "England" wurde durchgestrichen)

Sollen wir auch die Briefe vielleicht lieber in Deine Wohnung schicken, schreibe darüber.

Mein lieber Siegfried לא"ט

Auch ich möchte Dich herzlich bitten uns doch auf unsere diversen Anfragen zu antworten. Besonders gern wüsste ich, ob Du zu dem שיעור von Dr. Spitzer gehst. Wann geht man dort morgens in Schul, wenn Du regelmäßig hingehen könntest, würdest Du doch Zeit gewinnen. Ist in Eurer Nähe keine Synagoge? Onkel Elkan wird Schabbos 75 Jahre alt, ich denke, Du wirst ihm doch gratulieren. Wir haben Onkel Elkan und Tante Dora zu Schabbos Abend zum Abendessen eingeladen. Alles sonstige hast Du ja von Mama gehört, daher heute nur herzliche Küsse und Grüße von Deinem Päppchen

The Australia letters

[49] *This draft was made while Siegfried was in the Hay internment Camp in NSW and had to be sent through a censor.*

Siegfried Hirsch, Hut I, No. 7 Camp
Eastern Command, c/o District Censor
45 Reservoir Str., Sydney
6 February 1941

Liebe Musch, Lieber Peter

Ich hoffe, zuversichtlich, dass es Euch bei Empfang dieser Zeilen recht recht gut geht u. dass Ihr bei bester Gesundheit seid. Auch von mir kann ich Euch mitteilen dass ich ganz gesund bin und auch seit meinem letzten Brief an Euch gewesen bin und es mir gut geht. Ich war besorgt das Du lb. Peter vor einiger Zeit nicht ganz wohl warst. Was hast Du gehabt war es eine Erkältung? Jedenfals hoffe ich zuvedrsichtlich dass Du ganz wiederhergestellt bist, und dass ich bald darüber von Euch hören werde. Wenn meine täglichen Gedanken an Euch immer Zeilen von mir wären dann würdet Ihr soviel Briefe von mir erhalten, wie die Woche Tage hat. Es ist die grosse Sehnsucht von der man hier lebt, immer die selben Gedanken und Gebete, dass man seine Lieben bald wieder sieht. Man hat sehr viel Zeit nachzudenken und so bewegen sich auch die Gespräche zwischen Addi und mir immer nur den selben Punkt. Wann werden wir unsere Lieben in USA wieder sehen, wir hoffen zuversichtlich zu G'tt dass dies recht bald sein wird. Ich freue mich schon unendlich auf den Moment von dem an ich wieder beginnen kann zu arbeiten für meine lieben und Euch all das Gute vergelten, dass Ihr für mich getan. Euch all die Liebe wiedergeben kann, die ich durch das augenblickliche Fernsein hindurch von Euch empfinde. Die Hauptsache ist nur dass Ihr Euch auch gesund erhält, wie ich schon schrieb braucht Ihr Euch gar keine Sorgen um mich zu machen u. könnt guten Mutes sein. Mit herzlichen Küssen u. inniger Liebe, Euer

Siegfried

[50] *This is the first of three typewritten extracts of letters received from David Hirsch in New York. The others are dated 6 April 1941 (No. 53) and 8 May 1941 (No. 54). David Hirsch reports the contents of letters he had received from Pincus and Adele, who appear to be aware of details of Siegfried's life though considerably after the events.*

(From) *David Hirsch*, 19/2/41
73.Keap Street, Brooklyn.

I have two letters from your parents of 21/1.and 30/1. They would be glad if you could join us soon to have one care less. They got information that your papers have been transferred to the Consulat in London since July of last year. They want, to know if your address is the same as that of Addy because your uncle Max of Rio wanted to-write you. I asked why your father did not write so much. It is because he cannot work on the thin air mail-paper. Always his pen hooks on it. Now he has written with inkpencil. He is well th.Gd. He does not walk so much because it is very cold and snowy. But regularly he attends the services in the morning end in the evening.Your mother comes daily to my parents to bring them the newspaper.

[51] *The letters from Hamburg that Siegfried is acknowledging here will have come to him in Australia via the USA.*

28 Februar 1941
Liebe Musch, lieber Peter

Mit dem Inhalt Eurer Briefen vom 10 Dezember 40, den ich am 7/2 erhielt, habe ich mich unendlich gefreut u. hoffe ich, dass auch meine Zeilen vom 6 Februar inzwischen angekommen sind. {……} Ich nehme täglich drei mal am öffentlichen G'ttesdienst teil, zu dem sich stets eine grössere Anzahl von Personen anfinden. Heufiger bete ich auch vor und am vorletzten Sabbath wurde ich zur Thoravorlesung aufgerufen u. trug danach den Wochenabschnitt aus den Profeten vor. {......}Es freut mich auch dass Onkel Manfred u. Tante Else Euch jetzt wieder heufiger besuchen können, grüsst sie bitte herzlich von mir auch Tante Harriet und Hanna.

Ich wünsche Euch heute schon herzlich angenehme Osterferientage und bin mit herzlichsten Küsse in inniger liebe

Euer Siegfr.

[52] *This letter appears to have been sent to Martha Wittmund in Chicago for onward transmission to Hamburg.*
21 März 1941
Mrs M Wittmund
Chicago

Liebe Musch, lieber Peter

Ich hoffe dass Ihr inzwischen meine Februar schreiben Erhalten habt und dass Ihr besten Gesundheit seid. {........} Wie geht es übrigens Tante Henny u. Tante Aly, ich hoffe dass auch sie gut durch den Winter gekommen sind. Wohnen sie noch in der selben Pension? Grüsst sie bitte herzlich von mir.

{.............}

Auch ich bin mit Studien beschäftigt Sprechen, Stenographie mit Büroarbeit u. manchmal mit Zahnärzslichen Assistenz. Ich sorge also dafür dass ich immer etwas zu tun habe, damit der Tag ausgefüllt ist. Auch im Reinmachen u. Wäschewaschen habe ich Uebung bekommen.

{............}

{............} mit herzlichen Küssen u. inniger Liebe Euer S.

[53] *See headnote to No. 50. Siegfried's letters seem not to have reached Pincus and Adele but they were receiving his news through David Hirsch. This letter gives a small insight into conditions in Hamburg.*

From David Hirsch
6/4/41

I have got 2 letters from your parents of February 26th.and March 11th.

They are glad to have heard about you and that you are allright. They hope you will go on this way. They regret that your things have gone lost, but you should not be discouraged because it is the fate of many of us. Please Gd. better times will come for you too. They always thought how you will care that they have not heard from you. Now it is good that you are quiet. The news that your coming to the States may be delayed has them rather dejected. They think that would delay at the same time to meet you one day but they hope that the Almighty may improve conditions that life may be worthwhile bearing. They are glad that Adolph and the other ones take care of you and thank them. It may be better perhaps if your coming will be delayed for some time, They think we are in a better position to judge the matter. They are th.Gd. in the best of health, although other sorrows are plenty. Your mother comes every day to see my father, she wished she could give more help. Also your mother is convinced that Elkeles has too much cares of his own, otherwise he would help more as he did in former times. She advises me to communicate with Ernst, though he also did not show much interest when your mother saw him the last time. Your mother's siblings (Geschwister) hope to come over here still this year so that they will have the pleasure to see again their Addi. They do not know if they can live during the holidays according the dietary laws. They send their most cordial regards for you and hope to hear about you very soon again. Your father adds some lines telling that he feels happy to read about your wellbeing. He is okay and hopes same from you. He wishes you all the best especially that you may meet us soon.-In the other letter they regret that the informations are lying so far behind. Some weeks ago your mother went with your father to his former business. It was affecting to see the joy all former colleagues displayed when they met and shook hands with your father.

[54] *See headnote to No. 50. The first two sentences are addressed by David Hirsch to Siegfried. The remainder of the letter was transcribed by David Hirsch from a letter dated 16 April 1941 mainly by Adele and responding to a letter from David Hirsch.*

From David Hirsch
75 Fort Washington Ave., Apt. 42., New York City. 8/5/41.
(16/4/41.)

Many thanks for your letters of 26.2.and 3. I wanted to answer them before the holidays but I was too tired and exhausted by the work that fatigued in this year more than ever because I did not have the real help.

I was pleased to hear again from you and your dear ones, hope they will be allright. As to your report of Siegfried's passage it is regrettable in every respect if it has to be delayed, but it is up to you of course as you are in a better position to judge what will be good. As you write it is hard for both sides to put up with it but we almost do not mind for more or less hardship. I am confident that you all will hasten whatever and whenever something can be done. I hope, Siegfried will understand it, even if it is special bad for him to have setbacks again and again. Hope he will follow your advice to write more personally and that he is okay. So far we have spent the holidays well. The first nightsi we were alone, we could not have visitors. We thought back with woefulness of the fine nights in your house. The first day at lunch Gustav Heineman was with us, Berta is in the Hospital for some weeks to be observed. Yesterday Loebels have left for there, next week Zinners will leave. I hear that also your mother-in-law may leave soon, so it gets more and more lonesome round us. The dear Papa is somewhat better during the last days. Hope it will last this time a little longer. Now, dear D. hope to hear from you soon again. Love for all your dear ones and for Siegfried as well.

Your auntie Adele.

The most cordial regards for you and Siegfried, yours uncle Pincus.

[55] *This letter appears have come to Siegfied in Australia directly from Hamburg, probably by prisoner mail.*

Hamburg 27. 4. 41

Mein geliebter Siegfried

Durch Sally Cohn, der auch dort ist und der seinem Vater schrieb, erfuhren wir Deine Addresse und beeilen wir uns Dir mitzuteilen, dass wir G.s.D. gesund sind. Wir dachten auch einmal von Dir zu hören, Du kannst Dir wohl denken in welcher Sorge wir um Dein Ergehen sind, hoffentlich bist Du wohlauf. Es hat uns sehr interressiert aus den Brief an Herrn Cohn etwas über Euer dortiges Leben zu erfahren. Wir haben die Osterfeiertage gut verlebt, in (*sic*) nehme an und hoffe, dass auch Ihr alles in gewohnter Weise hallten konntet. Der l. Vater geht nach wie vor Morgens und Nachmittags seinen gewohnten Weg in die Nachbarschaft und auch mehrere Male in der Woche zu sdeinen Schwestern, und auch ich mache täglich wie Du weisst auf Wunsch meiner Ärzten meinen täglichen Spaziergang.

Ich hoffe nun mein liebes Kind, dass Du uns gleich nach erhalt dieser Zeilen antwortest, es wird ja ohnehin lange Zeit vergehen, bis wir Deine Antwort erhalten. Leb wohl für heute und nimm innige Grüsse und Küsse

Von Deiner

Mutter

Mein lieber Siegfried

Auch ich würde mich unendlich mit einem Lebenzeichen von Dir freuen. Ich bin G.s.D. gesund und hoffe ich ein Gleiches von Dir. Schreib bitte gleich nach erhalt dieser Zeilen.

Für heute die herzlichsten Grüsse und Küsse von

Deinem Dich liebender Vater

[56] *The significance of the two dates at the beginning of this draft is not clear. 'Osterfeiertage' is a reference to Passover. Addi is Adolf Nussbaum, Siegfried's cousin, who had also been on the Dunera and was also an internee in Australia. Onkel Elkan is Pincus's brother, who was suffering from cancer of the bladder. Else and Manfred are Addi's parents.*

2/5.41 30.04.41

Meine liebe Musch, mein lieber Peter

Unendlich habe ich mich wieder gefreut mit dem Inhalt Euerer Zeilen von Ende Januar den ich Ende März erhielt. {……} Ich hoffe dass Ihr die Osteferientage gut verbracht habt. Auch bei mir war dass der Fall, soweit dass in diesem Jahre möglich war, jedenfalls war allen religiösen Belangen Rechnung getragen. - Wie ich frührer schon erwähnte bin ich immer mit Addi zusammen u. wohnen wir auch wieder unter dem selben Dach allerdings mit noch anderen zusammen. Ich war sehr bestürzt von David zu hören dass Onkel Elkan's Krankheit garnicht so leicht ist. Im letzten Brief schrieb er dass es ihm etwas besser geht. {……….}

{………..} Dass Du trotz der nun beendigten Kalten (unleserlich) wie gewohnt regelmässig den Morgen und Abendg'ttesdienst besucht hast freute mich zu hören lb. Peter auch dass Du lb. Musch täglich die Geschwister besuchst [?--? Auch Else + Manfred ?--?lich]. {…….} In der

Hoffnung von Euch in Kürze zu hören bin ich mit herzlichsten Küssen in Liebe Euer Siegfried

{.........}

[57] *'Pfingstfeiertage' is a reference to Shavuot (Pentecost). The new address refers to Siegfried's move from Hay to Tatura. The documents Siegfried needed, presumably for his immigration to the USA, is not clear.*

5/6.41

Meine liebe Musch, lieber Peter

Ich hoffe zuversichtlich dass Ihr beide vollkomender Gesundheit seid. {..........} Wie Ihr aus der adresse ersieht bin ich jetzt an einem anderen Platz. Ich lebe hier ähnlich wie vorher, nur ist das Klima ein besseres. {..........} Ich brauche von Onkel Adolf Salomon dringend neue Unterlagen da die alten wertlos sind. Bisher bin ich nicht in dem Besitz der selben gelangt trotzdem ich ungeduldig darauf warte. Ohne dieselben werde ich meine Reise nicht antreten können. {.........}

Lasst umgehend per Luftpost von Euch hören u. seid in inniger Liebe herzlich geküsst von Eurem Siegfried

[58] *This draft letter dated 11 June 1941 has been omitted as they are almost identical to other letters.*

[59]
Siegfried Hirsch
Camp No.3, Sector B
Tatura, Victoria, Australia
17 June 1941

Meine sehr Lieben, Ich warte immer noch darauf von Euch zu hören und schreibe Euch daher heute per Clipper-Post.

Ich bin sehr unruhig das der Consul noch nicht den Eingang des neuen Affidavits von Chicago bestätigt hat. Ich hoffe das es endlich dahin kommt, dass die Angelegenheit beschleunigt wird. Ich denke dass meine Zeilen von 21/3 und 30/4 inzwischen eingetroffen sind dass ich in Kürze auf meine Briefe Antwort erhalten werde.

{.........}

Diese Woche hatte ich endlich den ersten Brief von Elkeles und eine Antwort wegen der Einwanderung nach USA. Er bestätigt meine ersten zwei Briefe.

{................} Seid heute innigst gegrüsst und geküsst von

Eurem Euch l. Siegfried

[60] *Undated letter to David Hirsch in New York, probably October 1941. The "Ehrenämtern dieses Tages" refers to the chatan Torah and the chatan Bereshit of Simchat Torah (For an explanation see Appendix 3).*

Lieber David

Herzlichen Dank für Deine l. Zeilen und Eure guten Wünsche wir waren glücklich nach längerer Pause wieder von Dir zu hören Wie Du Deiner Mutter schreibst hast Du viel Arbeit, ich meine die Arbeit ist heute ein Segen, kommt man doch nicht soviel zum Nachdenken über alles Schwere. Die Feiertage haben wir gut verbracht, ich bin froh,dass ich nun auch wieder mehr zu tun habe, aus den schon vorher erwähnten Gründen. Wir sind G.s.D. gesund, ich hoffe, dass dies auch bei Euch der Fall ist, man muss schon hierfür dem Allmächtigen danken. Onkel Pincus war am letzten Freitag zusammen mit seinen früheren Geschäftskollegen Aron zu den beiden Ehrenämtern dieses Tages ernannt. Am Nachmittag waren alle mit diesen Ämtern betrauten Herrn zusammen und wurden nette Ansprachen umrahmt von Chorgesang gehalten. Dass aus dem Besuch Deines Vetters nun vorläufig wieder nichts wird, ist sehr zu bedauern, nun heist es, sich auch damit wider abzufinden. Dass mein Bru. Max Dir mit Einlage geschrieben hat, wussten wir schon, wir hatten letztens Post von ihm.

Nun lieber David sende ich Euch beiden ebenso al deinen lieben, auch Hans und Erna die allerherzlichsten Grüsse, wir hoffen bald wieder etwas zu hören.

Lebt wohl für heute alles Gute

Deine Tante Adele

=====

Lieber David

Auch ich danke Dir herzlichst für Deine lieben Zeilen, habe mich mit demselben sehr gefreut, und sende Euch beiden die allerherzlichsten Grüsse.

Dein Onkel Pincus

[61] *Original draft of this letter was written in English – marked at the top "letter David"*

27/10/41

My dear Peter and Musch, I confidently hope that you are quite healthy, thank G'd I can tell you the same about me. I have not heard about you since the middle of August and I trust to get your news very soon again. With David's last letter I got the grievous notice that uncle Elkan passed away, redeeming him from great suffering. I am very upset by this report. I still hoped all the time it will be possible to cure his illness. It may be comforting tom you all that he didn't know he was seriously ill. I learn that he has been buried at the side of his Selma, that many friends attended the funeral and that our Rabbi, who was a sincere and ardent friend, delivered the speech. Dear Peter please tell also dear aunt Dora, Siegmund and the aunties that I am very sad with you over the bereavement which all of you have sustained. I heard that you, dear Musch, were present almost every day during uncle Elkan's sickness and I am sure you will further on assist auntie Dora and be at her side as she is so alone now.

I hope you spent the autumn holidays as well as possible and that both of you got well over the Fast. On those days I had only one prayer to the Almighty that he may give you a constant health and that we can join again before long. I also trust that my hearty wishes for your this year's birthday, dear Peter, arrived in time and I am waiting to hear whether this was the case. Have you been once again with your doctor and was she satisfied with you, dear Musch? How are auntie Else and uncle Manfred and the other aunties? (The following is deleted in the draft: As for me I wrote already earlier that my present life runs very monotonous and the days are exactly alike. For the last half-year I have only been engaged with office work and I am doing a lot of daily typewriting. Except that I have to do my own washing and mending. As I have had very little physical exercise during the year past I have grown bigger and when my weight was taken some time ago it showed an increase of about 20 pounds.) Some friends of mine and a number of other people are now holding their own daily divine services where the prayers are recited according to our customs and I have been entrusted with the same office during prayers as you were, dear Peter. I am also sometimes conducting the prayers.

The following was written between large crosses as shown below and was probably omitted from the letter that was ultimately sent.

X I passed the holidays as it was possible under prevailing circumstances. On the High Festivals we had good readers in our service and I got well over the Fast. We had also a big Tabernacle and the weather was fine all the days. X

Now my dear ones keep well, hoping to hear about you shortly. I am for to-day, with hearty kisses and much love

Yours Siegfried

[62] *See headnote to No. 55. This letter may have come by the same route.*

Hamburg 10.11.41

Mein gel. Siegfried

Durch einen Brief des Herrn Sally Cohn an seinen Vater erfuhren wir, dass du unseren Brief von 27.4 erhalten hast, und bedauern wir unendlich, bis heute noch keine Antwort von Dir erhalten zu haben. Du kannst Dir doch wohl denken, mit welcher Sehnsucht wir auf ein Lebenszeichen von Dir warten. Wir hoffen dass Du gesund bist auch wir befinden uns G.s.D. wohl, und dafür müssen wir schon dem l.G'tt danken. Leid und Freude haben wir inzwischen gehabt. Leid durch den Tod des l. Onkel Elkan, den Du wohl schon durch seine Kinder erfahren hast. Er fehlt uns allen sehr, aber ihn ist wohl, denn er hat zuletzt sehr viel schmerzen aushalten müssen. Freude durch den 80 jährigen Gebutstag des l. Papa's. Die Freude an diesem sonst so schönen Tag war natürlich sehr gestört, erstens durch das eben erwänte traurige Ereignis, hauptsächlich aber da durch dass Du geliebtes Kind nicht bei uns sein konntest möge doch der Almächt'ge geben, dass wir uns noch einmal wider sehen, unsere Sehnsucht ist gross. Wir beten täglich für dich, aber tu Du es auch für uns.

Nun wünsche ich Dir für heute noch alles alles Gute, bleib recht gesund und schreib uns gleich wieder. Nimm tausend innige Grüsse und Küsse von Deiner Dich innig liebender

Mutter

Mein lieber Siegfried!

Nachdem wir gehört haben dass Du Dich mit unserem Brief sehr gefreut hast, möchte ich Dich herzlich bitten auch uns mit einem Brief zu erfreuen. Wie die liebe Mutter schon schrieb, sind wir G.s.D. gesund, nur die Sehnsucht nach Dir is gross. Hoffentlich geht es auch Dir gut. Für heute noch innige Grüsse und Küsse

Dein Dich liebender

Papa

[63] `This is the first of a number of very short messages that may have been sent via the International Red Cross Prisoner of War Mail.*

5 Januar 1942
Pincus & Adele Hirsch
Hamburg 13
Kielortallee 16
Germany

Siegfried Hirsch
Internment Camp No. 4, Section C
Tatura, Victoria, Australia

Meine Geliebten

Lange nicht von Euch gehört hoffe Ihr seid gesund. Nur Brief April erhalten schreibt häufiger. Innige Küsse

Euer Siegfried

[64] *It seems that the paragraphs marked X – X in the draft were omitted from the final letter.*

4/2/42

Meine lieben Eltern

Ich habe leider lange nichts von Euch gehört und ich warte von Post zu Post einmal wieder einen Brief von Euch zu erhalten. Viele Leute hier bekommen regelmässig Post von ihren Eltern. ?---? hingegen ist niemals ein Brief für mich dabei. Euren lieben Brief den ich Ende Juli bekommen habe ist Euch bestätigt und gebeten häufiger zur (*sic*) schreiben, eventuell per Luftpost da dies manchmal schneller geht. Der Sohn von meinem früheren Collegen Aron, lieber Papa, hat in letzter Zeit Karten u. auch Briefe von seinen Eltern bekommen. Vor allem hoffe ich zuversichtlich, dass Ihr Beide ganz gesund seid. Von mir kann ich ich Euch GsD. das Gleiche berichten.

X Mein augenblickliches Leben ist sehr eintonig, wie Ihr Euch denken könnt, und ein Tag ist gleich dem anderen. Ausser den Arbeiten die ich im Lager für die Gemeinschaft mache habe ich für meine eigenen Sachen wie Wäsche washen, nähen u. stopfen, zu sorgen. Ausserdem ist gelegenheit zum lesen und lernen und täglich ?-? in der ?---?schule Unterricht zu nehmen. Das Essen das aus drei Mahlzeiten pro Tag besteht und von unserem Leuten gekocht wird ist gut und reichlich.

Augenblicklich ist, wie Ihr woll wisst, hier Sommer der in diesem Erdteil viel heisser ist wie in Europa. Hingegen kühl (ist) es abends (häufig) und sehr (--) und manchmal sind die Nächte richtig kalt. Man gewöhnt sich jedoch an die Tempwraturunterschiede wenn man längere Zeit in dem Klima lebt. Natürlich muss ich dann abends warmes anziehen besonders wenn man am Tage infolge der Hitze nur Hemd & kürze Hose getragen hat manchmal sind allerdings auch die Nächte sehr warm, und dann lässt man alles offen was an Fenstern und Türen verhanden ist. X

Ich war sehr betrübt über Davids bericht von sel. Onkel Elkans ableben. Ich hoff(t??)e die ganze Zeit, in der ich über seine Krankheit hörte dass es möglich sein wird dieselbe zu heilen. Es ist gut dass er selbst nicht wusste, dass er so ernslich krank ist. Wie ich hörte ist er an Selmasi Seite bestattet worden, und hielt Dr Carlebach, der einen aufrechtigen u. wiklichen Freund verloren hat, ihm den Nachruf. Der lb. Tante Dora und Euch allen möchte ich mein herzliches Mitgefühl sagen. Ich hoffe dass es den Tanten sowie auch Onkel Manfred u. Tante Else gesundheitlich gut geht. Das weiteren hoffe ich dass die wünsche zu Deinem Geburtstage lb. Papa Dich seinerzeit rechtzeitig erreicht haben. Ueber den Tag habe ich vor einiger Zeit einmal von Leo gehört. Bist Du in letzter Zeit einmal wieder bei Deinem Artzt gewesen u. war er zufrieden mit dir lb. Mutter? Ich hoffe über alles recht bald von Euch zu hören. Auch ich werde Euch in Kürze wieder schreiben, indessen erwarte ich bestimmt dass Post von Euch an mich unterwegs ist und ich in Kürze einen Brief erhalte denn bis zur Antwort auf diese Zeilen wird ja längere Zeit vergehen. Für heute bin ich mit herzlichsten Küssen und in inniger Liebe, Euer, Siegfried

[65] *This letter is probably acknowledgement of Adele and Pincus's letter of 10 November 1941 (No. 62).*

12/2/42

Meine geliebten Eltern

Ihr könnt Euch vielleicht vorstellen wie unbeschreiblich meine Freude war als vor zwei Tagen bei der Post einen Brief von Euch ---- nachdem ich unendlich lange auf einen solchen gewartet habe. Ich beeile mich daher Euch Eure lieben Luftpostzeilen vom 10/11 sofort zu bestätigen und hoffe dass es nicht so sehr lange Zeit dauern wird bis Euch dieser Briefv erreicht. Gerade vorige Woche habe ich Euch geschrieben wie sehr ich auf Zeilen von Euch warte und ich hoffe dass Ihr auch diese Zeilen von 4 ds. recht bald bekommt. Ich ?--? Euch auch dass ich Euren seiner Zeitigen Brief vom 27/4 den ich ende Juli erhielt sofort bestätigt u. gebeten habe dass Ihr häufiger schreibt Ich hoffe dann auch, dass Ihr auch(?nicht) erst auf eintreffen meiner jetztigen Zeilen (?warte) bis Ihr antwort, sondern auch inzwischen schon schreibt sodass ich recht bald wieder einen Brief von Euch erhalte. Vor allen (?---?) war ich sehr dankbar aus Euren Zeilen zu ersehen dass Ihr G.s.D. gesund seid und hoffe ich zuversichtlich dass dies auch jetzt und wenn dieser Brief eintrifft der Fall ist. Von mir kann ich auch G.s.D. dass selbe mitteilen, nur ist auch bei mir die Sehnsucht nach Euch so sehr gross. Ich bitte Euch nur eines, tut alles um Euch gesund zu erhalten, damit wir uns gesund wieder sehen können. Ich bete jeden Tag (?----?) für Euch, wie ich auch wuste dass Ihr für mich täglich betet u. es besteht keine minute in der ich nicht an Euch denke. Wie ich am Tage Deinen 80 jährigen Gerbutstages, geliebter Papa, mit meinen Gedanken bei Euch war könnt Ihr Euch wohl vostellen und wie mir ums Herz war dass ich nicht mit Euch ----- verleben konnte. Mein gebet zum Allmächtigen war dass er Dich diesen Tag noch recht recht lange erleben lassen möge. Füt heute wünsche ich Euch noch alles Gute. Nehmt tausend innige Grüsse u. Küsse von Eurem Euch innig liebender

Siegfried

[66] *This short message of 25 February 1942 has been omitted. See headnote to No. 63.*

[67] *The airmail letter of 10 November referred to is No. 62.*

11/3/42

Meine geliebten Eltern

Hoffentlich habt Ihr zwischenzeitlich meine beiden Briefe von 4 u. 12 Februar erhalten. Euren lieben Luftpostbrief vom 10/11 den ich mit so grosser Freude erhalten habe, habe ich Euch bereits bestätigt. Hoffentlich seid Ihr auch jetzt gesund und warte ich ungeduldig darauf einen weiteren Brief von Euch zu erhalten – Auch mir geht es gesundheitlich gut nur ist meine Sehnsucht nach Euch gross, und denke ich dauernd an Euch ganz einerlei womit ich mich gerade beschäftigt bin wie Ihr Euch bedenken könnt ist mein augenblickliches Leben sehr einförmig und ein Tag ist gleich dem anderen. Ausser den Arbeiten die man im Lager für die Gemeinschaft macht, hat man für seine eigenen Sachen wie Wäsche washen, nähen u stopfen zu sorgen. Ausserdem ist gelegenheit zum lesen u. lernen u. möglichkeit in der Lagerschule unterricht zu nehmen. Das Essen das aus drei Mahlzeiten besteht ist gut u. wird von unseren eigenen Leuten gekocht. Augenblicklich ist wie Ihr wohl wisst hier Sommer der allerdings dem Ende entgegengeht. Der selbe ist in diesem Erdteil viel heisser als in Europa. Allerdings kühlt es Abends häufig sehr ab und manchmal sind die Nächte richtig kalt. Anfangs sind diese ungewöhnlichen Temperature unterschiede sehr unangenehm es gibt sich aber wenn man längere Zeit in dem Klima lebt. Man muss sich dann abends wärmer anziehen besonders wenn man am Tage infolge der Hitze nur Hemd und kurze Hose getragen hat. Manchmal sind allerdings auch die Nächte sehr warm und dann lässt man alles offen was an Fenstern und Türen vorhanden ist.

Hoffentlich höre ich nun in Kürze auch wieder von Euch. Für heute wünsche ich Euch noch alles von Herzen gute. Mit tausend innigen Küssen bin ich Euer Euch innig liebender Siegfried

[68] *This short message of 25 March 1942 has been omitted. See headnote to No. 63.*

[69]

5/4.42

Meine geliebten Eltern

Nachdem fast zwei Monate wieder vergangen sind seit dem ich Euren lieben Brief von November erhalten und Euch gleich beantwortet habe, hoffe ich nunmehr in kürze wieder Zeilen von Euch zu erhalten. Hoffentlich wartet Ihr nicht mit Eurem nächsten Brief bis meine Zeilen eingetroffen sind, da es in diesem Falle so lange dauern würde bis ich wieder von Euch höre. Ich hoffe indessen zuversichtlich, dass meine beiden Briefe von Februar u. meine Zeilen von März Euch zwischenzeitlich erreichen und dass Ihr Beide gesund seid. Auch mir geht es GsD. gesundheitlich gut. Allerdings sind Sehnsucht u.

Gedanken mir lieben Dinge die standige Begleiter sind. Bei schreiben dieser Zeilen ist gerade Osterwoche u. ich brauche Euch nicht zu sagen wo mein Denken an den beiden Oster-Abenden war, wenn wir zusammen sassen die üblichen Feiertags Gebete zu verrichten. Im übrigen haben wir die bezüglichkeit der Feiertage wie üblich zu verbringen und ?--? wie im vorigen Jahre allen Erfordernissen Rechnung getragen.

Bis ich Eure Oster-Zeilen erhalte wird ja leider auch noch eine ganze Zeit vergehen.

Der Sommer ist hier nun zu ende gegangen und sind die Tage jetzt wesentlich kühler, indessen behält die Sonne hier doch soviel Kraft dass sie an klaren Tagen in den Mittags stunden eine angenehme wärme ausstrahlt. Überhaupt sind die Tage mit klarem blauen Himmel auch im Winter in diesem Erdteil viel zahlreicher als in Europa.

Wie geht es Tante Dora, ist sie schon etwas ruhiger über den verlust den sie durch das ?--? des lieben Onkels erlitten hat: und wie geht es den anderen Tanten?

Warst Du in letzter Zeit einmal wieder beim Artzt, liebe Mutter, und was hat er zu Dir gesagt, hast Du noch eine ständige Behandlung? Und wie ist es mit Deinem Geh-Beschwerden, lieber Papa.

Für heute nehmt tausend Grüsse u. Küsse in inniger liebe von Eurem

Siegfried

Viele Grüsse für Hanna,

Wie geht es ihr

[70] *This short message of 24 April 1942 has been omitted. See headnote to No. 63.*

[71]
28 April 1942

Geliebte Eltern

Ich hoffe zuversichtlich, dass meine vormonatlichen Zeilen in Eurem Besitz gelangt sind u. Euch auch mein letzter Brief vom 5 April bald erreicht. Ich selbst warte noch immer auf den nächsten Brief von Euch und erwarte nunmehr ungeduldig dass der selbe in aller Kürze eintrifft. Ich will hoffen dass Ihr beide gesund seid was ich Euch GsD. auch von mir berichten kann. Hoffentlich habt Ihr mir zwischenzeitlich etwas heufiger und in kürzeren Abständen geschrieben damit ich nicht so sehr lange warten muss bis ich wieder von Euch höre, da die Post naturgemäss unregelmässig eintrifft manchmal mit kürzerer laufzeit denn wieder ----- viel längerer.

Im letzten Brief habe ich Euch über die Osterwoche geschrieben. Wir konnten Ostern gleich dem vorigen Jahre wie gewöhnlich verbringen. An den beiden Abenden sasen wir zu den üblichen Feiertagsgebeten zusammen, aber ich war die ganze Zeit mit meinen Gedanken nur bei Euch.

In meinen letzten Zeilen habe ich Euch angefragt ob Ihr in letzter Zeit einmal wieder bei Eurem Artzt gewesen seid und was er zu Euch gesagt hat. Hast Du noch Deine ständige Behandlung liebes Mutterchen, und wie ist es mit Deinen Geh-Beschwerden lieber Papa? Wie geht es Tante Dora und den anderen Tanten? Vor einiger Zeit hatte ich einen Brief von Onkel Max und Tante Hedwig. Sie schreiben recht zufrieden und haben wie Ihr wisst gutes Ankommen. Habt Ihr in letzter Zeit von ihnen gehört?

Augenblicklich ist es hier wieder viel wärmer, die Herbsttage sind hier manchmal so warm wie in Europa die Sommer Nächte.

Meine Tage sind nach wie vor mit den gleichen Arbeiten ausgefüllt, Reinmachen, ?--? Nähen sowie lesen, lernen, schreiben. Für heute schliesse ich Euch alles gute Wünschend, mit tausend innigen Küssen in Liebe

Euer Siegfried

[72] *This is the draft of No. 73. Words and text in brackets were omitted from the letter that was finally sent.*

24 Mai 1942

Meine lieben geliebten Eltern

Ich nehme bestimmt an, dass meine früheren Briefe inzwischen in Euren Besitz gelangt sind und hoffe, dass auch meine Zeilen vom 5 und 29 April Euch bald erreichen. Leider habe ich auch in den letzten Wochen noch keinen weiteren Brief von Euch erhalten und warte ich mit jeder Post darauf von Euch zu hören nachdem dies nun schon so lange (Zeit) wieder her ist. Vor allen Dingen hoffe ich zuversichtlich dass Ihr beide gesund seid. Auch mir geht es GsD gesundheitlich gut und habe ich von der Vorstellung wie es sein wird wenn ich wieder mit meinem Lieben zusammen sein werde. Inzwischen sind auch die Pfingsttage vorüber, so vergeht ein Monat nach dem anderen. Am ersten Abend sassen wir mit einer Anzahl Freunden zusammen und lernten in gewohnter Weise. Unserer Abend u. Morgen Gottesdienst schmückten wir mit grünen Zweigen aus. Es ist natürlich hier ganz anders grün wie in Europa und zwar hauptsächlich von Gummi und Eucalyptus Bäumen die hier überall wachsen. In den letzten vierzehn Tagen regnet es ziemlich viel im Gegensatz zu dem vorausgegangenen Sommerhalbjahr ein Zeichen der begonnenen Wintermonate. Der Himmel ist bedeckt und die Sonne kommt selten durch die Wolken, während die Temperatur auch jetzt häufig wechselt von kalt auf wärmer. Die Temperaturunterschiede bleiben auch in dieser Jahreszeit hier stark.

(Während es gestern und die Tage vorher noch sehr nasskalt war ist es augenblicklich wieder milde trotz der abwesenheit von Sonne. Letzte Woche wurde ich durch einen Brief von Arthur Rubin überrascht von dem ich Jahre nichts gehört habe. Er hat bei Leo u. Martha besucht u. dort meine Addresse erfahren. Er hat nach neunjähriger Ehe eine Tochter bekommen die jetzt 2 Jahre alt ist.)

Ich hoffe zuversichtlich dass ich Euch das nächste mal einen Brief bestätigen kann und in dieser Erwartung bin ich für heute mit Küssen in inniger liebe Euer

Siegfried

[73] *This letter, of which No. 72 is the draft, reached Hamburg by an unknown route. A stamp on the outside of the letter (Fig 6.4) shows that it was sent by Prisoner of War mail. In Hamburg it was opened by the censor of the Wehrmacht. It was returned from Hamburg on 9 September 1942 with a sticker saying, "Abgerist ohne Angabe der Adresse" (Moved away without leaving an address). On its return, either in Australia or in the United Kingdom it was once again subject to a censor. By this time Siegfried was back in Britain andtThe letter was returned from Australia to Siegfried at the address of his aunt, Mrs Henny Landau, 38 Northolme Road, London N5. This was the address Siegfried had given at the time of his internment in Australia.*

24 Mai 1942

Meine lieben, guten Elterrn

Ich nehme bestimmt an dass meine früheren Briefe inzwischen in Euren Besitz gelangt sind und hoffe, dass auch meine Zeilen vom 5. u. 28 April Euch bald erreichen. Leider habe ich auch in den letzten Wochen auch keinen weiteren Brief von Euch erhalten und warte ich mit jeder Post darauf von Euch zu hören, nachdem dies nun schon so lange wieder her ist. Vor allen dingen hoffe ich zuversichtlich, dass Ihr Beide gesund seit. Auch mir geht es GsD gesundheitlich gut, und lebe ich von der Vorstellung wie es sein wird, wenn ich wieder mit meinen Lieben zusammen sein werde. Inzwischen sind auch die Pfingsttage vorüber, so vergeht ein Monat nach dem anderen. Am ersten Abend sassen wir mit einer Anzahl Freunden zusammen und lernten in gewohnter weise. Unseren Abend- u. Morgen G'ttesdienst schmückten wir mit grünen Zweigen aus. Es gibt natürlich hier ganz anderes Grün wie in Europa und zwar hauptzächlich von Gummi- und Eucalyptus Bäumen, die hier überall wachsen. In den letzten vierzehntagen regnet es ziemlich viel im Gegensatz zu dem vorangegangenen Sommerhalbjahr, ein Zeichen der begonnenen Wintermonate. Der Himmel ist, bedeckt und die Sonne kommt selten durch die Wolken, während die Temperatur auch jetzt häufig wächselt von Kalt auf wärmer. Die Temperaturunterschiede bleiben auch in dieser Jahreszeit hier stark und sind typisch für das Klima. – Ich hoffe zuvedrsichtlich, dass ich Euch das nächste Mal einen Brief bestätigen kann, und in dieser Erwartung bin ich für heute mit tausend Küssen in inniger liebe Euer

Siegfried

[74] *A short message of 26 May 1942 has been omitted. See headnote to No. 63.*

[75] *At about the date of this letter, Jews were progressively compelled to live in Judenhäuser (Jew houses). David Hirsch's mother, Dora Hirsch, had informed him that she was now living in the Altersheim (the Jewish Home for the Aged) in Sedanstrasse, Hamburg, while Siegfied's parents were living in the Jewish Orphanage. Emil and Bella Badrian, brother-in-law and sister of Dora Hirsch were about to move to the Hamburg Jewish Boys Orphanage at 3 Papendam. The rabbi referred to is the Hamburg Chief Rabbi Dr Joseph Carlebach.*

From David Hirsch
75 Washington Ave
New York City
May 28, 1942

My dear Siegfried

I'm glad to tell you that I had a letter from my mother reporting that your dear parents are living now in the same building and on the same floor with her. Badrians are going to live in the orphanage Papendam. My mother wrote I should tell you that Peter is longing for some lines from you. Uncle Julius celebrates his 80th birthday. Almost all our family is now in the home for aged people.

Your questions about dates when letters has been sent by or received me I cannot answer. Life here is very quite. I cannot hold my letters longer than I have answered them.

I wrote you almost from the beginning that I was not optimistic about the conditions to enter this country. I did not yet change my opinion. You know that I didn't succeed in bringing out my folks.

Should I advise you I would try to volunteer there in defense work or civil service. I cannot agree with sailing over the ocean in this time.

Our Rabbi is now in Riga. Benny Meyer's widow got married to the old Mr Offenberg.

Else wrote that your things are standing with Dr Levy. Lazar Lanzkron has a job somewhere in the country, as it seems to me. He is now father of boy-twins.

Adolf asked this week for your address. He will send you a little money-order. Sulzbacher told in London from you. You did not change yet your nature. Why not?

I had to register. I don't care about exemption. We all have changed our nature.

There is no way to bring people here from oversea. Should I not succeed in bringing my family to this country during the war, I would rather prefer to go back to England.

Elkeles' father-in-law arrived here recently. I did not see him yet. ~In the course of time you get indifferent to all the former friends.

Keep well, good luck. I wish you a little more courage and resoluteness

Regards and love, Yours David

[76] Many Jewish internees in Australia came from Germany and some appear to have received post from Germany, which is referred to as 'dort' ('*there*').

16 Juni 1942

Meine gel. Guten Eltern, Trotzdem in der letzten Woche viel Post von dort angekommen ist, teilweise, schon von ende März, war für mich leider nichts dabei, und warte ich täglich darauf von Euch Post zu erhalten. Ich hoffe zuversichtlich dass Ihr meine Briefe inzwischen erhalten habt und dass Ihr Euch beide wohl fühlt. Auch kann Euch mitteilen, dass ich GsD. gesund bin. Mir ist eingefallen, dass ich Euch zu Eurem Geburtstagen schon in meinem vorigen Brief von 24.5 hätte schreiben müssen, da dieser Brief nicht mehr rechtzeitig eintreffen wird. Nichtsdestoweniger will ich dies heute tun, und wünsche ich Euch, gel. Papa u. gel. Muttchen, aus tiefsten Herzen innigst alles alles Gute. Möge der gütige G'tt Euch im Kommenden Jahre nur Gesundheit geben und möge er es geben, dass wir uns einmal wiedersehen werden. Ich bete täglich zu G'tt und dies Gebet gibt mir Stärke. Ich denke soviel an Euch und dann kommen mir meine glücklichen Kinderjahre in Erinnerung, die ich unter Eurem Schutz u. Eurer Leitung verbracht habe. Dann denke ich an die schönen Jünglings- u. späteren Jahre, die ich so sehr glücklich im Elternhaus verbringen durfte, in dem ich mich sonnen konnte in Eurer Liebe, Eurem Verständnis, Eurer elterlichen Kammeradschaft. All dies ist mir ständig lebhaft vor Augen und erfüllt mich mit unendlicher, tiefer

Dankbarkeit.zu Euch. Auch die Sorgen u. die betrüblichen Stunden, die ich Euch in meinem Leben verursacht, habe ich nicht vergessen, u. nur das Bewusstsein mildert die Reue, dass das Kind u. der junge Mensch noch nicht übersicht, wie unrecht es ist Eltern Gram zu bereiten, und die Hoffnung alles nochmal wieder gutmachen u. denken zu können. Für heute seid innigst gegrüsst u. geküsst von Eurem Euch lb. Siegfried

[77]
26 Juni 1942

Meine geliebten Eltern, Es ist diese Woche wieder Post von dort eingetroffen ohne dass für mich etwas dabei war von Euch. Ich hoffe zuversichtlich, dass Ihr meine Briefe inzwischen erhalten habt und auch die letzten von Mai und Juni recht bald eintreffen. Ich hoffe weiter, dass Ihr beide gesund sind und kann ich Euch berichten, dass es auch mir gesundheitlich GsD. Gut geht. Ich habe Euch im vorigen Brief geschrieben, dass ich Euch zu Eurem Geburtstagen eine Post früher hätte schreiben müssen, damit meine Wünsche rechtzeitig eintreffen. Ich möchte diese für alle Fälle nochmals wiederholen und Euch gel. Papa und gel. Muttchen innigst alles vom Herzen gute wünschen. Möge der liebe G'tt Euch im kommenden Jahre gesund erhalten und möge er es geben, dass wir uns einmal wiedersehen werden. Ich bete täglich hierfür und weiss mich im Gebet mit Euch vereint, das gibt mir Stärke. Wenn ich an Euch denke, und dass is fast immer, dann erinnere ich mich meiner glücklichen Kinderjahre, die ich unter Eurem elterlichen Leitung verbracht habe. Dann denke ich an die so schönen späteren Jahre, die ich so glücklich im Elternhaus verbringen durfte, und Eure Liebe, Euer Verständnis, Eure väterliche und mütterliche Kammeradschaft ist mir selbst vor Augen und erfüllt mich mit so unendlicher Dankbarkeit zu Euch. Ich weiss auch, dass Euch auch Sorgen und betrübliche Stunden durch mich nicht erspart geblieben sind, jedoch erfuhr ich, dass Eltern sofort verzeihen, wissend dass der junge Mensch noch nicht so das Unrecht empfindet Eltern etwas anders als nur Freunde zu bereiten. Ich hoffe zuversichtlich alles noch einmal danken zu können. Hoffentlich sehe ich bald Eure Zeilen und in dieser Erwartung bin ich mit innigsten Küssen und Grüssen Euer Euch lb

Siegfied

[78] Draft letter

8 Juli 1942

Meine geliebten Eltern

Ich will hoffen dass Ihr zwischenzeitlich meine früheren Briefe erhalten hast und dass auch meine Zeilen von Mai und Juni recht bald bei Euch eintreffen, die letzteren mit meinen Geburtstags wünschen. Ich hoffe zuversichtlich dass Ihr Euch gesundheitlich wohl fühlt und kann ich Euch auch von mir GsD das gleiche mitteilen. – Vorige Woche war es ein Jahr her, dass sel. Onkel Elkan [das zeitliche gesegnet? hat] und gedenke Deiner lb. Papa, Tante Dora anlässlich dieses Tages. Auch David habe ich ?----??---? geschrieben, und möchte auch Siegmund mein Gedenken zum Ausdruck bringen. Trotzdem die Tage und Wochen hier so gleichmässig ablaufen und ein Monat wie der andere geht vergeht auch so ein Jahr sehr schnell, jedenfalls erscheint es so, wenn man darauf zurückblickt. Ich hoffe nur, dass bald Jahre kommen in denen man nicht mehr so getrennt von seinen lieben leben muss und alles schwere vorüber sein wird. – Neulich bekam ich von dem Sohn Deines alterskollegen lb. Papa Grüsse von Euch ausgerichtet mit denen ich mich sehr gefreut habe. Leider war der Brief den er von seinem Vater bekam von Ende vorigen Jahres, also ? 3 words?. Wie Euch schon letztens geschrieben hoffe ich ?----? bald neue Post von Euch zu bekommen. Kürzlich wurde ich durch einem Brief von Arthur Rubin überrascht von dem ich sehr lange nichts gehört hatte. Er hatte bei Leo und Martha besucht uns dort meine Adresse erfahren. Er hat nach neun Jahren eine Tochter bekommen, die jetzt 2 Jahre alt ist. X Ich hoffe, dass die alten Tanten und auch Tante Dora wohl sind. Habt Ihr einmal Post von Onkel Manfred & Tante Else Harriet gehabt, hoffentlich geht es ihnen gut. – Ich muss für heute schliessen und bin gel. Papa & gel. Mutter, mit tausend Grüssen & Küssen in inniger Lieben Euer Siegfried

X Auch von Ernst hatte ich diese Woche einmal einen Brief als Antwort auf meine Zeilen zum ableben seiner Mutter. X

[79] *David Hirsch wrote the following letter to Siegfried.*

David Hirsch
75 Fort Washington Ave
New York City
August 28, 1942

Dear Siegfried!

Your letters of June 3 and July 10 I received with the same delivery of post. You are impatient to hear from your parents. So was I up to now. On the 13th of August I received a letter from the Red Cross that reads as follows: Lieber David, hope you and Siegfried well, worried, we are well, live Sedanstrasse. Affectionate regards to you and Siegfried, hope news soon, Pinkus Adele. Immediately after receipt I answered on the same way: My Dears, Siegfried quite well. He hopes to return to Else. Only then he can write to you by Red Cross. His return still undecided. DavidI took my information about a prspective return to England from newspaper reports that our friends in England sent me. If it will come true, I do not now, of course. But it may be a little heartening for your parents to live in this belief. Anyway, I wish this letter should not reach you anymore in Australia but in England. Haven't you an opportunity to write your parents by the way of the Red Cross?

It is very easy to blame me for not writing you often. But believe me, it is not so comfortable for me either to live here alone. Sometimes you lose all the courage to go on. Unfortunately, I had no opportunity to write you important news. Things you wanted to know never came up in the meantime. I do my work only and do not care about anything else. Would you be in this country, you might understand med beter

My family lives now together with family Sussmann. They rented a furnished house in Queen Elizabeth Walk and seem to feel quite comfortably. There are always problems as to the education of the children and as to providing facilities for a job for Joseph and a good school for Gotthelf. Hans is working at Dr Bondy's. In his trade he could not find a position.

Of course, I registered for the army. Whether they will grant me exemption as minister, I do not know yet. Whatever will come, we have to take it. I had several times Red Cross letters from m y mother. Naturally she cant write much.

I am anxious to get my family over. The necessary documents are now in Washington. The proceedings will take about a year. Even then there is the question how to accomodate a passage.

I do not understand what you have written about pending decisions you will have to take. Do you mean joining the army or returning to England? An emigration to the U.S.A. seems to be possible again. However I do not know whether I shall advise you to do so. It seems to me more reasonable, for the time being, when you will return to England.

Wishing you a better and more prosperous New Year than the last one.

Yours, David

(*According to a note made on the letter, it arrived in March 1943*)

Appendix 2

PEOPLE AND PLACES

Carlebach, Rabbi Dr Joseph Zwi (Hirsch), was born in Lübeck in 1883, the eighth child of Rabbi Salomon Carlebach, the Rabbi of Lübeck. After attending the Katharineum in Lübeck, he studied physics, mathematics, philosophy and history of art at Berlin University from 1901 to 1905. After his early Jewish education he attended the Hildesheimer Rabbinical Seminary in Berlin. In 1905 he passed the teacher's examinations in physics and mathematics and from 1905 to 1907 he taught at the Simon von Lämel School in Jerusalem. He continued his studies in Leipzig and in 1908 he was awarded a doctorate at the University of Heidelberg for a dissertation entitled Lewi ben Gerson as mathematician: A contribution to the history of mathematics amongst the Jews. From 1908 he taught at the Margareten Lyceum in Berlin and in 1914 he was given semichah (ordination) at the Hildesheimer Seminary. At the beginning of the First World War he volunteered for military service and was a commissioned officer in the German army. He was posted to Lithuania, where he was to set up Jewish schools to be run according to the German model. The Gymnasium he founded in Kovno later became the exemplar of schools in Vilna, Riga and Memel. In 1920 he was appointed rabbi in Lübeck in succession to his late father but a year later on appointment as Director of the Talmud Tora School he moved to Hamburg. Under his leadership, the school underwent far-reaching educational reforms. In 1925 he was called to the post of Chief Rabbi of Altona. In 1936 he returned to Hamburg and took up the post of Chief Rabbi there in succession to Rabbi Dr Samuel Spitzer. Pincus and Elkan Hirsch and their families were close friends of Rabbi Carlebach and his family. On 6 December 1941 Joseph Carlebach, his wife, his son Salomon (Peter) and daughters Rudi, Noemi und Sara were deported to Riga. In the Jungfernhof concentration camp, near Riga, he gathered teachers and organised the education of the children. He also succeeded in continuing Jewish life, to celebrate festivals and to conduct services. On 26 March 1942 (8 Nissan 5702) he, his wife Charlotte (Lotte) née Preuss and three young daughters were murdered (see Gillis-Carlebach 2009). His son Shlomo (Peter) Carlebach survived.

Colm, Heinrich owner of a ladies clothing store, the Ostindienhaus, 13/15 Neuer Wall, Hamburg. The fate of the firm is described by Bajohr (2002).

Danglow, Jacob (1880-1962) Rabbi of the St Kilda Hebrew Congregation, Melbourne. He was born in England and studied for the ministry at Jews' College, London. He was appointed to the Melbourne community in 1905 and became a member of the Melbourne Beth Din in 1911. He studied arts subjects at the University of Melbourne, graduating B.A. and M.A. He was commissioned into the Australian Military Forces and later appointed Jewish chaplain. In 1942 he was appointed senior Jewish chaplain to the Australian Army. He was appointed O.B.E. in 1950 and C.M.G. in 1956 and retired in 1957. Danglow visited the Dunera internees but seems not to have been very understanding of their plight (Levi, 1981; Patkin, 1979).

Lanzkron a Hamburg family with connections to the Möller family (see below Gottfried Möller). Lazar Lanzkron was born in Hamburg in 1903. He was married to Regina née Fröhlich of Würzburg. They moved to England at the end 1936 or the beginning 1937. Their daughter Betty was the wife of Willi Stern (see below). The Lanzkron and Stern families were friends of the Hirsch family; a friendship that continued in London when in April 1939 Siegfried found accommodation in the Stern home in North London.

Minden, Ernest (1898-1972) was born in Hull, Yorkshire to Max Minden and Sophie née Feitler of Hamburg. In 1894 the family moved to England where Max Minden carried on a successful egg exporting business in Kingston upon Hull. The family moved back to Hamburg in 1904. Ernest Minden worked at the Warburg Bank in Hamburg until he left for England in the mid-1930s. In London he remained closely connected with the Warburgs and worked for Siegmund Warburg's early enterprises in England. Ernest Minden's brother, Henry (1890-1971), a Hamburg lawyer, came to England on 1 November 1938 and was the second husband of Erna Sussman née Hirsch. Ernest Minden died in 1972.

Falk, Leib Aisack (1889-1957). Born in Latvia, he attended yeshivot in Kovno and Telsch, and from 1912-15 he was Minister in Dundee. From 1915 he was Minister in Plymouth and in September 1922 he was second reader at the Great Synagogue, Sydney. During a visit to Palestine in

1936 he received semicha. During World War II he was chaplain to Jewish internees in; though he made efforts to secure their release, he was criticized for lack of sympathy (Rutland, 1981).

Heinemann, Gustav (1883-1941), a businessman, was born in Hamburg. His wife, Bertha, was a née Wittmund. He was a member of the Jewish Community and of the Burial society. They had one son (born 1921), who went to Holland to train in agriculture with the intention of going to Palestine. In 1942 he got married according to the evidence of his wife, who survived the Shoah, he was deported to the concentration camp at Arnheim in 1943 from where he was taken to the camp at Westerbork and from there to Sobibor, where he was murdered on 14 May 1943. All trace of his parents is lost after their deportation to Minsk.

Möller Gottfried (1899-1977) was a member of a very large Hamburg Jewish family descended from Juda Möller (born 1805) of Fackenburg; he later settled in Altona [see www.angelfire.com/ny/oferiko/Family/Moeller/Moeller3gen.rtf]. Juda Möller's wife Eva née Peine (1804-1868) may have been related to Feitel Hirsch's wife Ella née Peine (see Volume 3). Juda's second son Pinkus was married to Esther née Hesslein who may have been related to Hanchen née Hesslein the wife of Pincus Hirsch's cousin Salomon Levy (see Volume 3). Gottfried Möller and his family came to England in the 1930s and were well-known and active in the Adath Yisroel congregation in Hendon, North-West London, to which after 1946 Siegfried Hirsch also belonged.

Möller Herman (Hamburg 1904-1994 Queens, New York) was an acquaintance of the Hirsch family. His parents were Markus Mordechai Möller (1861-1923) and Augusta Lanzkron (Hamburg 1869- 21 September 1942, murdered in Treblinka).

Nachrichtenblatt (1938-1943), the Jüdisches Nachrichtenblatt ('Jewish Newssheet') replaced other Jewish newspapers after these had been banned by the Gestapo. The Israelitisches_Familienblatt of Hamburg had moved to Berlin in 1935 and was closed down by order of the Gestapo. Its last number was that of 3 November 1938, the edition of 10 November could no longer appear and it was replaced by the Jüdisches Nachrichtenblatt, which was edited by Jews and included items of Jewish interest but was controlled by the Gestapo. Its purpose to a large extent was to publicise to the Jewish population the inreasing number of anti-Semitic laws and regulations that institutionalised Nazi persecution after the Pogroms of November 1938 [see https://archive.org/details/juedischesnachberlin].

Nathan, Nathan Max was born in 1879 in Emmerich, a small town on the north bank of the Rhine in North Rhine-Westphalia, north-west of Duisburg. After studying philosophy and oriental subjects at the universities of Bonn and Berlin he attended the Hochschule für die Wissenschaft des Judentums where he was ordained as a rabbi. In 1905 he was awarded a doctorate in philosophy at the University of Strassburg for a thesis entitled Ein anonymes Wörterbuch zur Mišna und Jad hahazaka.

Fig. App. 2.1. Rabbi Dr Nathan Max Nathan

Nathan had academic inclinations and in 1906 he was appointed general secretary of the Gesellschaft zur Förderung der Wissenschaft des Judentums in Berlin. At the same time he was active in the Gesamtarchiv der Juden in Deutschland, as well as teaching in religion classes and acting as a rabbi. In 1912 the Hamburg Deutsch-Israelitische Gemeinde appointed him Syndicus (Authorised Scretary), though he did not have the legal training usually regarded as necessary for such an appointment. On 28 May 1914 (3 Sivan 5674) he married Dora née Rieger and presented his bride with a German prayer book, Beruria, intended for women and girls, edited by Rabbi Dr Max Grunwald, rabbi of the Neue Dammtor Synagogue, Hamburg, from 1895 to 1903.

This prayer book was in the possession of Erna Sussman née Hirsch, before her move to Britain and it has been placed in the custody of the Hamburger Gesellschaft für jüdische Genealogie. Amongst Erna Sussman's papers is an undated family photograph in which Dora Nathan appears with Elkan Hirsch and his wife Dora née Hanover together with a young unidentified woman member of the Heimann family.

Fig. App. 2.2. The inscription reads, "As a memento of our
wedding 3 Sivan 5674 Dr N. M. Nathan and Dora Nathan".

It appears that the Hirschs and Nathans were close acquaintances. In 1916
Nathan published Das Israelitische Vorschuss-Institut in Hamburg 1816-
1916 a detailed study of a charitable society dedicated to making loans
to impecunious members of the Hamburg Jewish community to support
craftsmen wishing to establish their own businesses. In the decades after
Dr Nathan's appointment as Syndicus of the Community he continued
with his literary work and wrote or published numerous studies about
Hamburg. He was particularly interested in youth activities and in 1921
founded an organisation for this purpose. He also pursued editorial
activities and founded the Gemeindeblatt der Deutsch-Israelitischen
Gemeinde from 1925 until it was banned by the Nazis in 1938.

Fig. App. 2.3. Undated photograph. 'Nathan' is Dora Nathan, Breuer is unknown, ‚Mama' is Dora Hirsch, ‚Papa' is Elkan Hirsch, Heimann is unknown

In 1922 he became a member of Verein für Hamburgische Geschichte (Association for the History of Hamburg) from which he was excluded in 1934. He frequently acted as rabbi at the Neue Dammtor Synagoge. Dr Nathan was a member, often in leading positions, of many societies and institutions, including the Cemetery Commission of the Chevra Kaddishah and the Gesellschaft für jüdische Volkskunde, the Jüdischen Mittelstandshilfe (an association that offered financial assistance to the needy of the middle class) and the Franz-Rosenzweig-Gedächtnisstiftung (Franz Rosenzweig Memorial Trust). Jewish institutions respected him for the discretion with which he conducted himself. In the face of the tensions between different religious trends in the community during the difficult and changing conditions after 1933, he was a source of stability in the community. In about June 1939 Dr Nathan took a Kindertransport to England (Letter No. 23 of 13 June 1939) and then returned to Hamburg. It appears that at about this time he was contemplating emigration and there is a record in the archives of the Central British Fund for German Jewry (CBF now World Jewish Relief) about his emigration to Britain (Home Office No. N5108). On 19 July 1942 he and his wife Dora née Rieger were deported to Theresienstadt and from there on 23 October 1944 to Auschwitz, where they were murdered about two days later. (After Ina Lorenz with additional information)

Plaut, Dr. Max (1901-1974) was born in Sohrau in Upper Silesia (now Żory, Poland) the oldest of five children of Raphael and Else Plaut. After high school in Marburg, he moved to live with his parents in Hamburg. Here he began his further education and an apprenticeship to M.M. Warburg and Co. To pursue his studies he temporarily left the company to take a doctorate in law, which he was awarded in 1928 by the University of Rostock for a thesis entitled Der Gebrauch der Urkunde. He then returned to Warburg & Co., where he remained until 1930. Plaut then acted as a volunteer in the Jewish community until, in 1933, he was appointed secretary to the Deutsch-Israelitische Gemeinde. When the various Jewish communities were forcibly centralised to form the Jüdischen Religionsverband Hamburg e.V., Plaut oversaw the whole Jewish Community of Hamburg. He was inducted into the position by Rabbi Leo Baeck. Later, in 1942, when the Gestapo forcibly merged the Jewish Communities of north-West Germany to form the Bezirksstelle Nordwestdeutschland of the Reichsvereinigung der Juden in Deutschland, Plaut was placed in charge.

The following is summarised from a memoir dictated by Max Plaut in 1968 (Leo Baeck Institute, Max Plaut Collection, Call No. ME 743). On 10 June 1943 Heinrich Himmler ordered the dissolution of the Reichsvereinigung and all remaining community officials, including Plaut, were to be deported to Theresienstadt by 30 June 1943. Though Plaut already had notice to attend for deportation, he received information from Geneva that there was a certificate for him to go to Palestine. The Swiss Consul-General in Hamburg, Zehnder, informed Plaut that he was on an exchange list with the British Embassy in Bern. The Red Cross arranged for his name to be removed from the transport to Theresienstadt. He, his mother and Mrs Emma Levi of Hamburg, were then sent first to a camp at Vittel in France and then to a camp in Vienna. From here they and 268 others, including some from Auschwitz, Belsen, Gurs etc., were sent by train via the Balkans to Palestine. Apparently the exchange that had been arranged was for German Templers living in Jerusalem.

It appears that the Hirsch family were well acquainted with Dr. Plaut. Thus, Adele wrote to Siegfried on 23 June 1939 that Plaut had visited her and reported on his visit to London during which he had seen Siegfried (letter 26). Further evidence of Dr. Plaut as a family acquaintance comes from a postcard Bella Badrian sent to Dr Berthold Hannes (1882-1955; von Villiez 2009), a doctor in Hamburg. She wrote to him from Theresienstadt on 2 August 1944, in acknowledgement of a food parcel and asked him to convey regards to Max Plaut. Plaut returned from Israel to Germany in 1950 and lived in Bremen, where he was elected vice-president of the Jewish Community. He lived in Bremen until 1965, when he moved back to Hamburg. Max Plaut died in Hamburg in 1974.

Spitzer, Dr Alexander (1899-1991) was a lawyer and rabbi, and the son of Rabbi Dr Samuel Spitzer (1872-1934) Chief Rabbi of Hamburg 1910-1934. In 1922 Alexander Spitzer was awarded a doctorate of law by Hamburg University and practised as a lawyer. In the 1930s he came to England where he worked as a rabbi.

Stern, Willi (Wilhelm) (sometimes St. in the letters) was born on 7 May 1902 in Fulda, Hessen, Germany, the son of Menachem and Henriette Stern. He was the youngest of seven children. Before WW2 one brother died in Germany and one went to Palestine. The three other brothers Simon, Fritz and Willi, finally lived in Cardiff. The two sisters were Else and Amalie (Mali), who was married to Isaac Levy, a dental surgeon and grandson of Rabbi Samson Raphael Hirsch. Isaac Levy was the first translator into English of the S. R. Hirsch Pentateuch commentary.

The Stern family had owned a paint and lacquer factory in Fulda since the 19th century. As a young man Willi moved to Hamburg, where he worked in engineering and banking and set up a business in the course of which it is said that he had occasion to travel, including to India.

Pincus, Adele and Siegfried Hirsch were close acquaintances of Willi Stern and the Lanzkron family and they are frequently mentioned in the correspondence.

On 30 June 1933 in Hamburg Willi married Betty, the daughter of Abraham Alphons Lanzkron and Flora Frumet of Hamburg. She was born on 20 May 1902 in Hamburg. On the occasion of their marriage the Franz

Rosenzweig Gedächtnis Stiftung in Hamburg (The Franz Rosenzweig Memorial Trust in Hamburg) presented the couple with a copy of the 1930 edition of Die Fünf Bücher der Weisung (The Books of Instruction, i.e. The Pentateuch) translated by Martin Buber and Franz Rosenzweig (Fig. App. 2.4). The inscription reads:

"On the day God created man

He made him in God's likeness

He created them male and female

And he blessed them

And gave them the name humankind on the day of their creation".

(Genesis 5:1-2)

Franz Rosenzweig Gedächtnis Stiftung in Hamburg.

..... „Am Tag, da Gott den Menschen erschuf, machte er ihn in Gottes Gleichnis, männlich und weiblich schuf er sie, und segnete sie, und rief ihren Namen: Mensch! am Tag ihrer Erschaffung."

Diese Worte sind dem biblischen Buch „Im Anfang" entnommen. An dem heutigen Tage, da Sie im Anfang Ihrer Ehe stehen, überreicht Ihnen die Franz Rosenzweig Gedächtnis Stiftung eine Uebersetzung der Thora.

Mögen Sie alle Tage Ihres Lebens vereint danach trachten, des Segens inne zu werden, als „Gottes Gleichnis" Mensch zu heissen.

Herrn *Wilhelm Stern*

und Frau *Betty* geb. *Lanzkron*

überreicht am *30. Juni* durch

Fig. App. 2.4. Presentation page of the Buber Rosenzweig Translation of the Torah

These words are taken from the book "In the beginning". On this day, as you stand at the threshold of your marriage, the Franz Rosenzweig Memorial Trust presents you with a translation of the Torah.

May you all the days of your life be united in striving to become part of the blessing to be human in the "image of God's likeness."

In 1933, soon after his marriage, Willi came to Britain, where he settled in London; two of his brothers, Simon and Fritz, followed in 1937. In London he ran an import/export business, Stern (London) Ltd and had a stake in another company, Mercantile Oils Ltd. At first after moving to Britain, Willi Stern lived at 84 Queen's Drive, London N4, where he later accommodated Siegfried for a time after his arrival in London.

To deal with the severe unemployment in Britain in the 1930s, the UK government established two so-called trading estates in 1936, one in Team Valley, Gateshead, in County Durham just south of Newcastle and the other at Treforest in the Rhondda valley of Wales, north-west of Cardiff. The object of these trading estates was to encourage light manufacturing. Here, in 1939, at the suggestion of the young Harold Wilson, then a senior official in the Ministry of Labour, the Stern brothers established Pearl Paints Limited as the first manufacturing enterprise on the Treforest Trading Estate. The paints and lacquers they produced, based on research and technical expertise in the company, were specialist paints, such as fire resistant paint, and of a very high quality, some for military use. One customer of Pearl Paints was Dinky Toys, a company that produced scale model die-cast toys of motors cars, aeroplanes and the like. Willi was the Chairman of Pearl Paints Ltd.

The Stern brothers were active members of the Cardiff United Synagogue and Willi was Chairman of the Building Committee of the Cardiff Penylan Synagogue. Betty Stern, who had been ill for some time, died in Cardiff on 26 January 1961.

On 8 October 1961 Willi married Erica Hakesberg in London in the garden of Fred Rosenberg and his wife Tirza née Lanzkron at 2 St. Georges Close in Golders Green under the aegis of the Golders Green Beth Hamedrash. Erika was born on 24 April 1907 in Hofgeismar north of Kassel, the

Fig. App. 2.5. Willi Stern (left) and his second wife Erica (wearing spectacles), at Jonathan Sussman's Bar Mitzvah, Cardiff, 17 November 1974 [from left to right, Mrs Anita Slyper, Willi Stern, Edna Frey, Erica Stern, Karl Frey, Erna Minden-Sussman, Eliot Fine and Jean Sussman]

daughter of Felix Hakesberg, a master butcher, and his wife Hedwig. She came to Britain as a domestic servant together with her sister Else (http://www.alemannia-judaica.de/hofgeismar_synagoge.htm). On 3 November 1939 a Metropolitan Police Tribunal exempted her from internment and special restrictions as an Enemy Alien. In 1949 Erika was the Manageress of Grodzinski's bakery in Willesden Lane, London NW2 and later at the Golders Green branch where she was friendly with the Lanzkron family. Erika became a naturalised British subject on 8 November 1949.

The following throws light on the life of Jews in Germany in the 1930s. During his final illness, a brother of Erika, who died in 1933, was being treated by a Nazi, Dr. Karl Heinrich Christian Wilharm. Erika told post-war investigators that Wilharm had been in her home treating her terminally ill brother when men with revolvers came to their door. She told the investigators that Wilharm "allowed the men to haul our father from the house. He was taken to the factory and beaten beyond recognition". An oil portrait, Girl from the Sabine Mountains, probably by Franz Xaver Winterhalter, famous for painting a portrait of Queen Victoria, had belonged to a Jewish art collector, who had been forced to sell it. After the war it was in the possession of the 84-year-old German baroness Maria-Luise Bissonnette, the step-daughter of Dr Wilharm. The picture had belonged to Julius Stern, not a relative of Willi, a textile mill owner who specialised in Dutch, Flemish and German painters. In 1934, Max Stern inherited the business from his father and in 1937 he was forced to sell his property and his art gallery. More than 200 paintings were sent to a Cologne auctioneer, whose sale catalogue included Girl from the Sabine Mountains. Karl Wilharm bought the painting at auction and Bissonnette was in possession of the painting and of the purchase receipt when, after the war, the ownership of the painting came into contention (http://www.foxnews.com/printer_friendly_wires/2008Feb02 /0,4675,APainfulPortrait,00.html). The picture was eventually returned to the Max Stern estate and is now in the Montreal Museum of Fine Arts (http://www.cbc.ca/news/arts/nazi-victim-s-art-holdings-unveiled-at-montreal-museum-1.806556).

Shortly after moving to Cardiff in 1964, to take up an academic post at the Medical school there, Max Sussman met the Stern brothers and got to know 'Uncle Willi' and 'Uncle Fritz' particularly well. At the time he was unaware of the earlier family connection in Hamburg. Willi Stern and Erika attended the Bar Mitzva reception for Jonathan Sussman at his home in Cardiff in November 1974 (Fig. App. 2.5). Also, Fritz Stern's second wife, Ruth, was the widow of James Marcus a close friend of Hans Sussman, the editor's late father; the two friends are buried side by side in the Adath Yisroel Burial Ground, Carterhatch Lane, Enfield London.

In about 1968, in view of Max Sussman's interest in Franz Rosenzweig, the Jewish existentialist philosopher, Willi presented him with the Rosenzweig bible translation referred to above.

On 1 March 1972 Ellis Pruchnie of Cardiff became Sales Director of Pearl Paints Ltd., and later the Managing Director. He told Arthur Harverd, a friend of the editor from his university years in Leeds, the following story. Apparently, at some time, probably in about 1942, Willi Stern advised the

UK Government that it would further the war effort if the dams to the east of Dortmund were destroyed. This may have been the origin of Operation Chastise in which the Möhne, Eder and Sorpe dams were destroyed ('The Dambusters'). In 1977 Willi was awarded the M.B.E. (London Gazette, 30 December 1977). In November 2014 a Freedom of Information Request (FOI320238) was made to the Cabinet Office for details of the citation of Willi's MBE. Unfortunately, in the reply all useful information had been redacted. It may be that the advice to HM Government about the Ruhr dams was the information that was removed.

Willi died in Cardiff in 1983.

Streim, Dr Siegfried (1896-1944) was a Hamburg dental surgeon married to Johanna née Hausmann (1897-1944) of Wilhelmsburg. They had three children, Kurt Salo (born 1927), Werner (born 1930) and Sulamith (born 1932). The family were friends of the Hirsch family probably based on their common membership of the Hamburg Jewish Community, the fact that he was their dentist and, perhaps, also Siegfried's business interests in supplying dental equipment and medicines. In 1942, the family were compelled to live at Dillstrasse 15, a Judenhaus that had previously been Zacharius and Ranette Hesse, and Mathilde and Simon Hesse Stiftung, a Housing Trust. This is now once again a residential building owned by the Jüdische Gemeinde in Hamburg (Hamburg Jewish Community).

The Streim family were deported from Hamburg to Theresienstadt on 20 July 1942 (Transport VI/2). Dora Hirsch, Pincus's sister-in-law records in a letter of 24 October 1945 from Switzerland to her family that she attended the Bar Mitzvah of Siegfried Streim's son, Werner, which will have taken place, on 25 December 1943 (28 Kislev 5704). The Streim family were deported from Theresienstadt to Auschwitz on 1 October 1944.

Warburg, the Hamburg bank M. M. Warburg & Co., sometimes simply W. or M.M.W. in the letters. Sometimes W. is the Warburg Bank in London. Pincus's life-long association with the bank meant that he was closely acquainted with its senior members. A full account of the Warburg family and the bank was published by Chernow (1995).

Warburg, Dr Fritz M. Warburg (1879-1964), Younger brother of Max M. Warburg, partner in the Warburg bank. He moved to Sweden in 1939 and then to Israel in 1957, where he died.
Max Warburg (1867-1946), also Max or Max W. in the letters. He was the senior partner in the Warburg bank and, in 1939, moved to the USA.

Warburg, Siegmund (1902-1982), a Director of the Warburg Bank. In May 1934 he left for London where he continued with his banking interests with the assistance of Ernest Minden. (Ferguson 2011)

Wertheimer, Dr Max (1883 Munich – 1961 USA) was in private practice as a general practitioner at Grindelberg 77 and was the school doctor of the Talmud-Tora School. From October 1938, having been deprived of his licence to practice, he was a Jüdischer Krankenbehandler (literally "One who treats the Jewish sick"). In August 1939 Wertheimer and his wife Rosa née Meyer went first to London and in January 1940 to New York, where he was apparently no longer in practice (von Villiez 2009).

Wigderowitsch, James (1902-1993), was a member of a Hamburg family related to the extended Möller family (see above) and a teacher in the Jewish school in Hannover. He moved to London, where in 1945 he taught Max Sussman for his Bar Mitzvah.

Wilhelminerhöhe was at Rissener Landstraße 127, Rissen, AItona-Rissen, north-west of Blankenese a pleasant small town on the estuary of the Elbe near Hamburg that is still known as a local resort. Pincus and Adele stayed there from Friday, 16 June to Sunday, 2 July 1939. Wilhelminerhöhe was primarily a kibbutz (collective) for the training (hachshara) of pioneers planning to go to Palestine (see www.rrz.uni-hamburg.de/rz3a035/borchardt.html). In view of the increasing difficulties for Jews in Germany and their exclusion from other holiday resorts, it was made possible for them to take holidays at Wilhelminerhöhe.

Wolffson, Dr Ernst (1881 Hamburg – 1955 Hamburg) was an evangelical Christian of Jewish descent and a General Practitioner. He received his licence to practise medicine in 1907 and was then an assistant at Eppendorf General Hospital (AK Eppendorf) until 1910. He then went into private practice at Rothenbaumchausee 52 and was active in a number of important medical associations. In 1938 he was arrested and deported to Sachsenhausen Concentration Camp. His licence to practice was withdrawn and, after his release, until 1943, he was Medical Director of the Hamburg Jewish Hospital (Israelitisches Krankenhaus) during a most difficult period. He made great efforts to delay the discharge of patients from the hospital in order to prevent their deportation. After the War Wolffson became a member of the Hamburg Chamber of Physicians (Hamburger Ärztekammer) and a member of the Commission for the Denazification of Hamburg doctors, which worked with the British Military Government. After 1945 Wolffson was once again in private practice in Hamburg (von Villiez 2009).

Appendix 3

ABBREVIATIONS AND GLOSSARIES

Abbreviations

StaH – Staatsarchiv Hamburg

N.A.A. - National Archives of Australia

Glossaries

Invocation of God in the Letters
At the beginning of letters written by Jews it is traditional in any of a variety of ways to express gratitude to God. In the case of the letters in this book, the abbreviation ב"ה (for ברוך השם *barukh hashem*, Blessed be the Name, i.e. of God) appears at the top left of the letter in most but not every case. In this way the writer gives praise to the Divine. The form used here was the one commonly used by German Jews.

Salutation
When addressing a person in writing it is also conventional, immediately after their name to add a wish for their long life. The abbreviation used in these letters is לא"ט (*le'orekh yomim tovim* לאורך יומים טובים, for a length of good days). This invocation was added immediately after Siegfried's name in most but not all of the letters and postcards. In most cases, as judged by the handwriting it seems that Pincus added the invocation to his wife's letters. To give the reader an impression, the invocations and salutations are shown only in the first five translations of the letters; they are added in each case in the German texts in Appendix 1.

Use of Divine names
The use of names of the divine were generally avoided by Pincus and Adele and were rarely written in full. Though, in principle, there is no objection to writing out the names of God in German or English, this has long been avoided by religious Jews mainly because such manuscript texts might later be mishandled or inappropriately destroyed. Writing in German, Pincus and Adele would write G'tt for Gott (God) or Allmächt'ger for

Allmächtiger (Almighty).

Use of Hebrew in the letters

Pincus Hirsch frequently used Hebrew words or expressions either in Hebrew cursive script or as transliterations. Adele did not use Hebrew, only transliterations; Pincus would add abbreviated Hebrew expressions to Adele's letters.

In the following glossaries Hebrew words and transliterated Hebrew words are listed alphabetically. Since the spellings are occasionally idiosyncratic, words are listed as they appear in the letters with an indication of the correct spelling. The identity of the writer, P for Pincus or A for Adele, with the letter Number and dates of the letters in which the words first appear are given in square brackets.

Hebrew Glossary

אבֿל [P, 23.6.39] (*avel*) – mourner.

אמן [P, 23.6.39] *amen*.

הצלחה u. ברכה [P, 31.3.39] (*berachah vehatzlachah*) – Blessing and success.

הבדלה [P, 11.7.39] (*havdalah*) 'Separation'. Ceremony to mark the end of Shabbat.

ה"י [P, 18.4.39] = השם יתברך (*hashem yitbarach*) 'May the Name be blessed'. One of the terms to designate God.

הספד [P, 25.8.39] (*hesped*) eulogy.

ז"ל [P, 25.8.39] = זכרונה לברכה 'May her memory be a blessing'. Unusually the feminine form is used here with reference to a man.

חן [23.6.39] (*chen*) grace.

יום טוב [P, 3.4.39] often abbreviated as י"ט [P, 6.4.39] literally 'Good day', refers to a Jewish festival.

מגלת רות [P, 30.5.39] (*Megillat Ruth*) The biblical 'Book of Ruth', which is read in the Synagogue on Shavuot (Pentecost).

מוצה שבת, should read מוצאי שבת [P, 11.7.39] (*motzaei shabbat*) literally 'The going out or departure of the Sabbath', i.e. the conclusion of the Sabbath.

מנחה [P, 15.8.39] (*minchah*) the afternoon service.

מעריב [P, 25.8.39] (*ma'ariv*) the evening service.

פסח [P, 3.4.39] (*pesach*) Passover.

קדיש [P, 25.8.39] (*kaddish*) literally sanctification, the doxology recited in the synagogue by mourners.

רב [P, 30.5.39] (*rav*) literally, teacher, now has the common meaning of Rabbi.

שבת [P, 31.3.39] (*shabbat*) Sabbath.

שיעור [P, 6.9.39] (*shiur*) literally 'measure', term used for a study period.

תענית [P, 28.7.39] (*ta'anit*) fast day.

ט"ב = תשע באב [P, 21.7.39] (*tisha be'av*) Ninth day of the Hebrew month of Av, which commemorates the destruction of the first and second Jerusalem Temples.

Transliterated terms and expressions
Some of the transliterations used are affected by the particular manner in which Ashkenazi German Jews pronounced Hebrew. The glossary is arranged alphabetically according to the transliteration as it occurs in the letters. The transliteration as it would be in Modern Hebrew is given in italics.

Al tiftechu bin Divim [P, 28.8.39] (Ps 146:3) should read *Al tivtechu benedivim*, usually translated as "Put not your trust in princes" but *nediv* (pl. *nedivim*) means *benefactor*.

Anbeissen [A, 25.7.39] German, usually refers to fish 'to bite, nibble, take a bait', refers to breaking a fast.

Arba Minim [P, 31.7.39] 'Four species', the palm branch, citron, myrtle and willow that were paraded in the Jerusalem Temple and now in the synagogue during the Festival of Tabernacles.

Auneg Schabbos [P, 4.7.39] (*Oneg Shabbat*) words for Sabbath enjoyment generally but also refers to a light Sabbath afternoon meal often with singing of hymns.

Aslo Geresch [A, 18.7.39] (*azlo geresh*) One of the musical forms used in the cantillation of the Bible when read in the Synagogue. It is very characteristic series of notes and can easily be whistled. It was used by the Hirsch family when attracting the attention of a relative in a crowd.

Barmitzwoh [A, 18.7.39] (*bar mitzvah*) the celebration of the 13th birthday, when a boy reaches his religious majority.

Bimharo Bjomenu [P, 12.4.39] (*bimherah beyamenu*) 'Soon in our days'.

Drei Wochen [A. 11.7.39] The three weeks between the 17th of Tammuz and the 9th of Av, a period of mourning, first, for the breaching of the walls of Jerusalem and finally the destruction of the two Temples in Jerusalem.

Fast of the First Born [P, 31.3.39] takes place on the day before Passover and commemorates the plague of the first born [Exodus 11.1ff.] when the Egyptian but not the Israelite first born died.

Fast of Tammuz [P, 7.7.39] recalls the breach of the city walls before the Roman assault on Jerusalem in 70 CE.

Fasten, ausfasten [P, 4.7.39] 'To fast' and 'to complete a day of fasting' as distinct from fasting only part of such a day.

Genäwe [P, 9.5.39] (גנבה) (*genevah*), theft.

G'tt [P, 3.4.39] Abbreviation for 'Gott'. For secular purposes the name 'God' was generally not written or spoken in full.

Jaumtouw [A, 30.5.39] (*yom tov*) for Hebrew see above, alternatively, Jom Touw [A, 6.4.39] or Jontef [A, 9.4.39].

Kille [A, 25.7.39] (*kehillah*) (קהילה) community, sometimes congregation.

Matzot [P, 6.4.39] the plural of Matzah, the unleavened bread eaten during Passover.

Minhag Paulin [P, 13.6.39] (*minhag polen*) the religious customs of the majority of German Jews as distinct, for example, from the customs of Frankfurt-am-Main, which was called Minhag Askenaz.

Mizwoh [31.3.39] (*mizvah*) (מצוה) lit., 'commandment' but usually refers to a religious obligation, hence "to do a mitzvah" means to fulfil a religious obligation.

Parnohse [A, 31.8.39] (*parnasah*) (פרנסה) livelihood.

Rausch Chaudesch [P, 13.6.39] (*rosh chodesh*) (ראש חודש). The 'new moon' of a lunar month.

Rausch-haschonoh [A, 31.7.39] (*Rosh Hashanah*) (ראש השנה) the New Year festival.

Schabbos [A, 31.3.39] *Shabbat* (שבת) Sabbath.

Schabbos Nachmu [A, 18.7.39] the first Sabbath after the 9th of Av. The name is taken from the opening words of Isaiah 40, *nachamu nachamu ami* 'Be comforted, Be comforted my people'. It refers to the reading of the prophets in the synagogue on the Sabbath after the Fast of Av.

Schiur [P, 9.5.39] (*shiur*) see above lesson.

Schwuaus [A, 19.5.39] (*shavuot*) Pentecost.

Seder [A, 6.4.39] the formal festival meal that takes place on the first and second evenings of Passover.

Simchat Torah [A 10.41 Footnote] Rejoicing of the Law, the festival at the end of Tabernacles.

Sukkaus [A, 29.6.39] (*succot*) Tabernacles.

Tanis [A, 7.7.39] (*ta'anit*) fast day.

Vorzuoren [P, 23.6.39] Leading prayers in the synagogue; derived from '*oren*', 'to pray', used exclusively by German Jews. Derived from Latin '*ora*' pray.

ACKNOWLEDGEMENTS

The following is an alphabetical list of those I consulted and who assisted me in a variety of ways during the lengthy editing process. I am most grateful to all of them. Any omissions are entirely inadvertent and I offer my sincere apologies here.

Rabbi Raymond Apple, Israel

Rabbi David Freedman, Sydney Australia

Arthur D. Harverd, London

Joseph Hirsch, Oak Park Michigan

Lurline and Arthur Knee, Tatura Wartime Camps Museum.

Gillian & Romi Lanzkron, Petach Tikva, Israel

Astrid Louven, Hamburg

Adele Lustig, London

Dr Linda Nussbaum, Santa Monica, California

Patricia Thoburn, Customer Services Desk, Robinson Library, Newcastle University

Warburg Archive

Golders Green Beth Hamedrash Synagogue, London

BIBLIOGRAPHY

The persecution of the Jews during the Nazi period is the subject of a very extensive literature. No attempt has been made in this book or this Appendix to support all the facts reported in the text. The reader will find much useful additional information on the internet, in general libraries and particularly libraries that specialise in the holocaust and related subjects, such as the Wiener Library, 29 Russell Square, London WC1B 5DP.

The Hamburg address books were useful to identify people, occupations and addresses. They can be accessed via the Landesbibliothek Hamburg, University of Hamburg via http://landesbibliothek.sub.uni-hamburg.de/en/service-hh/english.html.

Bajohr, F., '*Aryanisation in Hamburg: The Economic Exclusion of Jews and the Confiscation of their Property in Nazi Germany*. New York: Berghahn 2002.

Chernow, Ron, *The Warburgs: A family saga*. London: Pimlico 1995.

Duckesz, Eduard, *Ivoh Lemoschaw: enthaltend Biographien und Grabstein-Inschriften der Rabbiner der drei Gemeinden, Altona, Hamburg, Wandsbeck*. Krakau: Josef Fischer, 1903.

Duckesz, Eduard, *Chachme AHW: Biographien und Grabsinschriften der Dajanim, Autoren und der Sonstigen Hervoragenden Männer der Drei Gemeinden Altona, Hamburg, Wandsbek*. Hamburg: Goldschmidt Verlag 1908.

Ferguson, N., *High Financier: The Lives and Times of Siegmund Warburg*. London: Penguin Books 2011.

Gillis-Carlebach, M., *Jüdischer Alltag als humaner Widerstand 1939-1941*. Hamburg: Verein für Hamburgische Geschichte 1990.

Gillis-Carlebach, M., *Jewish Everyday Life as Human Resistance 1939-1941*. Frankfurt am Main: Peter Lang. 2009.

Astrid Louven/Max Sussman, Pincus und Adele Hirsch In: Lohmeyer, S., *Stolpersteine in Hamburg-Eimsbüttel und Hamburg-Hoheluft-West*. Volume 1, pp. 295-299. Hamburg: Landeszentralle für politische Bildung. 2012.

Patkin, B., *The Dunera Internees*. Cassell Australia, Stanmore N.S.W. 1979.

Pearl, C., *The Dunera Scandal*. Angus & Robertson Publishers, London 1983.

Rutland, S. D., Falk, Leib Aisack (1889-1957). *Australian Dictionary of Biography*, Volume 8. Melbourne University Press 1981

von Villiez, Anna, *Mit aller Kraft verdrängt: Entrechtung und Verfolgung "nicht arischer" Ärzte in Hamburg 1933 bis 1945*. Dolling und Gallitz Verlag 2009.

INDEX

The names and 'familiar' names of family members are very frequently mentioned in the letters by Pincus and Adele. Readers searching for a particular name or connection in the letters are unlikely to find it useful to search for these in the index. Family relationships are provided in the Dramatis Personae (Chapter 3). Names of family members as they appear in the letters have, therefore, been omitted from this index. The entries in this index usually exclude the letters themselves.

Lightning Source UK Ltd.
Milton Keynes UK
UKOW06f0907120116

266238UK00004B/80/P

9 781845 496654